Played in Tyne and Wear

Charting the heritage of people at play

Played in Tyne and Wear
© English Heritage 2010

English Heritage is the
government's statutory advisor
on all aspects of the historic
environment

Bessie Surtees House
Newcastle upon Tyne NE1 3JF
www.english-heritage.org.uk

Series designer Doug Cheeseman

Series editor Simon Inglis

Production and additional research
Jackie Spreckley

For image credits see page 198

Maps by Mark Fenton

Malavan Media is a creative
consultancy responsible
for the Played in Britain series

www.playedinbritain.co.uk

Printed by Zrinski, Croatia

ISBN: 978 1905624 744
Product code: 51341

Played in Tyne and Wear

Charting the heritage of people at play

Lynn Pearson

Editor Simon Inglis

Twenty first century casual meets 1960s chic at the Jesmond Cricket Ground in Osborne Avenue, Newcastle, former base of the Northumberland County Cricket Club and home of one of the most striking examples of 1960s pavilion architecture in Britain.

Page One Collars, ties and a good throwing arm are the necessary requisites on summer evenings at the Hawkey's Hall Quoit Club, tucked away behind a wooden fence next to the Tynemouth Golf Club. The members have a minute book going back to 1863, but believe that the club may actually have formed three years before then, thus making 2010 their 150th anniversary.

Page Two Sunderland fans queue outside Roker Park in February 1964 for tickets for a fifth round FA Cup tie v. Everton. Despite being in the Second Division that season, Sunderland's average gate of over 41,000 was the fifth highest in English football. But it is important not to gloss over the harsher realities of our sporting past. For the club's sixth round replayed cup tie v. Manchester United a few weeks later, although the official gate was 46,727, an estimated 100,000 were said to have converged on Roker Park, leading to a crush in which two fans died.

Contents

Foreword

1. Played in Tyne and Wear.........................8

2. Town Moor, Newcastle 26
3. Gosforth 50
4. Hillheads 62
5. Wearmouth 72
6. Ashbrooke..90

7. Clubhouses and pavilions 96
8. Grounds and grandstands....................108
9. Stadiums and tracks 114

10. Cock fighting 128
11. Quoits 132
12. Bowls..136
13. Real tennis...142
14. Running...146
15. Pigeon racing 150

16. Rowing..156
17. Model boating 162
18. Swimming..168

19. Conclusions 192

Links...194
Credits...198

'Geordies' or 'Mackems', black and white or red or white, the football fans of Tyne and Wear are renowned equally for their passion. One such supporter was Harry Hutchinson, whose garden, in the village of Sherburn, was visited by photographer Julian Germain in 1992. Alas Harry had just died, leaving it in the care of his long suffering wife Vera (who also at Harry's request had scattered his ashes on the pitch at Roker Park). Tyne and Wear is unusual in having its two main rivals play in stripes (Sheffield being the only other example in Britain). But it was not always like that, and nor were the colours as we know them today. Sunderland originally wore blue, while before 1894 Newcastle actually played in red.

Foreword

Sporting roots are deep in the north east, and nowhere more so than in Tyne and Wear.

The superb modern facilities at Sunderland Aquatic Centre, Gateshead International Stadium, Tyne United Rowing Club, St James' Park and the Stadium of Light are well known and represent the latest development in a long tradition of local sporting excellence.

At the other end of the scale, everyone is familiar with the pigeon crees that crop up just about everywhere, perching on inaccessible and unwanted areas of city land. Many of these are wonderful vernacular structures, expressing the skill and creativity of their builders.

The architectural and cultural heritage of other sports in Tyne and Wear is less familiar.

A strong tradition of model boating clubs thrives in Roker, Heaton, South Shields, Tynemouth, Saltwell Park and elsewhere.

Bowling clubs are often hidden from public view by tall hedges and walls, which conceal oases of calm green, yet fierce competition.

Some things have disappeared without trace. It is hard to imagine that White City Stadium, at the foot of Scotswood Bridge, or the outdoor pool on the front at South Shields, were ever there.

Each sport has a unique architectural and cultural heritage that is celebrated in this book.

This new research has also highlighted the importance of the Town Moors in Newcastle and Sunderland as the cradle of the sporting heritage of each city. Anything and everything has been staged on Newcastle's Town Moor, from horse racing and golf to baseball and rugby.

Some of the region's strongest and most enduring community traditions are centred on sport, not just the well known sports but also more unusual ones such as real tennis, as played at Jesmond Dene.

The quoits pitches at Hawkey's Hall Quoit Club, Tynemouth, and at the Lindisfarne Social Club, Wallsend, are survivors of a game which, in the 1980s, had about 700 pitches across the region.

Many historic facilities are now community run.

In working with English Heritage on this project we have discovered many riches, from our fabulous archives and library collections, to the surviving clubs and grounds being tended and used by sportsmen and women – not to mention international standard facilities hiding long histories behind modern facades.

We hope that this book will inspire you to support our many clubs and their traditions – perhaps to research the history of your local club, to try a sport you have never tried before, or to look behind those tall hedges to explore the rich architectural history of sport in Tyne and Wear.

Councillor **Mick Henry**,
    Leader, Gateshead Council
Councillor **David Faulkner** OBE,
    Leader, Newcastle City Council
Linda Arkley, Elected Mayor,
    North Tyneside Council
Councillor **Iain Malcolm**, Leader,
    South Tyneside Council
Councillor **Paul Watson**, Leader,
    Sunderland City Council

Identities and traditions in sport can soon establish themselves. Newcastle's team adopted the name Diamonds in 1938, yet there was uproar when for one season in 1949 the promoters tried to rename them the Magpies, the same as Newcastle United.

Chapter One

Played in Tyne and Wear

Their equipment may be state of the art and they may now have female members, but the Bowmen of Backworth, formed in 1961–62 and based at Backworth Hall, maintain a sporting tradition of target archery that goes back to the 18th century. Centuries before that, archery was a required skill for all males of fighting age. Indeed, much of our knowledge of medieval sport comes from lists of games that were banned because they distracted men from practising with their bows and arrows.

On Spring Bank Holiday Monday in May 2010, visitors to the Beamish Museum in County Durham were treated to an unexpected bonus – a cricket match on the museum's village green between the Rose Growers of Whickham and the Gentlemen of Percy Main.

But this was no ordinary match.

Some of the players wore bowler hats, cravats and waistcoats. Some appeared to sport false moustaches. Instead of six balls per over there were four, a number of which were delivered underarm.

Not village cricket as we know it today, perhaps, but pretty much how the game was played in 1860.

Why 1860? Because that was the year both Whickham and Percy Main cricket clubs were formed, and so this re-enactment was the clubs' way of celebrating their joint 150th anniversaries.

Sporting heritage is manifest in various different forms: in the survival of historic buildings and of historic places of sport, or 'sportscapes'; in the historic artefacts of sport (such as cups, medals, badges and caps); in

the intangible traditions and narratives of sporting history (the competitions, rivalries and recollections of great moments); in the memorials and artefacts of great sporting figures, and, not least, in the clubs themselves.

To readers who do not live in the area, the chances are that the two clubs in Tyne and Wear that they will know most about are not Whickham or Percy Main, but the footballing giants, Sunderland AFC and Newcastle United.

Formed in 1879 and 1881 respectively (although the name Newcastle United was not adopted until 1892), the Premiership duo may not have won the honours amassed by some of their counterparts, but the scale and loyalty of their support is a phenomenon in itself.

Yet the Black Cats and the Magpies, as the clubs are nicknamed, form only one part of our story. For while in 2010 Whickham and Percy Main celebrated their 150 years of existence – both, incidentally, having played on the same grounds on which they started life

in 1860 – five other clubs in Tyne and Wear are of a similar vintage.

The roll call is impressive.

Sunderland Cricket Club, the oldest club in the area, formed in 1834, and was followed by Tynemouth Cricket Club in 1847, South Shields Cricket Club in 1850, Tyne Rowing Club in 1852, and Hawkey's Hall Quoit Club, also formed in 1860.

Meanwhile, three other clubs are fast approaching their own 150th anniversaries; Whitburn Cricket Club (formed 1862), South Northumberland Cricket Club (1864) and the Gateshead Bowling Green Club (1865).

The latter is based in a clubhouse, a section of which itself dates back to the 1860s or 1870s, which may, our research suggests, be the oldest surviving sports related building in Tyne and Wear.

Longevity is not the only criterion that can be applied when considering sporting heritage.

For example, the sports event with probably the highest international profile in Tyne and Wear, the Great North Run –

Joseph Strutt sums up the *Played in Britain* ethos in his seminal study of 1801, *The Sports and Pastimes of the People of England*.

> In order to form a just estimation of the character of any particular people, it is absolutely necessary to investigate the Sports and Pastimes most generally prevalent among them.

which in September 2009 featured some 50,000 participants and was watched by thousands more lining the streets (plus millions on live television) – dates only from 1981.

Yet what is billed as 'the most iconic half marathon on the planet' did not simply emerge out of a void. Rather, it follows in a tradition that goes back to the early 19th century, when the north east was one of the cradles of distance running, first known as 'pedestrianism' – the province of hardened professionals, or 'peds' – and later dominated by amateur 'harriers', who established dozens of clubs, several of which are still, as it were, running today.

A similar provenance exists in the world of rowing.

The boat race that now takes place annually on the River Tyne between the universities of Newcastle and Durham may have been inaugurated only in 1997, but it is in fact an echo of the rowing races that from the 1840s onwards saw immense crowds line the river banks to urge on such local heroes as Harry Clasper, Bob Chambers and Jim Renforth.

These individuals' cult status, as we shall examine later, was arguably as great as any 20th century sporting star, the likes of Jackie Milburn, Alan Shearer, Brendan Foster or Steve Cram.

That said, *Played in Tyne and Wear* does not set out to present a straightforward narrative history of sport. There are plenty of other sources that already perform that purpose admirably, and which are listed in our Links section.

Instead, our aim, in the spirit of Joseph Strutt (*see opposite*) is to identify, record and, where appropriate, to celebrate those examples of sporting and recreational heritage that we feel

lead to a wider understanding of the character of modern day Tyne and Wear.

For the benefit of readers outside the north east, what do we mean by Tyne and Wear?

Historically, the area north of the River Tyne formed part of Northumberland, with the area to the south, as far as the River Wear, and immediately beyond, being in

Durham. However this all changed following major local government reform in 1974, which saw the creation of the Metropolitan County of Tyne and Wear.

The reform was not entirely welcomed, particularly in the world of sporting governance, in which previous county identities and allegiances held firm.

But then in 1986 the »

◀ In the Garrison Room of the 12th century **Castle Keep** on **Castle Garth, Newcastle**, this stone slab is a reminder of when the term 'sport' referred specifically to bloodsports and gambling. The iron ring was used to tie up a bull, which would then be baited by dogs; the aim being to bet on which dog was able to clamp onto the bull's nose for the longest period. This practice was endorsed by the authorities in the belief that meat from a bull that had been baited tasted better.

The bull ring seen here was dug up in 1821 on nearby Sandhill, where baiting had last taken place in 1768, when a young apprentice, Kenslyside Henzell, was fatally gored. Baiting carried on elsewhere in the town, however, before being banned nationwide in 1835.

From further back in our sporting past, the plaque on the left is at **Shieldfield Green**, off **Simpson Terrace, Newcastle**, and commemorates a game of golf played on the Shield Field by Charles 1 during his imprisonment in Newcastle in 1646. 'Goff' was, as a contemporary account stated, 'an amusement' the beleaugered king 'was very fond of'.

Shield Field was a small pleasure ground where an attempt to stage horse racing was made in 1658 before the authorities intervened. A block of flats called King Charles Tower now overlooks the site.

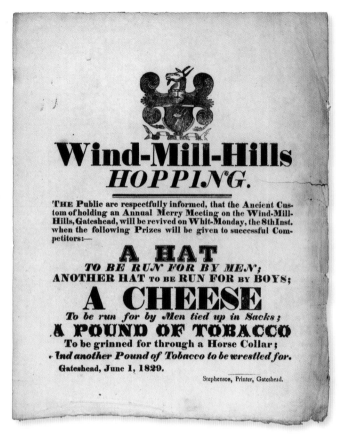

Wind-Mill-Hills
HOPPING.

THE Public are respectfully informed, that the Ancient Custom of holding an Annual Merry Meeting on the Wind-Mill-Hills, Gateshead, will be revived on Whit-Monday, the 8th Inst. when the following Prizes will be given to successful Competitors:—

A HAT
TO BE RUN FOR BY MEN;
ANOTHER HAT TO BE RUN FOR BY BOYS;
A CHEESE
To be run for by Men tied up in Sacks;
A POUND OF TOBACCO
To be grinned for through a Horse Collar;
And another Pound of Tobacco to be wrestled for.
Gateshead, June 1, 1829.

Stephenson, Printer, Gateshead.

▲ This handbill from June 1829 is a reminder that awareness of sporting heritage is no recent phenomenon. It advertises the revival of the 'Ancient Custom of holding an Annual Merry Meeting' or 'hopping' on **Wind-Mill Hills**, an area overlooking the Tyne, just west of **Gateshead** town centre.

The word hopping is thought to derive from an Anglo Saxon word for dancing, and was commonly used to describe fairs. Indeed it is still used for The Hoppings fun fair, staged every June on Newcastle's Town Moor (*see Chapter Two*).

Wind Mill Hills was itself the location of horse racing in the early 18th century, although clearly, as this planned revival confirms, it had ceased by 1829.

It will be noted that the prizes on offer were seemingly everyday items: a hat, a cheese and tobacco.

Yet such prizes were actually highly valued and helped to attract some serious competition, even if some of the events, such as the sack race and the grinning competition were more frivolous.

Another common feature of such gatherings were 'smock races', run by scantily clad women, typically with tea being offered as the prize.

In 1861 Wind Mill Hills became Gateshead's first public park, until it was eclipsed by Saltwell Park, opened 15 years later.

>> Metropolitan County Councils were abolished, to be superceded in Tyne and Wear by five unitary authorities: Gateshead, Newcastle, North Tyneside, South Tyneside and Sunderland.

Tyne and Wear does live on in certain respects however; for example for statistical purposes and in terms of postcodes. There also survive several joint bodies, governing transport, fire services, and, of most relevance in the present context, Tyne & Wear Archives & Museums (to which we are grateful for visual material in this book).

Compared with previous studies of individual cities in the *Played in Britain* series, *Played in Tyne and Wear* therefore covers a relatively large geographical area, incorporating two cities; Newcastle, which received its royal charter in 1882, and Sunderland, which gained its status in 1992.

Inevitably, the historic sporting rivalry between Northumberland and Durham, and more specifically between Newcastle and Sunderland – expressed in shorthand as 'Geordies' v. 'Mackems' – may lead some to look for evidence that the sporting heritage of one area is superior to that of the other.

(According to the Oxford English Dictionary, incidentally, the term Geordie was first applied to inhabitants of Tyneside in 1866, whereas Mackem is not cited in print before 1980. But for what it is worth, Mackem is popularly believed to derive from a sentiment expressed on Wearside that while their ship builders would 'mack'em', or make them, others, such as the Geordies, would then 'tack'em', or take them.)

Of course all sport is a matter of competition, for without an opposition there would be no sport at all. But in terms of sporting heritage there can be no doubt that the constituent elements of Tyne and Wear share a great deal in common.

In a spirit of celebration and friendly rivalry, therefore, let us now 'howay' (or even 'haway') and commence our survey of the fascinating sporting landscape of both Tyne *and* Wear.

Pre-Victorian 'sport'
As noted on the previous page, the word 'sport' traditionally referred not to games but to bloodsports and to any other activity related to gambling. As such it is no surprise that the earliest sport to be recorded in our study area, in the 12th and 13th centuries, was hunting, in Heworth 'chase' or park. This area, at the time heavily forested, lay in what is now Felling, in Gateshead.

One regular huntsman there was Hugh de Puiset, the Bishop of Durham, despite the fact that he had the run of his own deer park in Bishop Auckland.

Bloodsports were equally, if illicitly, enjoyed at the lower end of the social scale, in the form of rabbit coursing, cock fighting and, in later years, pigeon shooting.

Not all pre-modern sports involved the killing of animals.

In the county of Durham, for example, there are references to early games of Shrove Tuesday football, in which two teams would fight for possession of a stuffed ball. In Chester-le-Street, outside our area, Shrove Tuesday was known as 'football day'.

One such game on the Town Moor at Sunderland in 1667 resulted in the death of one Richard Watson.

The same Town Moor was also

the venue for regular bull, badger and bear baiting during the 17th and 18th centuries.

As we learnt earlier, the people of Newcastle enjoyed bull baiting too. In January 1768 the *Newcastle Courant* reported that the gentlemen of the town had graciously provided a bull for the amusement of the poor.

Not that the town's elite were above joining in. William Lawson's *Tyneside Celebrities* (*see Links*) recounts an occasion in 1774 or thereabouts when Newcastle's magistrates enjoyed a baiting to the accompaniment of 'ringing of bells and firing of guns'.

By the turn of the 19th century opposition to this cruel spectacle was starting to take effect.

Sunderland's last recorded baiting took place in May 1822, and in 1835 the practice was finally banned by government statute.

By contrast, cock fighting proved less easy for the authorities to ban. This was not only because cock fights were easily conducted in rural areas or in back street cockpits, but also because the sport had the enthusiastic backing of several eminent individuals.

In 1863, J Collingwood Bruce (*see Links*) wrote that a cock pit had flourished in Newcastle's Westgate 'even during the Commonwealth, when all public amusements were regularly interdicted'.

It also carried on in Newcastle after it had been banned by the government in 1849, with the last known active cock pit in England said to have been one on Gallowgate, eventually closed down by the police in 1874.

In Chapter Ten we visit the only site remaining in Tyne and Wear which is thought to have been used for cock fighting, hidden away in a Tynemouth cellar.

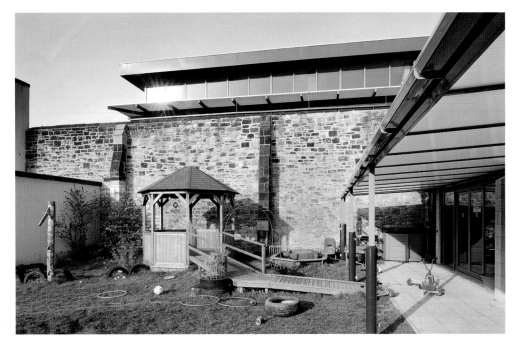

Equally enjoyed by gamblers was horse racing.

From 1621 Newcastle's annual races were held on Killingworth Moor, where the course extended from near the village of Murton to Benton Church (on what is now Station Road), where a grandstand was erected from scaffold. Today that course would cross the A19.

The meeting was suppressed during the Commonwealth of 1649–60, leading one royalist sympathiser, Daniel Collingwood, to opine that 'there were none now in power but the rascality, who envied that gentlemen should enjoy their amusements'.

These amusements resumed at Killingworth at the Restoration, after which the annual summer meeting transferred to Newcastle's Town Moor in 1721, a story we continue in the next chapter.

Other meetings meanwhile were recorded at Woolsington »

▲ This seemingly anonymous sandstone wall at the **Wallsend Children's Centre** on **North Road** was built for the once popular game of **handball**, in which two players, using their palms, would strike a small, stuffed ball against a tall wall in a fashion similar to the modern game of fives.

One prominent handball player in the north east was the early 20th century Sunderland and England footballer, Jackie Mordue, who apparently found the game a useful source of extra income.

Thought to have been introduced to England by Irish migrants in the early 19th century, handball became extremely popular among Northumberland and Durham miners, often being played for high stakes against the walls of pubs or churches.

Several walls used in this way can still be seen in rural south west England. However, this wall is a rare survivor in the north of England, and is also relatively late, having been built as part of the **Buddle Board School**, in 1877.

Initially it served simply as a dividing wall in the school's large playground. But as the game caught on amongst the pupils, it was later raised to its present height of 19 feet, and buttresses added along its 60 foot length.

The buttresses allowed six separate games to take place at any one time, three on each side of the wall.

In 1981 the Buddle School, now listed Grade II, was converted into an arts centre, although since 2008 it has lain empty. Meanwhile, in 2002 the Wallsend Sure Start centre (now the Wallsend Children's Centre) seen on the right, was built on the former car park area.

As may be seen, handball is not one of the games currently on offer at the centre.

▶ Held intermittently between 1811 and 1916, the legendary **Blaydon Races** are commemorated by three plaques in the area.

The brown plaque faces north over the site of the racecourse as it existed from 1861–65, and is on a brick plinth beside **Stella Road**, just before the junction with Stella Hall Drive. (It had originally been positioned on the Blaydon Races Hotel, which stood nearby.)

The blue plaque, recalling **John Brown**, the Blaydon bellman, is at the western entrance of the **Blaydon Shopping Centre**.

The third plaque, meanwhile (not shown), on the **William IV** pub on Gateshead's High Street, honours **George 'Geordie' Ridley** (1835–64), who once lived in a house on the site.

A music hall singer, Ridley was the man who composed the famous song, *The Blaydon Races*, whose lyrics are reproduced on the right, as written, in Geordie dialect.

The song was first aired at Balmbra's Music Hall in Newcastle on June 5 1862, on the occasion of a testimonial for the renowned rower, Harry Clasper, of whom we will learn more in Chapter Sixteen.

Nowadays of course Ridley's song is most frequently heard being belted out by Newcastle United's self-styled 'Toon Army'.

The chorus is sung between each verse.

The Blaydon Races, by George Ridley, 1862

Aw went to Blaydon Races, 'twas on the ninth of Joon,
Eiteen hundred an' sixty-two, on a summer's efternoon;
Aw tyuk the 'bus frae Balmbra's, an' she wis heavy laden,
Away we went alang Collingwood Street, that's on the road to Blaydon.

(chorus) Ah me lads, ye shud only seen us gannin',
We pass'd the foaks upon the road just as they wor stannin';
Thor wes lots o' lads an' lasses there, all wi' smiling faces,
Gawn alang the Scotswood Road... to see the Blaydon Races.

We flew past Airmstrang's factory, and up to the "Robin Adair",
Just gannin' doon te the railway bridge, the 'bus wheel flew off there.
The lasses lost their crinolines off, an' the veils that hide their faces,
An' aw got two black eyes an' a broken nose in gan te Blaydon Races.

When we gat the wheel put on away we went agyen,
But them that had their noses broke they cam back ower hyem;
Sum went to the Dispensary an' uthers to Doctor Gibbs,
An' sum sought out the Infirmary to mend their broken ribs.

Noo when we gat to Paradise thor wes bonny gam begun;
Thor was fower-an-twenty on the 'bus, man, hoo they danced an' sung;
They called on me to sing a sang, aw sung them "Paddy Fagan",
Aw danced a jig an' swung my twig that day aw went to Blaydon.

We flew across the Chain Bridge reet into Blaydon toon,
The bellman he was callin' there, they call him Jackie Brown;
Aw saw him talkin' to sum cheps, an' them he was pursuadin'
To gan an' see Geordy Ridley's concert in the Mechanics' Hall at Blaydon.

The rain it poor'd aw the day an' myed the groons quite muddy,
Coffy Johnny had a white hat on - they war shootin' "Whe stole the cuddy".
There wes spice stalls an' munkey shows an' aud wives selling ciders,
An' a chep wiv a hapenny roond aboot, shootin' "Noo, me boys, for riders".

▶▶ in 1713, on Sunderland's Town Moor from 1724 until the 1740s (*see Chapter Four*) and, as noted earlier, on Wind Mill Hills in Gateshead.

More famous were the Blaydon Races, as featured on the right.

One of the characteristics of those races, and indeed of most major sporting events in the area, was the sheer numbers of miners, or pitmen, in attendance.

Coal mining had begun to impose its presence upon the landscapes of Durham and Northumberland in the late 18th century, and in doing so unleashed upon the area a new breed of hardened sportsmen, playing quoits, potshare bowling, racing their dogs on any available open space, and of course all the while earning a fearsome reputation for drinking and gambling.

Pitmen were amongst those drawn to the Forth pleasure grounds in 1799 by a handbill advertising a boxing match.

According to MA Richardson, writing in the 1840s (*see Links*), they came from far and wide, only to realise that, the date being April 1, there was no boxing at all.

Perhaps the hoax had been the work of local publicans, for as Richardson added, they knew from experience that disappointment of this kind was enough to make any man thirsty.

19th century sport
Moving into the Victorian era, tangible examples of sporting heritage start to appear in greater numbers, in the form of clubs, buildings, grounds and artefacts.

As in all of Britain's growing urban areas, the key factors governing the development of sport in Tyne and Wear during the 19th century were urbanisation and rising population levels. ▶▶

▲ William Irving's painting **The Blaydon Races** drew huge crowds when unveiled in Newcastle in 1903, and continues to bring delight at Gateshead's **Shipley Art Gallery**, where it has been on display since being bought at auction in 2002 after a joint fund raising effort by Tyne and Wear Museums, Gateshead Council, the Heritage Lottery Fund and numerous private individuals.

The painting perfectly captures the spirit of 19th century racing.

Although Irving, who made his living as an illustrator for the *Newcastle Weekly Chronicle*, provided a key to the identity of several of the characters depicted, little is known about most of them.

Some say that the gentleman in the foreground with a whippet, identified as 'George the Plunger', is the lyricist George Ridley (*see opposite*). But in fact the figure bears more resemblance to one of Irving's well known cartoon characters, 'Geordie Pitman'.

As to the racecourse, a stand can just be made out in the distance, below Newburn Church and the chimneys of Spencer's Iron Works.

Largely owing to the changing course of the Tyne, Blaydon's racecourse occupied three different spots. Between 1811 and the 1830s it ran alongside the river. Then from 1861–65 (the period recorded in the song), it was laid out on Blaydon Island. Horses were walked across to the island from Lemington, on the north bank,

while spectators arriving at Blaydon station crossed from the south, using a bridge made up of barges.

From 1887, the final location was a mile or so west at Stella Haugh, until in September 1916 a riot amongst a boisterous crowd of 4,000 proved to be the final straw for the authorities.

Seeing Irving's painting, their unease can be readily imagined.

Stella Haugh was later occupied by a power station, and is now the Riverside Crescent housing estate.

▲ This intricately detailed trophy belt, held in the collection of the **Monkwearmouth Station Museum** in Sunderland, was awarded to the Newcastle professional cyclist **George Waller** in 1879, for winning the Six Day Championship of the World at the Agricultural Hall in Islington, London. In those six days Waller completed 10,500 laps of the small indoor track, the equivalent of 1,404 miles.

Such endurance races had become all the rage with the public since the invention in France of the 'High Bicycle' in 1869, and its refinement two years later by James Starley in Coventry.

Waller's own Coventry-made High Bicycle – only later was the name Penny Farthing applied – is now in the collection of **Beamish Museum**. It had cost him £20, a considerable sum considering Waller had been an apprentice stonemason. But, by winning the

Six Day Championship he returned to Tyneside as a cult hero, with a prize of 100 guineas in his pocket.

Some of these winnings Waller used to establish his own Bicycle and Recreations Grounds on Dalton Street, Byker, where he promoted races for both amateur and professional cyclists.

Known more commonly as Waller's, the Byker grounds had a cinder track and a small grandstand. It was not a success, and closed in 1884, but other tracks were more successful, including the one where Waller had trained, at the North Durham Cricket Ground (*opposite*).

Despite the fact that cycling was not yet seen as entirely respectable, a dozen cycling clubs had formed in the north east by 1877, each member being expected to buy his own machine and often kit himself out with a special club uniform.

Another cyclist of this era was **Harry Carr**, whose grave at **All Saints Cemetery**, **Jesmond**, depicts on one side his own High Bicycle, and on the other, the badge of the **Jubilee Rovers Athletic & Cycling Club** (*left*). This had been founded in 1887, two years before his death, probably from meningitis, at the age of 22.

» Newcastle grew from a town of some 33,000 in 1801 to a city of 247,000 by 1901, while over the same period Sunderland expanded from around 25,000 to 146,000.

Gateshead, meanwhile, grew more than tenfold, from less than 9,000 in 1801 to 110,000 by 1901.

This unprecedented rise in population was reflected in attendances at sports events. For example, by the mid 19th century attendances on Newcastle's Town Moor during Race Week in June rose to estimated levels of 50,000.

The nature of events changed too. We referred earlier to pedestrianism in the north east. In its earliest form this involved 'peds' racing not against each other but against the clock.

One such 'ped' was Peter Macmillan, who in 1828 managed to walk 110 miles in 24 hours around a half mile track roped off on Newcastle's Town Moor.

Even more remarkably, a fortnight later his mother Mary managed 92 miles over the same period, an extremely rare instance of a woman taking part in early professional sport.

She was, at the time, aged 63.

Events such as these proved so popular that pressure grew from the authorities to displace them from public spaces, which in turn led to the creation of purpose-built enclosed grounds, the forerunners of our modern stadiums.

All were run on a commercial basis, with payment at the gate and small grandstands built to attract a higher class of punter. Most were located in close proximity to pubs, whose landlords were often active in promoting events and acting as unofficial bookmakers.

One early example from the 1840s was the Wrestling Ground at Elswick (*see opposite*).

Others in Newcastle from later decades would include the Grapes Running Ground on Westgate Road, the Victoria Grounds, next to the Elswick Lead Works (roughly where the Metro Radio Arena now stands), the Fenham Park Grounds on Nuns Moor, and Waller's in Byker (*see opposite*).

For its part, Gateshead had a sports ground at Borough Gardens, while in Sunderland a similar venue was established at the Victoria Gardens.

No trace of any of these venues has survived. Most were swallowed up by development or fell foul of crackdowns on betting. Pedestrianism, which in the 1880s became increasingly tainted by race fixing (known as 'roping'), also lost its audience to football by the late 19th century.

But that was by no means the end of organised running. Far from it. The demise of professionalism paved the way for the rise of amateur athletics, and in particular a form of competitive running that has characterised sport in the north east ever since.

The first amateurs to form a running club in Tyne and Wear were the Newcastle Harriers, at the Lord Hill Inn on Barrack Road in 1887. They no longer survive, but the Elswick Harriers, who formed in 1889, do still exist, as do Saltwell Harriers and Heaton Harriers, both founded in 1890.

A similar backlash against professionalism occurred in rowing, starting in 1852 with the formation of the Tyne Amateur Rowing Club. Its members may have been middle class, but this alone was not the reason for them setting themselves apart. They also recognised that they would struggle to beat professional rowers who were, as working »

▲ Presumably dating from the 1860s or 1870s, this image of the **Wrestling Ground**, which lay south of **Pottery Lane** in Newcastle (where now lies the northern approach to Redheugh Bridge), is a rare glimpse of one of the many speculative grounds built in Tyne and Wear during the 19th century.

Cumberland and Westmorland style wrestling is first recorded in Newcastle during the 1830s, when it was staged on Meadows Island,

in the Tyne. It was then switched to the more central Forth ground, before being established in 1846 at the venue seen here.

Although other sports were staged there, its location was significant because the site belonged to the Newcastle & Carlisle Railway, which would have been the main conduit for those travelling from the Lake District to attend the annual Easter Wrestling and Great Northern Games.

There were three stands, one of which, perhaps the one seen here, was described in 1857 as being fitted out in an 'ornamental and tasteful' style with crimson drapery.

In 1875 the railway reclaimed the site, after which the annual wrestling event was staged at the Northumberland cricket ground (*see inside front cover*) and, from 1879, at the new Victoria Grounds, also in Elswick.

Shown left in July 1900 is the cement-lined, cambered cycle track at another multi-purpose sports ground, the home since 1866 of the **North Durham Cricket Club** (founded 1864), and of **North Durham RFC** (founded 1876), on **Prince Consort Road, Gateshead**.

Although the cycle track did not survive – very few of its ilk did once the cycle boom ended in the early 1900s – the pavilion and ground remained in use until the 1990s.

The site is now scheduled to be re-developed as a new 9,000 capacity stadium for Gateshead Football Club, due to open in 2012.

▲ Viewed from the Bewick Court tower block, the glass-roofed building seen here is one of the forgotten sports buildings of Victorian Newcastle. Designed by Hubert Laws and opened in 1888, the **College Street Rackets Court**, was built for members of the Union Club on Westgate Road.

Rackets, or racquets, a cross between real tennis (*see Chapter Thirteen*) and squash, had evolved, unusually, amongst inmates at the Fleet Prison in London in the 18th century, but was then taken up by gentlemen and the public schools.

An earlier court measuring 112' x 62', probably uncovered, had been built on Newgate Street in Newcastle in 1823. The College Street court, however, conformed to the new standard of 60' x 30', established by the Prince's Club in London in 1853.

Only the wealthy could afford this modernised form of rackets, largely because it required courts constructed with hard wearing, plastered walls, a set of robust rackets, and compressed cloth balls covered in white sheepskin. In a typical tournament match up to a hundred such balls might be used.

As seen here, the court is a plain, unadorned brick structure, lit from above. It has a viewing gallery on the fourth side, reached via an ornate spiral staircase.

Newcastle's court is one of only two in the north still extant. The other, at the Manchester Tennis and Racquet Club, dates from 1880.

Since squash became the more popular game, the College Street court has been used mainly for badminton, judo and as a crèche.

However, as of 2010 it lay empty, its future as yet undecided by its owners, the City Council.

》 rivermen, on the water every day; the sort of men who, in the 1840s, had challenged their counterparts from the River Thames in London to a series of high profile races for large stakes.

Besides which, joining a club, any sports club, was the ideal way for newly arrived urban dwellers to make friends and establish a sense of local identity.

This was particularly true when it came to team games, and of these, the first to become organised in Tyne and Wear was cricket. Of the ten oldest sports clubs operating today in the area, seven are cricket clubs, the oldest one of all being Sunderland CC, which formed in 1834 under the original name Bishopwearmouth CC. As mentioned previously, other early developers that are still in existence are the cricket clubs at Tynemouth (1847), South Shields (1850), and of course Whickham and Percy Main (both 1860).

In Newcastle the oldest surviving cricket club is South Northumberland, formed in 1864, and based since 1865 at Roseworth Terrace in South Gosforth.

Cricket was to prove of immense significance in the wider development of sport in Tyne and Wear. It was, for example, the first team game that would see clubs criss-crossing the Tyne to play each other on a regular basis.

It was the first game to take advantage of the growing railway network, and the first game to adopt and develop its own private grounds, from the 1830s onwards.

But this was only the start. For as the 19th century wore on, it was at cricket grounds that many of the area's first rugby and football clubs formed. Examples include Percy Park RFC, one of the earliest rugby clubs to form

in Tyne and Wear, who started out at Percy Main CC in 1872, Sunderland RFC, formed on the ground of Sunderland CC in 1873, and Westoe RFC formed at South Shields CC in 1875. Indeed in the second and third cases mentioned, the cricket and rugby clubs still share today, as do the cricket and football clubs at Hebburn and Whickham. Such groundsharing, once common across Britain, is now relatively rare in the modern sporting scene.

In Newcastle, the two clubs whose paths would ultimately lead to the formation of Newcastle United at St James' Park also owed their origins to cricket clubs.

East End FC were formed by members of Stanley CC in Byker in 1881, while a year later West End FC, who were the tenants of St James' Park when East End eventually took it over, were formed by members of West End Junior CC, originally known as the Crown Cricket Club.

We noted above how cricket benefitted from the railway network. Also key to broadening access to sport was the gradual reduction in working hours, in which respect mention must be made of the Nine Hours Movement in Sunderland, whose members' twenty week strike in 1871 proved to be a turning point in gaining shorter working days for workers not only on Wearside but across Britain.

Improved transport links and more free time explain only part of how sport was able to emerge as a major social and cultural force in Victorian Britain.

Three other developments would prove equally significant.

The first of these was the creation of public parks. For while the upper classes were

able to garner the resources to set up clubs and grounds, for the vast majority of middle class and working people the only spaces for recreation were areas like the Town Moors in both Newcastle and Sunderland, places where they were not always welcome and where there was often a good deal of jostling for space between different sporting interests.

In this respect the provision of public parks in Tyne and Wear represented a major leap forward. The first in the area was Mowbray Park in Sunderland, opened in 1857. But the first park to have a specific area set aside for organised sport was Saltwell Park,

Gateshead, where a bowling green was laid out in 1878. Three years later, in response to a petition, a recreation ground was laid out on the edge of Newcastle's Town Moor (where Exhibition Park is now), followed across the road in 1882 by the provision of the town's first municipal bowling green, in Brandling Park.

The green is still in existence today, as is one at Roker Park, Sunderland, dating from 1883.

So popular did these prove that by the end of the century virtually every park had a green, and just as importantly, a parks bowling club too. Indeed it was parks clubs that in 1892 established what

is thought to be the first county association in English bowls, the Northumberland and Durham Bowling Association.

This leads us to the second significant development of the late 19th century, and that is the growth in sporting governance.

In Tyne and Wear this resulted, *inter alia*, in the formation of the Durham County Rugby Football Union in 1876, the Northumberland Rugby Union in 1880 and the Northumberland Football Association in 1883.

The Northern Football League, meanwhile, established in 1889 with several clubs from the north east being represented, is now »

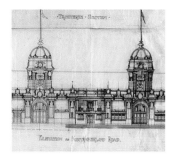

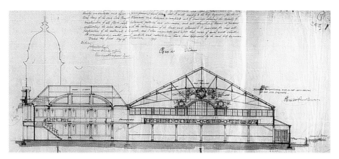

▲ Another craze to sweep Britain in various phases was **roller skating**.

Seen above and above right are the plans of one such rink at **The White City,** opened on Northumberland Road, Newcastle, in December 1909. (The name was adopted for several entertainment complexes around Britain at that time, inspired by London's White City exhibition, opened in 1908.)

'Rincomania', as the first phase of roller skating was dubbed, took off following the invention of the four-wheeled skate in America in 1863. One of skating's main attractions was that it allowed close contact between men and women.

In the north east the first known rink was at the Albion Assembly Rooms in North Shields, opened in 1873, followed by one built in conjunction with the Aquarium and Winter Gardens at Tynemouth in 1876. The building in which it was located is still extant, but is now occupied by shops (see page 189).

Rincomania then returned in the Edwardian period, thanks largely to improvements in skate design and to the use of maple, rather than asphalt flooring.

This phase saw roller skating offered at the Exhibition Hall on St Mary's Place, Newcastle and at the Olympia (later the Whitehall) Rink in Sunderland, both in 1908, and in 1909 at the Town Moor Grandstand Roller Rink (see page 33), at the Tynemouth Winter Gardens (in the former aquarium), a building later renamed The Plaza,

and at the Whitley Bay American Roller Skating Rink on Park Avenue in 1909. The latter was promoted by Gosforth builder George Parkinson, who was also behind The White City development.

The White City's architects were Joseph H Morton & Son, who adopted a similar imperial style for their **Olympia Skating Rink** on **Sea Road**, **South Shields** (above), opened in 1910.

Whereas most rinks had closed by 1914, the Olympia lasted the longest, partly because it hosted other attractions, including boxing.

Roller skating's third phase started in 1930, reappearing at **Tynemouth** (left), while at the Olympia, now renamed the Spa Roller Rink, a Yorkshireman called Arnold Binns broke the world endurance record by roller skating non-stop for 72 hours and 18 minutes in 1931.

Unfortunately the rink burnt down soon after, in January 1932.

the second oldest league in the world.

County associations and leagues galvanised team sports in the area, driving up standards, rooting out the weaker clubs and ultimately, leading to the integration of local clubs into national networks. In football, Sunderland were the first, being elected to the First Division in 1890, and winning the Championship three times during their first five seasons.

Newcastle followed in 1893, initially joining the Second Division, before rising to the First in 1898.

Thus within less than 20 years, Association football in the area had risen from almost nowhere to a position of near total domination of the local sporting scene.

The final factor in sport's inexorable rise during the late 19th century concerns technology.

The list of key inventions is a long one, but briefly it includes the invention of the lawnmower (thereby leading to improved turf management), and of vulcanised rubber (which led to improved balls that could be mass manufactured). Together these two breakthroughs led to the invention in the 1870s of a completely new sport, lawn tennis.

Other sports and games to benefit from new technology were billiards, roller skating (see left), golf, pigeon racing (see Chapter Fifteen), and of course cycling. By 1900 there were some 40–50 cycling clubs in Sunderland alone.

20th century sport

Despite the advances of the 19th century, there can be no denying that as the Victorian era gave way to the Edwardian there remained huge inequalities in the provision and nature of sporting life. »

ELEVATION TO ST ANDREW'S ST.

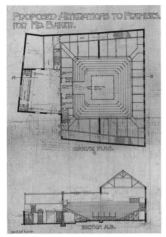

PROPOSED ALTERATIONS TO PREMISES FOR MR BAKER.

▲ Although little tangible heritage survives, **boxing** was once a thriving sport in Tyne and Wear. So much so that in the period 1886–1933, 38 venues have been identified in Newcastle, plus a further dozen or so in Sunderland. No doubt there were many others, the backrooms of pubs for example, such as the Lord Byron Tavern in Sunderland's east end, where bare knuckle fights were recorded in the 1830s. Boxing booths were also common at race meetings.

After the adoption of boxing gloves and tighter regulation under the Queensberry Rules of 1867, boxing grew in respectability, leading to the creation of several purpose-built boxing stadiums in major British cities.

Above are two details of **St James' Hall**, which lay directly opposite the Gallowgate End terrace at St James' Park, with its original entrance (*far left*) on St Andrew's Street. Designed by Percy Browne, and opened in 1909, the hall's capacity was 2,500–3,000.

The hall was then rebuilt on the same site, but with an entrance on Strawberry Place, and reopened as the **New St James' Hall** in May 1930 (*below left*). Designed by the Chester-le-Street architects Cowe & Lawson, it could seat 4,000, plus a few hundred standing at the back.

Its opening night featured one of the north east's leading boxers of the day, **Jack Casey**, the 'Sunderland Assassin' (*right*), who managed to avoid being knocked out throughout his entire career, from 1926–42.

A measure of how important Newcastle was as a centre of boxing, along with Liverpool, Birmingham and London, is that in the mid 1930s St James' Hall hosted fights on six nights a week.

Meanwhile in Sunderland, the largest venue was the Holmeside Stadium, which held 2,000 and operated from 1920–30. This was succeeded from 1934–36 by a 2,000 seat venue at the former Theatre Royal on Bedford Street.

Boxing was also staged in Sunderland at several open air venues, such as Roker Park, Hendon Cricket Ground, the Blue House Field and Ashbrooke (*see Chapters Five and Six*).

New St James' Hall staged its final bout in May 1967, after which it continued to host wrestling, then bingo, before being demolished in 1976 to make way for St James Station.

Boxing remains active in Tyne and Wear, albeit on a lesser scale, while the Sunderland & District Ex-Boxers Association and a number of enthusiasts do their best to keep memories of the golden era alive.

NEW ST. JAMES' HALL
NEWCASTLE UPON TYNE
Telephone 24932   Telephone 20521
Governing Director: SOL SHECKMAN
Booking Office open Monday to Friday 9 a.m. to 5 p.m.
Saturday Only 9 a.m. to 4 p.m.

Monday, March 16th, 1959
Doors Open 6 p.m.   Commence 7-0 p.m.

BOXING

6d.   PROGRAMME   6d.

Matchmaker: JOE SHEPHERD
Master of Ceremonies—BOBBIE LEIGHTON   Timekeeper—BILLY McCOLL
Ringmaster and Whip—GEORGE DAVIS   Referees Selected by the B.B.B.C
Official Seconds—Messrs W. RICHARDSON and W. EXLEY
Medical Officer—DR. H. BURNETT.   Resident Manager—G. R. WELCH
THE MANAGEMENT RESERVES THE RIGHT TO REFUSE ADMISSION
Free List Entirely Suspended

▶ Unlike other urban areas so far covered by *Played in Britain*, Tyne and Wear has not been home to a significant number of sports related manufacturers.

There is however one important sporting implement that largely owes its origins to Sunderland, and that is the aluminium golf club.

The man responsible for this innovation was the Sunderland engineer and inventor **Sir William Mills** (1856–1932), who set up Britain's first aluminium foundry at the Atlas Works in Bonnersfield, Monkwearmouth (near Wearmouth Bridge) in c.1885.

As a founder member of **Wearside Golf Club** in 1892, Mills first applied his mind to the design of golf clubs in 1896, registering two patents for aluminium heads.

He was not the first to come up with the idea, but he was the first to put his designs into production, setting up a subsidiary called the **Standard Golf Company**.

Between 1901 and the company's demise in 1939, Standard offered 135 different models across the full range of clubs – drivers, putters and so on – becoming the leading manufacturer of aluminium clubs in Britain, and more productive even than rivals in the USA. One estimate is that Standard produced 350–400,000 clubs, each, unusually, stamped with an individual number.

Mills himself moved in c.1905 to the Black Country, where he set up a foundry producing castings for the motor car and aircraft industries. It was there from 1915 onwards that he produced the hand grenade, or 'Mills bomb', for which he became best known, and for which he was knighted in 1922.

Meanwhile, back in Sunderland, former employees of the Standard Golf Company set up rival golf club workshops, both on a small scale, both based in Southwick.

One was the **Cowan Golf Company**. The other, much better known, was the **Imperial Golf Company**.

Seen below is a 1920s Medium putter made by Imperial, one of several historic clubs owned by Wearside Golf Club, where Mills had taken up the game. Note that its weight of nine ounces and two drams is stamped on the base.

Today there is a thriving collectors' market in Sunderland-made clubs. Lesser examples change hands for maybe £40–50. However in 2010 a rare Mills club was sold at auction for £1,500.

Also on display in the clubhouse of **Wearside Golf Club** at **Coxgreen**, is the crumpled piece of silverware seen below, all that remains of a trophy once awarded to the winners of an annual match between teams selected by the club captain and the secretary.

The trophy is a poignant reminder of the fate of so many items of sporting heritage, not only in Wearside but in Britain as a whole. Loss or destruction of historic assets is all too common a tale. Sometimes the loss is down to sheer negligence, a simple lack of understanding of how important certain items could be to a club or to the nation's wider sporting heritage.

The careless handling or storage of objects such as minute books or photographs is also common.

Vandalism is a further problem, particularly where pavilions are in isolated locations.

But by far the greatest damage has been caused by fire.

Wearside Golf Club have suffered twice on this account. Their original pavilion burnt down in 1909, while their second, from which this trophy was salvaged – a pavilion designed by George Brown and Joseph Spain, and in itself a sad loss – met a similar fate in 1956.

Fortunately clubs today are much more conscious of risk, and of the need to preserve their heritage.

But it cannot be denied that much has already been lost.

>> Most of all women were still excluded from all but a few sports. But even in those sports that did welcome them, such as tennis, swimming and golf, it was very much as junior partners. Tyneside Golf Club's committee, for example, decided in 1903 that they would admit ladies to membership, but that on no account would they be permitted entry to the clubhouse.

At Gosforth Golf Club, as we shall reveal in Chapter Three, these slights would take a sinister turn in 1913 when the clubhouse was targeted by Suffragettes.

But, as noted on the right, women did start to play a fuller role in sport after the First World War. Not in football, clearly, or cricket or rugby, but in 1921 a Women's Amateur Athletic Association was formed, and in 1928 female athletes were finally allowed to compete in the Olympics.

The 1920s also brought improvements to the sporting lives of Tyne and Wear's coal miners.

This was owing to the setting up of the Miners Welfare Fund in 1920. The bulk of this fund (raised via a levy on colliery revenues) went towards the provision of pithead baths. But it also resulted in the construction of community halls (as at Esh Winning), indoor swimming pools (Ashington), and a number of sports grounds too.

Several of these survive, such as the Wearmouth Colliery Welfare Ground on Carley Hill Road, Sunderland, opened in 1928 with a cricket pitch and bowling greens.

Though pleasant enough, it has no buildings of architectural quality. But as the following chapters show, that does not mean it lacks historical significance.

This is equally true of another strand of sporting development >>

▲ Of all the sports invented or codified in the Victorian period, none was embraced more readily by women than **lawn tennis**, as seen here at **Highfield Road, Westerhope**, in around 1905.

An evolution from the much older game that has since become known as 'real tennis' (*see Chapter Thirteen*), lawn tennis emerged in the 1870s and within a decade ousted croquet – itself introduced only in the 1850s – as the favourite summer game of the middle and upper classes. Ideal for the gardens of suburban villas, above all tennis allowed women to take part in competitive sport whilst also enjoying, in most cases for the first time, the social benefits of club life.

At private schools too, tennis joined hockey as an acceptable form of recreation, whereas at most state elementary schools, gymnastic drill and swimming were the most girls could expect.

All this changed as a result of the First World War.

As Patrick Brennan has noted (*see Links*), between 1916–19 several ladies football teams made up of workers from local munitions factories played at least 26 games at St James' Park alone. And perhaps many of the 500 or so women involved might well have played on in peacetime had the Football Association not banned them in 1921.

Between the wars another sport newly popular amongst women was netball, as seen at **Gosforth Secondary School** in 1930 (*right*).

Works teams provided a further outlet. Particularly active in the 1920s and 1930s were the Newcastle Business Houses Ladies Hockey League and the Tyneside & District Hockey League.

More recently, at least in the days before synthetic pitches became common, ladies hockey was a handy source of winter income for cricket clubs. For example when the men of St George's Hockey Club (founded in 1896) left Benwell's ground in the 1980s, the cricket club encouraged the formation of Benwell Ladies Hockey Club to take their place.

Of course apart from the inevitable social barriers women faced in gaining access to sports clubs, there was another obstacle.

However, as clubs came to realise, the cost of providing extra changing rooms was soon offset by the increase in membership.

▲ Sport can sometimes be the saving grace for historic buildings.

Since 1930 **Burnmoor Cricket Club** (formed in 1873) have used the former village school as their pavilion (*top*). Built in c.1870 and now Grade II listed, the building's polychromatic brickwork provides a spendid backdrop to the action.

Also from the late 18th century and listed Grade II is the clubhouse of **Arcot Hall Golf Club** (*above left*). The club had originally been known as **Benton Park Golf Club**, until in 1947 their course at Longbenton had been compulsorily purchased for housing (on what is now Hoylake Avenue, Gleneagles Close, Muirfield Road and Fairways Avenue). Coincidentally their clubhouse there had been another late 18th century mansion, so

Arcot Hall was very much a home from home.

A more recent conversion is **Close House** (*above*), a Grade II* building which again dates from the late 18th century. Until 2005 it was part of Newcastle University, whereas today it is a hotel and golf centre. We return to Close House in Chapter Seven to visit the estate's delightful former cricket pavilion.

» in Tyne and Wear, and that is the advent between the wars of the works ground.

Built predominantly by shipbuilding and engineering firms, their purpose mirrored that of the Miners Welfare grounds. For a few pence a week docked from their wages, workers could at last gain access to the sort of facilities that had hitherto been the reserve of private members' clubs.

Since the 1970s all Miners' Welfare and works grounds have become detached from their original owners. An example of this, as featured in Chapter Eight, is Hebburn, where four clubs, for football, cricket, tennis and bowls, jointly run the former ground of the Reyrolle switchgear company, the site of which is now owned by South Tyneside Council.

Because so much of what follows in this book concerns the 20th century, it is not necessary at this point to say more on how sport evolved during that period.

Three issues relating to heritage are worth noting however.

Firstly, in common with all parts of Britain, there are numerous historic pavilions and clubhouses in Tyne and Wear whose original design has been lost behind an array of modern extensions, alterations and replacement windows, as clubs have striven to maintain their viability by providing extra facilities for members and for hire.

Regrettable though this is, it is also entirely understandable.

Secondly, since the 1960s a significant number of historic sports buildings have been demolished. For example, only three pre-1914 swimming baths remain fully extant in Tyne and Wear. Of these, Wallsend (built in 1912) currently stands empty, while those at Byker (1886) and Gibson Street (1907), both in Newcastle, have been adapted for other sporting uses, climbing and badminton respectively.

On the other hand, as featured in Chapter Seven, Tyne and Wear has a number of pavilions that were built in the 1960s to replace Victorian and Edwardian buildings, but which can now be considered to have classic design qualities of their own.

The same could even be said of two buildings from the 1970s; the East Stand at St James' Park (featured in the following chapter) and the interior of Whitley Bay Waves (see Chapter Eighteen), one of the first leisure pools to have been built in Britain when it opened in 1974.

Finally there is the issue of those sports that as a result of social and economic changes, and of evolving tastes and fashions, have declined in the late 20th century or face decline in the present one.

In Chapter Eleven we look at quoits, once one of the area's most popular games but which is now down to handful of clubs.

In Chapter Nine we look at two sports that emerged in a flurry of stadium construction during the late 1920s and 1930s, greyhound racing and speedway, but which have also struggled to survive in the modern era. Again, these sports have not resulted in the construction of any buildings or venues of architectural merit. Yet their story – Brough Park in Byker in particular, dating back to 1899 – forms an inextricable part of the wider historical narrative.

On a positive note, the area's longer established sports appear to be in much ruder health, as is indicated both by participation levels – for example in running and rowing – and by attendance levels, not only for football but also for horse racing at High Gosforth Park and rugby at the new Kingston Park.

Played in Britain estimates that the Tyne and Wear area, with its overall population of just over one million, now has in the region of 800 active sports clubs, of which at least 200 are over 50 years old.

Of these, the three sports best represented are football (with around 300 clubs), bowls (130) and cricket (40). In addition, over 70 local homing societies take part in pigeon racing.

Played in Tyne and Wear
This book is divided into four sections. The next five chapters focus upon what we call 'sporting clusters'. These are followed by three chapters focusing on specific building types, followed by nine chapters on individual sports.

Inevitably some readers will be disappointed that their favourite sport has not featured as much as others, or even not at all. This is because, rather than cover the full range we have chosen those sports whose heritage we believe best represents the geography, history and character and, most of all, the people of Tyne and Wear.

Clearly, there is much to be proud of within this heritage.

Clearly, there is much to do to ensure that it is safeguarded.

But above all we hope to inspire readers to look afresh at the sites and buildings featured in this book. They may be new to some. They may be simply 'part of the furniture' to others.

But they do form a vital part of our historic environment, and should be celebrated as such, on whichever side of the Tyne or the Wear our colours may be laid.

▲ Built in 1778–80 for Ralph William Grey, the High Sheriff of Northumberland, the Grade II listed **Backworth Hall** is another historic property that would in time come to serve the very people whose toil and sweat had brought riches to men like Grey.

More than that, when the **Backworth Colliery Miners' Welfare Scheme** bought the house and its 85 acres in 1934, for £8,500, they brought it back to life after years of neglect.

The buildings were restored and in the grounds were laid out a golf course, the use of which was made available to the colliery's 3,000 workers, in return for 6d a week deducted from their wages.

Alas a fire in 1960 destroyed

much of the hall's interior, but it was eventually restored and continues to serve as the clubhouse.

Seen here in 2010, hosting a youth tournament, are the **Backworth Bowling Club**.

They share the hall and grounds with the **Backworth Golf Club** and **Backworth Cricket Club**.

No doubt the High Sheriff of Northumberland would have been horrified at his house being taken over in this way by working folk.

But Robin Hood would surely have approved, especially as the fourth club to use the grounds are the **Bowmen of Backworth**, the archers whom we encountered at the start of this chapter.

Between them these four clubs have around 1,000 members.

▲ Although our focus is buildings of historic value, it is interesting to consider which sporting venues of the modern era may yet be considered worthy of celebration.

One contender is the **Lightfoot Centre** (top), **Wharrier Street, Walker**, designed for Newcastle City Council by the locally-based sports and leisure architects, Williamson, Faulkner Brown & Partners (now FaulknerBrowns) whose work we will encounter throughout this book.

Conceived in the wake of the Wolfenden Report of 1960, which urged the construction of multi-purpose sports centres, when it opened in 1965 the Lightfoot Centre's 61m diameter 'flying saucer' dome was the largest in Europe. Moreover, its laminated timber ribs were covered in prefabricated reinforced fibreglass panels, a form of cladding that had never been used before on a building of this scale.

Beneath the 14m high dome is a clear expanse of 2,300 square metres, enough for two tennis courts, eight badminton courts, or a number of other spectator events.

Multi-functionality was also the key thinking behind Newcastle's **Metro Radio Arena** (above).

With a maximum capacity of 11,000 for concerts, the £10m Arena – brainchild of the former Animals bass player and impresario Chas Chandler – was larger than any indoor facility yet seen in the north east when it opened on the site of a goods yard in 1995.

Music is its staple, but it has also hosted boxing, wrestling, basketball (the Newcastle Eagles) and several ice hockey clubs (most recently the Northern Stars).

Experience tells us that design quality alone is never enough for a sports building to be loved. So it will be fascinating to see how these two venues come to be regarded by the historians of the future.

1. **Close House Golf Club** Heddon-on-the-Wall (*22, 98*)
2. **Tyneside Golf Club** Westfield Lane, Ryton (*99*)
3. **Tyne Rowing Club** Water Row (*160*)
4. site of **Blaydon Races** 1887–1916 (*12-13*)
5. **Fenham Swimming Pool** Fenham Hall Drive (*178*)
6. **Newcastle Falcons Kingston Park** Brunton Road (*113*)
7. **Arcot Hall Golf Club** Cramlington (*22*)
8. **Northumberland Golf Club** High Gosforth Park (*60*)
9. **Newcastle Racecourse** High Gosforth Park (*50-57*)
10. **Northern Football Club McCracken Park** Great North Road (*61*)
11. **City of Newcastle Golf Club** (*59*)
12. **Gosforth Golf Club** Broadway East (*58*)
13. **South Northumberland Cricket Club** Moor Road North (*107*)
14. **Gosforth Squash Club** Moor Court, Westfield (*33*)
15. **Jesmond Dene Real Tennis Club** Matthew Bank (*142-145*)
16. **Jesmond Swimming Pool** (*178-179*)
17. former **City of Newcastle Golf Clubhouse** Claremont Road (*34*)
18. **St James' Park** Strawberry Place (*36-49*)
19. **Summerhill Bowling Club** Winchester Terrace (*138, 141*)
20. **Metro Arena** (*24, 152*)
21. former **Rackets Court** College Lane (*16*)
22. **City Pool** Northumberland Road (*170-1, 176-7*)
23. former **Gibson Street Baths** New Bridge Street (*173-5*)
24. site of **City Stadium** Warwick Street (*116*)
25. **Portland Bowling Club** Portland Terrace (*137, 140-141*)
26. **Jesmond Cricket Ground** Osborne Ave (*2, 102-103*)
27. **Medicals RFC** Cartington Terrace (*100, 109*)
28. **Heaton & District Model Power Boat Club** (*164-167*)
29. **Cochrane Park Pavilion** Etherstone Avenue (*100*)
30. **Novocastrians RFC Sutherland Park** The Drive Longbenton (*101*)
31. **Brough Park** Fossway (*120-122*)
32. **Lightfoot Centre** Wharrier Street (*24*)
33. former **handball wall North Road** Wallsend (*11*)
34. **Wallsend Boys Club** Station Road (*104-105*)
35. **Backworth Welfare Club** (*8, 23*)
36. **Rockcliffe Bowling Club** Helena Avenue (*139*)
37. **Hillheads Rockcliff RFC Whitley Bay FC & CC Ice Rink** (*80-89*)
38. **Tynemouth Model Boat Club** Tynemouth Park (*164-165*)
39. former **Tynemouth Open Air Sea Water Swimming Pool** (*189*)
40. **Hawkey's Hall Quoit Club** off Preston Avenue (*1, 134-5*)
41. **South Shields CC and Westoe RFC** Dean Road (*101,108*)
42. **Gateshead International Stadium** Neilson Road (*126-7*)
43. **Gateshead Bowling Green Club** (*97, 136, 192*) / **North Durham Cricket Ground** Prince Consort Road (*15*)
44. **Gateshead Leisure Centre** Shipcote Lane (*180-1*)
45. **Sunderland Greyhound Stadium** Newcastle Road (*124-5*)
46. site of **Roker Park Sunderland AFC** (*70-73*)
47. **Stadium of Light Sunderland AFC** / **Aquatic Centre** (*74-79, 186-187*)
48. **Ashbrooke Sports Club** West Lawn (*90-95*)
49. **Ryhope pigeon cree** Back Ryhope Street (*154*)
50. **Wearside Golf Club** Coxgreen (*20*)

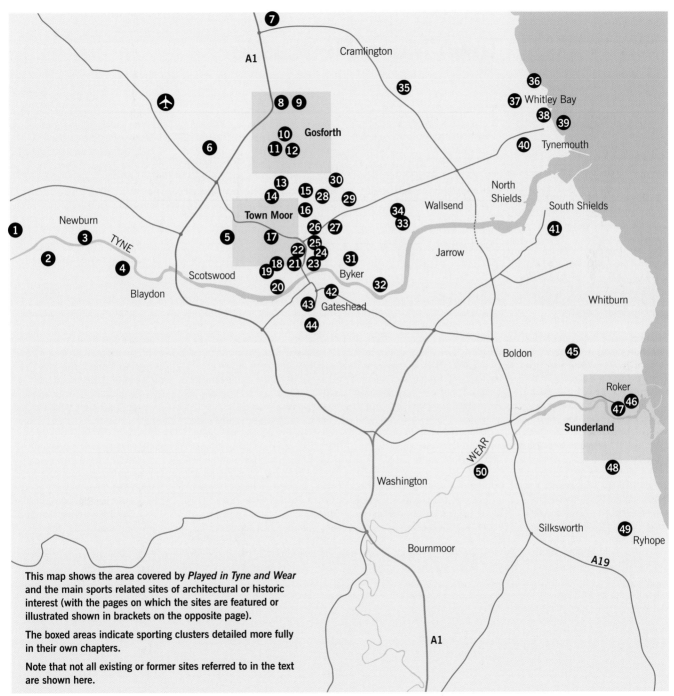

This map shows the area covered by *Played in Tyne and Wear* and the main sports related sites of architectural or historic interest (with the pages on which the sites are featured or illustrated shown in brackets on the opposite page).

The boxed areas indicate sporting clusters detailed more fully in their own chapters.

Note that not all existing or former sites referred to in the text are shown here.

Chapter Two

Town Moor, Newcastle

Before enclosed sports grounds started to appear in the mid 19th century, the Town Moor was the scene of many a foot race. This is George Wilson, one of a breed of local professionals known as 'pedestrians'. Rather than race against each other, the early 'peds' raced against the clock. In 1822 an estimated 40,000 crowd gathered on the Moor to see the 56 year old Wilson walk 90 miles around a half mile circuit in 24 hours. Despite rain and sleet he managed it with ten minutes to spare.

Town Moor has had many uses over the centuries, but might equally be described as the cradle of Newcastle sport.

No fewer than 29 individual sports and forms of recreation have been recorded on its wide open spaces since the 18th century.

These range from the most common, such as football, rugby, cricket, hockey, golf and running, to some of the more unlikely, such as skiing and wrestling.

Several sports have drawn massive crowds to the Moor, among them horse racing, rabbit coursing, potshare bowling and professional foot races (*see left*).

One of the earliest sports recorded on the Moor was archery, when in August 1792 the Bowmen of Chevy Chase held the first annual competition to win a silver quiver. This, however, was a sport only for the elite. One of its patrons, for example, was the Duke of Northumberland.

The aristocracy were also great patrons of horse racing. Originally racing took place on Killingworth Moor, but from 1721 onwards the Town Moor was favoured.

Race weeks, initially held at Whitsun, then in June, saw the Moor invaded by tens of thousands of pleasure seekers, gamblers and showmen. Horse racing formed only part of the fare. There were also boxing booths, cock fights, foot races and quoits matches.

Such was the popularity of Race Week that in his 1894 *History of Newcastle-on-Tyne*, RJ Charleton described it as 'the occasion of the great saturnalia of the North of England'. And although the races would move to High Gosforth Park in 1882, the Race Week gatherings on the Moor would evolve into the Hoppings Temperance Festival, an annual fair that has continued ever since.

The early Hoppings included a wide range of sports. In 1892 three baseball teams, named City of Newcastle, Wallsend and Elswick, played in a national tournament organised by the North Terrace Hotel. The pub, still extant, was one of the most popular spots at the Hoppings. In 1896 Wallsend became national baseball champions, before interest tailed off in the early 20th century.

Boxing, meanwhile, remained a feature of the Hoppings until 1995.

But what of team games?

Cricket, we know, was played on the racecourse during the 1830s, before a superior field was laid out beside the newly opened Northumberland Baths in 1839 (as shown on the inside front cover).

In 1848 a club called the Early Risers met on the Town Moor every fine morning at six o'clock to hear a lecture, play a little cricket, quoits or football, before repairing to a nearby inn for breakfast.

From the mid 1870s a number of fields by Burdon Terrace (north of what is now Brandling Park) were rented out to rugby, cricket and (later) football teams. In 1881, however, the poor quality of the turf persuaded a deputation from the Northumberland County Rugby Union to ask that a section of the Moor that had been set aside for recreation (under the 1870 Town Moor Improvement Act) be enclosed specifically for team games. The deputation was said to represent 750 players, of whom 250 lived in Newcastle and a further 120 worked in the city. »

▲ Viewed from the north west in 2008, the **Town Moor** covers an expanse of nearly 960 acres.

Although not the largest stretch of urban green space in Britain – Richmond Park (London), Sutton Park (Birmingham) and Pollok Park (Glasgow) are greater in area – the Town Moor is the largest to be located so close to a city centre. It is, for example, more than double the size of London's Hyde Park.

Although it lies within the definition of a common under the Commons Registration Act, Town Moor is technically not a common.

In 1213 the original Moor, much smaller than today, was part of land granted to the town by King John.

But the rights to its 'herbage' (that is the grazing of livestock) were retained by the **Freemen of the City**, a body whose origins pre-date the Conquest and which is now run as a charity.

Since the Moor was sold to the Town Council in 1885, for the sum of £2,200, the Freemen and the Council have managed it jointly, a relationship most recently defined under the 1988 Town Moor Act.

The Moor is split into several parts. Seen top left is the **Town Moor**, where the racecourse lay, with **Exhibition Park** in its south east corner. Since 1882 this area, next to the Great North Road, has hosted the annual **Hoppings** fair.

To the right of this, the expanse seen in the foreground is **Nuns Moor**, part of which is occupied by a golf course, the home of the **Newcastle United Golf Club**.

Beyond this, closest to the city centre lies **Castle Leazes**, a corner of which is occupied by **Newcastle United** (no relation to the golf club), whose **St James' Park** stadium is the prominent white block just visible in the middle distance.

Being on moorland, Newcastle United are tenants of the Council, with part of their rent going to the Freemen for the general upkeep of the Moor as a whole – a symbiotic, if not always easy relationship that is unique in senior British football.

Also on the south side is **Hunter's Moor**, part of which is occupied by the former Fenham Barracks, while not seen in this view are two smaller areas to the north of the Town Moor, known as **Dukes Moor** and **Little Moor**.

Over the centuries the usage of all these parts has varied under the 'intake system'. This allows the Freemen to designate up to 100 acres to be used for purposes other than grazing, on a lease no longer than 99 years.

Intakes can then be returned to grazing, as happened with Hunter's Moor, which until the 1980s served the barracks and Newcastle United as a sports and training ground.

>> The outcome was the creation of a recreation ground in part of what was later renamed Exhibition Park.

That said, some of the original pitches opposite Burdon Terrace, now much improved, are still in use today, by local schools.

Elsewhere, on Castle Leazes, a pasture set aside for football in 1880 evolved into the largest sporting venue of all on Town Moor land, St James' Park, while in 1891 a group of golfers similarly persuaded the Town Council to allocate a designated area to the west of the new recreation ground.

Since then, only Newcastle United FC and Brandling Park Bowling Club have remained on their original grounds.

In contrast, by 1914 most of the cricket and rugby clubs, and two of the original golf clubs had moved out to the suburbs; frustrated by overcrowding, by potshare bowlers (see right), by a sometimes hostile public (who wished to enjoy the meadows without being hit by a ball), or by the Freemen, wishing for their cattle to graze in peace. Understandably, cattle droppings were also an issue.

But new sports have arrived too. As shown right, croquet players have recently taken over two former bowling greens. Basketball at Leazes Park, jogging and cycling are also now commonly enjoyed.

Perhaps the greatest change to the character of the Moor has been the widening of the surrounding roads. It was road developments on the southern edge, for example, that forced the last remaining golfers to move west in 1973.

On the other hand, that same road provides an ideal starting point for the largest sporting gathering now seen on the modern Moor, the Great North Run, inaugurated in 1981.

▲ 'Ware the Bool' was the cry on Town Moor as two men shaped up to see who could hurl a small bowl the furthest distance along a roped off course known as 'the mile' (although it was said to have measured only 875 yards).

This was the popular miners' sport of **potshare bowling.**

Top potshare bowlers could cover 100 yards in a single throw of a 15 ounce bowl. Underarm was preferred, as this made the bowl skim across the turf and therefore travel longer distances.

Two theories exist as to the origin of the name; that the bowls were originally made from pot sherds, or more likely, that the winner took a share of the stake money, or 'pot'.

Potshare bowling is recorded

across the Northumberland and Durham coalfields throughout the 19th and early 20th centuries.

But as the sport was gradually forced off roads by magistrates and discouraged by colliery owners, the Town Moor, with its wide open spaces, became a particular favourite for more important duels.

Several accounts mention how thousands of spectators would gather to watch and place bets on the best bowlers, with some matches taking days to resolve.

As a result there were efforts to ban it from the Moor in 1855, 1870, and 1880; in the latter case owing to incidences of 'most blasphemous language', and on other occasions after complaints from rival sportsmen on the Moor.

None succeeded though, largely because local businesses complained about the loss of trade.

Potshare's heyday was between 1870 and 1914, and although it carried on sporadically until the 1930s, as a working class sport organised primarily amongst miners and later by publicans, little tangible evidence of it has survived.

Certainly no action photographs have been traced, leaving us only with a few static portraits, such as this one from around 1920. Note that Robert Armstrong, the bowler on the right, is posing in his underwear, which is apparently how many men played the game.

1. **Newcastle United Golf Club** (1973-)
2. **Town Moor golf course** (1892-1973)
3. **Moor Court Squash Court** (1938-) / **Gosforth Squash Club** (1953-)
4. **Racecourse grandstand** (1800-81) / **Grandstand Roller Skating Rink** (1909-12)
5. **Turf Hotel** (c.1800-81)
6. **Racecourse** (1721-1881)
7. **Burdon Terrace playing fields** inc. Northern FC (c.1876-)
8. **Brandling Park Bowling Club** (1882-)
9. **Tyneside Croquet Club** (1994-)
10. **Newcastle Model Yacht Club** (1882-2007)/**pavilion** (1894-)
11. **North East Coast Exhibition stadium** (1929)
12. **Great North Run** starting line (1981-)
13. **City of Newcastle Golf Club** (1892-1907) and **Newcastle United Golf Club clubhouse** (1907-73)
14. **Newcastle University sports centre** (1984-)
15. **Hunter's Moor sports ground / Military Recreation Ground** (c.1960s - c.1980s)
16. **Nuns Moor Park quoits ground** (1930s)
17. **Brighton Rutherford Bowling Club** now used by **Tyneside Croquet Club** (see page 9)
18. **Benwell Cricket Club, Garrison Ground** (1963-97)
19. **Springbank Bowling Club, Leazes Park** (1984-)
20. **Black Bull public house** (1850s-1938, rebuilt 1938) (see page 146)
21. **St James' Park, Newcastle United** (1880-)
22. **St James's Hall** (1909-29) and **New St James's Hall** (1930-68) (see page 19)
23. **West Walls bowling green** off Bath Lane (1827-97)

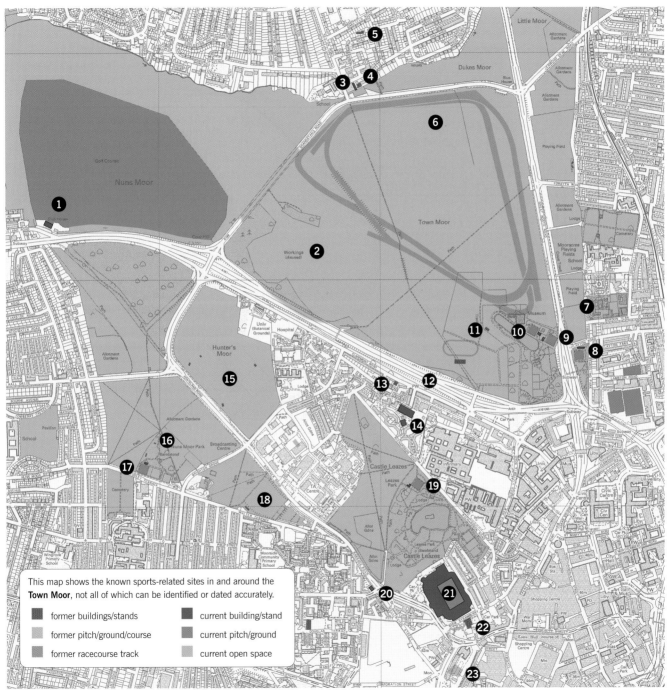

This map shows the known sports-related sites in and around the **Town Moor**, not all of which can be identified or dated accurately.

- former buildings/stands
- former pitch/ground/course
- former racecourse track
- current building/stand
- current pitch/ground
- current open space

Held in the collection of the Robinson Library at Newcastle University, this handbill from July 6–10 1829 dates from shortly after the **Town Moor racecourse** had been improved.

Seven years earlier, in order to ease a sharp turn followed by an uphill climb on the west side of the course, a cutting was excavated to create a gentler turn into a more level straight, heading south towards the town.

This resulted in a course of one mile, six furlongs and 132 yards, with the horses running in an anti-clockwise direction towards the finish on the north side, just east of where Grandstand Road now meets Kenton Road.

For those readers able to make out the small print it will be seen that the most valuable and also the longest race on the card was His Majesty's Plate, worth 100 guineas and run along four miles.

Also of note is that four of the runners were sired by a horse owned by Ralph Riddell of Felton Park, north of Morpeth. Dr Syntax, or The Doctor, as he was commonly known, later also sired a filly called Beeswing, who won the Newcastle Gold Cup six times, the Ascot Gold Cup in 1842, and was hailed as the greatest mare in Britain.

Both stewards named on the handbill were of similar good stock.

Sir Edward Blackett was the sixth baronet and son of the late MP for Northumberland, while Charles John Brandling, the wealthy coal magnate, was himself a former MP. Brandling Park, on the east side of the Town Moor, was named after his family, whose seat was at Gosforth House, now known as Brandling House, the headquarters of the present day racecourse in High Gosforth Park (*see Chapter Three*).

From the collection of John Somerville and shown at its actual size, this racing fob – a form of entry token worn on a chain – was one of many issued to subscribers who paid 15 guineas towards the cost of the Town Moor grandstand in 1800, thereby gaining free entry in perpetuity. On the reverse can be seen the name of its owner, Sir Thomas Liddell, whose seat was at Ravensworth Castle and whose colliery at Killingworth was famous as the place where the engineer George Stephenson first developed safety lamps and steam power. Coincidentally or not, Killingworth was also where race meetings had been staged until 1794.

▲ This unsigned etching, dating from the early 19th century, shows the first permanent grandstand to have been erected on the **Town Moor racecourse**, in 1800.

It replaced an earlier timber stand, built in 1776 by the first Clerk of the Course, William Loftus.

Loftus appears to have been a typical entrepreneur of the Georgian era. Apart from his involvement in racing he also ran the nearby Turf Hotel, and may well have operated coach services in the area too. The name Wm Loftus also appears as Clerk of the Course on the 1829 handbill shown opposite, although given the date that could well have been his son.

The structure seen above – after which Grandstand Road was to be later named (*below*) – was also typical of the period.

Built by subscription and described as being 'as convenient and commodious as could be wished', it was in effect a standard two storey building with balconies on the first floor and on the roof top. It also served as a hotel.

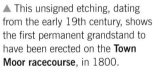

For the majority of racegoers, however, the facilities were of a more basic nature. In fact in June 1812 a temporary stand belonging to the White Hart Inn collapsed, causing serious injury to 40 people.

Overcrowding became an even greater issue following the introduction of the annual Northumberland Plate meeting in 1833. On these occasions, the infield of the largely unfenced course – to which entry was free of charge, mostly from the south, or town end – became a sea of tents, marquees and temporary wooden stands. Naturally the patrons of these areas were kept well clear of the grandstand.

GRAND STAND
TOWN MOOR
NEWCASTLE ON TYNE
Published by
W. RATCLIFFE JUNR
in aid of Charity.

▲ This Edwardian postcard shows the **Town Moor racecourse** as it was in about 1881, shortly before it closed after 160 years of racing.

In the centre is the grandstand, which had been rebuilt after a fire in 1844, as can be seen, with a raised and raked viewing area on its roof and a canopy added to the first floor balcony.

To its left, the smaller stand dated from 1867.

Its architect was William Parnell, who in the same year also designed the Tyne Theatre and Opera House on Westgate, Newcastle, a building that still operates today and is Grade I listed.

The small white tent seen to the side of Parnell's elegant stand (*right*) served as a ticket office for punters wishing to take a seat on its upper tier.

After the Town Moor racecourse closed, the stand was re-erected at High Gosforth Park, where it remained in use until the Second World War (*see Chapter Three*).

Meanwhile the main grandstand and its neighbouring stables were converted for use as the Bishop Chadwick Memorial School, an industrial school for boys.

This operated until 1905, after which the grandstand was finally demolished in 1909.

Grand Stand Skating Rink, Town Moor, N. C on Tyne.

◀ Straddling the site of the Town Moor grandstand and that of the former stables' courtyard next door, this was the **Grand Stand Skating Rink**, a 300 feet long corrugated iron building, designed to capitalise on the latest fad to have struck Edwardian Britain.

In fact there had been an earlier outbreak of what was dubbed 'rincomania' during the 1870s. But improvements made to the design of skates and to the construction of rink floors, now made from maple rather than asphalt, had given roller skating a new lease of life.

Opened in November 1909, the Grand Stand roller rink was one of several in the north east. But like most of them it was also short lived and in 1913 the building was bought by Armstrong Whitworths of Elswick and converted into an aircraft factory. Dukes Moor, immediately to the east, served as its airfield.

After the First World War, aircraft production gave way to the manufacture of motor cars, until the building finally closed in 1920.

In its place arose a quite different edifice. Opened in 1938 and designed by a Jesmond architect, Clarance Solomon, this was a splendid Art Deco block of flats, suitably named **Moor Court**.

Normally *Played in Britain* would not concern itself with residential buildings, but Moor Court was somewhat innovative in that for the benefit of its residents it had an adjoining block of twelve garages, described on the plans as 'motor houses', above which was built a squash court.

Squash was another sport that had become a fad in Britain. Derived from the game of rackets – played in Newcastle on a court in College Street (*see page 16*) – it caught on during the 1930s, and led to the construction of around 60 courts attached to hotels.

Both the squash court annexe and Moor Court are locally listed, while in 1953 the courts became the home of the newly formed **Gosforth Squash Club** (*left*).

The cosy bar of this club is actually a perfect place to look southwards across the Town Moor and gain an idea of what the panoramic view must have been like from the top of the old grandstand. Look hard and one can almost discern some earthwork traces of the racecourse.

Meanwhile, to the immediate west of Moor Court, on the junction of Grandstand Road and Kenton Road, there are still some surviving elements of the racecourse's old stable block. In 1926 these were taken over by Lawsons, the sweet manufacturers. Since then they have been converted into a garage, serving the needs of today's horseless carriages.

▲ Watched by fellow members of the newly formed **City of Newcastle Golf Club**, club president John William Pease tees off to mark the official opening of the **Town Moor golf course** on September 21 1892, before the party proceeded to enjoy a celebratory banquet in the clubhouse on Claremont Road.

This clubhouse was, and remains, a most unusual building.

Called **Chimney Mill** and dating from 1782, it had been designed by the engineer John Smeaton as Britain's first ever five-sailed smock mill, with its sails mounted on an octagonal rotating tower on the roof. Converting the mill into a clubhouse and adding a rooftop observation gallery had cost the club the then considerable sum of £1,500, an indicator of the social status of its founding members.

Pease, for example, was a well known Quaker and banker.

Golf had first been played on the Town Moor informally a decade earlier after the Council had laid out a recreation ground, subsequently renamed Exhibition Park (*see opposite*), in 1881. But cricketers and footballers had crowded them

out, and so in 1891 a group of gentlemen golfers petitioned the Freemen and the City Council to provide an alternative area.

Despite objections from members of the public who warned of the danger of flying golf balls, the petition proved successful, and so in October 1891 the City of Newcastle Golf Club came into being. Paying an annual rent of ten guineas for the site (*see page 29*), the club called in one of the leading course designers of the era, Tom Morris Snr of St Andrew's (himself a four times Open winner).

The result was an 18 hole course of over 6,000 yards, which Morris declared 'could become one of the best inland courses in England'.

But its promise was not fulfilled, and several members quickly grew restless. Not only did the greens have to be fenced in order to keep out the cattle which grazed the Moor, but the gentlemen members had to share the course with members of an artisan club, set up in June 1892 and known as the **Newcastle United Workmen's Golf Club**. (Interestingly, the football club on the other side of the Moor

did not adopt the name Newcastle United until December 1892.)

Unhappy at having to share the course, not only with other golfers and the cattle, but also with potshare bowlers, in 1898 130 members of the City of Newcastle club broke away to set up the Northumberland Golf Club (*see page 58*), followed in 1907 by the remainder, who decamped to form the Gosforth Golf Club (*page 60*).

Meanwhile the Newcastle United Golf Club bought the clubhouse for a token £13, and remained there until road developments during the early 1970s split the clubhouse from the course.

A new Newcastle United course was then laid out on Nuns Moor, to the immediate west, where it has remained since 1973.

The sails and fantail of the old Chimney Mill on Claremont Road may have been removed (between the wars), while the last golfing occupants moved on in 1973. But the sign above the door, added in 1892, survives, and today the Grade II listed building serves as a dental practice.

▲ The south east corner of the Town Moor, known as **Exhibition Park**, has hosted two exhibitions; the Royal Jubilee Mining, Engineering and Industrial Exhibition in 1887, and, as shown here, the **North East Coast Exhibition of Industry, Science and Art**, which drew over 4.3 million visitors in 1929.

Although the main aim of this exhibition was to promote trade and boost confidence at a time of economic hardship, sport played a role, being staged in a temporary stadium, seen at the top edge of the exhibition site by the fun fair.

Reportedly holding 20-30,000 spectators with a 2,000 seat stand on the south west side, the stadium hosted a variety of events, including a Highland Games and sheepdog trials. Traces of its turf banking remained visible until the 1990s.

Of the exhibition buildings only two survive, the 1887 bandstand and the 1929 Palace of Arts (just out of view, north of the lake).

Designed by Stanley Milburn of architects W & TR Milburn, in recent years the Palace has housed a museum of military vehicles.

The lake itself was until 2007 used by a model yacht club (*see page 163*), whose 1894 clubhouse still stands. The park's sports facilities include the tennis courts seen here in the centre, and, east of the lake, two bowling greens, one of which has been used since 1994 by the Tyneside Croquet Club.

As noted opposite, the area of the Town Moor seen beyond the exhibition grounds was, until 1973, the Newcastle United golf course.

▶ Almost wherever one goes on the **Town Moor** – from the level meadows of Exhibition Park to the rugged grassland of the former racecourse (*right*), from Dukes Moor in the north to the tree-lined lakeside of **Leazes Park** in the south (*below*) – there is no escaping the looming bulk of **St James' Park**, the home of football in Newcastle since 1880.

For years barely discernible above the hedgerows and treetops, then from 1958 onwards marked out on the skyline by its four 190 foot tall floodlight pylons, today the stadium's towering roof structures dominate the horizon. Even from as far afield as Gosforth Park, or the Rising Sun Country Park in Wallsend, or from across the Tyne in Dunston or Whickham, the stadium is a constant visual presence.

Moreover, because the majority of fans attending St James' Park approach it from the city centre or via the main roads, these views of the stadium – stunning to some, incongruous to others – are known only to those for whom the Moor remains a glorious haven.

A mixed bunch they are too.

Joggers and dog walkers (this writer included) are perhaps the most numerous. At other times they include cyclists commuting to and from the city, and, when conditions permit, model aeroplane enthusiasts and even skiers and sledgers. In June, during Race Week (when the Northumberland Plate is staged at Gosforth Park), the eastern edge of the Moor is transformed by the massive fair known as the Hoppings.

Yet none of this appears to unsettle the Moor's summertime residents, 500-600 or so cattle whose right to 'herbage' is said to have been established prior to the Norman Conquest.

▲ It might seem odd in a city with so much open space on its doorstep that by the mid 19th century demand for 'ready access to some open ground for the purpose of health and recreation' should result in a petition signed by 3,000 people.

Yet over the previous half century Newcastle's population had more than tripled, to nearly 90,000, while in 1853, in the third outbreak since 1832, a cholera epidemic killed over 1,500 people.

It was a similar tale across urban Britain, and one which gave rise to a new movement, for the creation of public parks.

The earliest parks, such as Birkenhead Park, opened in 1847, made little or no provision for sport. But by the time plans were finally approved to lay out a park on a part of the Town Moor known as Castle Leazes, in the early 1870s, sporting provision was very much to the fore. Indeed plans drawn up in 1871 were rejected largely because they ignored this need. Hence, the Council commissioned a new design from John Laing, a former steward to Lord Armstrong.

Opened in December 1873, **Leazes Park** – Newcastle's first ever public park – had a boating lake that in winter could be used for skating, and allowed space for the eventual creation of a croquet lawn and bowling green.

Shortly after, work started on laying out another part of the Town Moor as a recreation ground that, opened in 1881, would become popular for cricket and football and would later be named Exhibition Park (*see page 35*).

Thus began a new era in the city of publicly funded and publicly accessible sporting facilities.

In Leazes Park the first bowling green, still in use today by the **Springbank Bowling Club**, was ready by 1887. Croquet proved less popular, however, and by 1894 the lawn was reconfigured as a second bowling green. A pavilion was built alongside, being replaced between the wars by the present **Springbank Pavilion** (*right*), which also serves the **Leazes Park Angling Association**.

Meanwhile, in 1892 an extra portion of land was added to the park on Richardson Road. On this section a second lake was created, for ice skating. This would later be infilled and replaced by

six tennis courts and, as part of a £5m refurbishment part funded by the National Lottery in 2001, a basketball court (*above top*).

Since 2006 Leazes Park has also become the venue of an annual cycling event known as The Leazes Criteriums, raced around a mile circuit that threads its way through the very same paths and walkways laid down by John Laing in 1873.

▶ Before we turn our attention to the final area of sporting life on the Town Moor, it is worth noting from this map just how much of the land surrounding the Moor was undeveloped in 1810, and then compare it with the map on page 29 to illustrate how much of the area to the south, east and west of **Castle Leazes** has been swallowed up by development since.

It is in this context that we may appreciate how significant have been the efforts of the Freemen to preserve the rest of the Town Moor up till the present day.

Seen in the top right corner is the southern part of the racecourse.

Almost in the centre are two mills, one of them being the Chimney Mill that would later become the golf clubhouse.

On the western edge, in the centre, are the Fenham Barracks (after which Barrack Road is named), built in 1806 in the lead up to the Napoleonic Wars. Parts of the barracks still stand, as do parts of the building north east of it, the lunatic asylum, which dates from 1751 and is now private housing on Belle Grove West.

On the southern edge is Gallowgate, which as its name suggests, led to an area just south of the barracks where there was a set of gallows. Hundreds of felons met their end on this spot, some watched by crowds of 20,000 or more. The last person hanged there was a 35 year old wife murderer, Mark Sherwood, in August 1844.

The area that many in the crowd would have crossed in order to witness this gruesome spectacle lay in the tongue of Castle Leazes bordered in yellow, east of Spring Gardens and north of Gallowgate.

In 1880, this plot was to become the magnet for yet more mass gatherings...

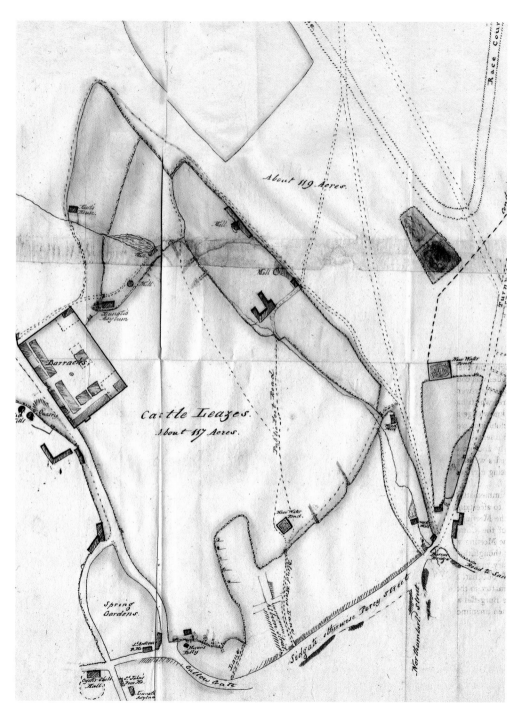

▶ There are several reasons why **St James' Park** is unique. But perhaps the most important one is that the building seen in this 1841 engraving is its neighbour.

This is **Leazes Terrace**, designed by Thomas Oliver for the influential builder-developer Richard Grainger, and completed in 1834, at a time when Grainger was engaged in the wholesale remodelling of the city centre. Offering unhindered views over Castle Leazes, Pevsner described it as 'probably the grandest terrace on Tyneside'.

Half a century after the scene shown here it was still an exclusive address, albeit with a public park to its north, and, to its west, a 'fine tract of pasture land' that, according to a local guidebook, was 'much frequented by football clubs and cricketers' and afforded 'ample scope for the juvenile population for games and pastimes'.

What the guidebook did not mention was that the pitch sloped 18 feet from north to south.

Newcastle United historian Paul Joannou, to whom we are indebted (*see Links*), records that the first club to lease this sloping pasture were **Newcastle Rangers**, who first played there on October 16 1880.

They stayed only two years, and there would no further tenant until May 1886, when a club called **West End FC** moved in, renting the site from a Leazes Terrace resident, William Neasham (sometimes also given as Nesham), who, being a keen sportsman, had himself leased the land from the Town Council.

For the next six years West End vied for supremacy with another Newcastle club, **East End FC**. On a few occasions up to 6,000 fans squeezed in to what was still a rudimentary enclosure. Quite what Neasham's neighbours thought can only be imagined.

LEAZES TERRACE

Then in 1892 West End fell into debt, paving the way for East End to take over the lease that summer.

The new tenants were warned that they would never be able to buy the site, or build any stands without permission. But they signed up all the same, and in December that year adopted the name **Newcastle United**, just like the golf club across the moor.

Seen above is Lord Beresford, about to kick off a United v. Sunderland match in 1904.

Note the residents looking down from St James' Terrace (the houses on the right), and the proximity of Leazes Terrace itself. Both these historic buildings are extant.

Truly, there has never been a setting for a football ground quite like this one.

▲ Given the drawbacks of the site it seems odd that United kept faith with **St James' Park**, and that the Freemen allowed them to stay.

For the players, the pitch was not just sloping but bumpy and often muddy. For the fans there were precious few facilities, not even urinals on the Leazes Terrace side, and, as attendances shot up to 30,000 or so, not enough room either. Twice during United's first decade there were near disasters caused by overcrowding.

Meanwhile the local residents grew so fed up with what they described as the 'intolerable nuisance' of match days that in 1898 they lobbied the council to evict United on the grounds that their tenancy breached the laws governing use of Town Moor land.

But with councillors now seeing how popular United had become, football fever won out, thus paving the way for limited development to commence.

This postcard from c.1904 shows the first stand to have been built on the Barrack Road side.

Interestingly, for some years United historians had dismissed the artist's portrayal as a work of fancy. But in 2005 a clip from the Mitchell & Kenyon film archive, showing a match in 1901, suggested that the postcard was actually not far off the mark. Then a hitherto unknown photograph also turned up and proved that the stand did indeed look like this.

Not for long though. After only half a dozen years it was demolished in 1905.

▲ This hand tinted postcard shows **St James' Park** as it looked following a £16,000 rebuilding programme in 1905, the year that United won the first of three League titles recorded during the Edwardian period.

Between 1905 and 1911 they also reached five FA Cup Finals.

If there had been any doubts before about United's viability, or of the need for the city to have a modern stadium, this run of success sealed the issue. Not only were United able to secure a further seven year lease from the Freemen, but they also negotiated the rental of an extra four acres.

Crucially, this allowed the club to shift the pitch westwards, thereby adding more standing room on the Leazes Terrace side.

On the left is the new Main Stand, which held 4,655 seats and had a distinctive rooftop press box under an arched central gable. It was clad entirely in corrugated iron.

Overseeing the works was a Scottish engineer, Alexander Blair, who at the same time was working on the newly built Hampden Park in Glasgow, a ground that by 1910 would become the largest in the world, with a capacity of 120,000.

The new St James' Park was only half that size, but that was still double its pre 1905 limit.

Some of Blair's designs were flawed. For example he installed wire rope barriers instead of rigid ones, while access routes within the stand were poorly planned.

As can be seen, the pitch still needed improvement too.

Thanks to Paul Joannou and other collectors, Newcastle United have a superb archive and collection of historic artefacts. Unfortunately the club museum at St James' Park was closed in 2008. But an interesting selection of items can still be viewed in an atrium area in the Milburn Stand, along with a collection of memorabilia loaned by the late Sir Bobby Robson.

▲ These aerial views from 1929 and 1968 show how little **St James' Park** changed during the interim, especially compared with other leading grounds in Britain.

But then, this was no typical ground. Firstly, there was the presence of Leazes Terrace, a major obstacle to development.

Secondly, in 1922 United tried and failed to buy the freehold, following objections not from the Freemen, who had agreed to sell, but from Newcastle Corporation.

Some improvements were made.

Under the direction of another Scottish engineer, the specialist ground designer Archibald Leitch (whom we will encounter later at Sunderland), the terraces were upgraded, the Main Stand modernised and, in 1929, a basic roof built over the Leazes Park end.

But this still left some 48,000 standing spaces uncovered, and fewer than 5,000 seats overall.

Yet Leitch's other proposals for covering the east terrace and

building a double decker stand at the Gallowgate End both failed to get approval from the Corporation.

During the 1950s the only major addition was the installation of floodlights, firstly on wooden poles, then in 1958 on four towering pylons in each corner, said to be the tallest in Britain.

That same year United again put forward proposals for a stand,

but after two years of wrangling these too were refused. This time, however, as the local politician T Dan Smith stated, it was not the height of the stand but its lack of aesthetic merit. He called United's designs 'practically historic'.

Not just a football ground, St James' Park now became a virtual battle ground, between the club and its landlords.

▲ In the immediate post war period, when crowds at football and indeed at most other sporting events reached record levels, **Newcastle United** were the best supported club in the Football League for three seasons running, their highest average being over 56,000 in season 1947–48, when this photograph was taken.

But the all time record gate at St James' Park for a single match was even higher: 68,386 attending a League match v. Chelsea in 1930.

In other words, the 'Toon Army', as the club's followers have become known in recent years, is no new phenomenon.

Another name for United is the Magpies, adopted after they changed their strip from red and white to black and white in 1894.

▶ Unveiled in November 1967, this model for a completely new 63,000 capacity **St James' Park** was designed by the engineers Ove Arup. The idea was that United's administration would be based in a new office block on Strawberry Place, which itself would become an urban motorway, while the new West Stand would house a multi-sport centre for shared use with the University of Newcastle.

Certainly a bold plan, and at an estimated £2.6m, a costly one too. But there was one major drawback.

The plan had been drawn up by the City Council and the University without involving Newcastle United.

How this came about is a long tale. But in brief, in 1962 St James' had been selected by the FA as a venue for the 1966 World Cup, providing an extra stand and other facilities were built. However the Council would only sanction these works if United agreed to become more accountable to the public. For their part, the club refused to invest in a site for which they had only a short lease.

At its root, the impasse boiled down to a stand off between the local Labour supremo T Dan Smith and the Conservative chairman of United, William McKeag.

Middlesbrough were the beneficiaries of this spat, as they got to stage the World Cup. An angry United, meanwhile, identified a site by Gosforth Park (*see Chapter Three*) which had room for a stadium but even better, lay outside the City Council's jurisdiction.

Of course neither the Gosforth nor the Ove Arup schemes ever left the drawing board. Instead, perhaps nervous of any backlash should the football club leave town, in 1971 the Council gave United what they had been seeking for decades, a 99 year lease.

Seen below is the result of this reconciliation, the first major piece of construction to have been carried out at the ground since 1929.

Opened in 1973 (shortly after T Dan Smith had been arrested on corruption charges) the £420,000 **East Stand** was designed by a local practice, Faulkner Brown Hendy Watkinson Stonor (now known as FaulknerBrowns).

Today the stand looks modest; a simple, reinforced concrete and steel cantilevered stand with a terrace in front. But for Toon fans in 1973 it appeared to be ultra modern.

Moreover, its design had at last satisfied the planners of its credentials as a worthy neighbour for the Grade I listed Leazes Terrace. Now that was progress.

▶ Sixteen years after the opening of the East Stand, this was the scene at **St James' Park** in 1989 – not quite what Faulkner Brown had intended, nor indeed their clients.

Instead, the new East Stand was to have been the first phase of a four sided redevelopment.

But the 1970s and 1980s were trying times in English football, and in the wider economy too.

First came the Safety of Sports Grounds Act, passed in response to the 1971 Ibrox disaster. Then building prices rocketed following the fuel crisis of 1973 and a series of industrial disputes.

Just to meet the immediate requirements of the new safety legislation United had to spend £300,000, including reinforcement of all the crush barriers.

Most other clubs preferred to use traditional steel to perform this task. But United's newly concreted barriers (*right*) did at least give the Gallowgate End a distinct, almost brutalistic character.

But the consquences of all this expenditure were fairly brutal too.

Following further delays caused by yet more arguments with the planners, in 1978 United took down the old and much lamented roof over the north terrace, built a new terrace, with behind it the foundations for a new North Stand, to match up with the East Stand.

Or at least that was the plan.

Except that in only seven years the costs had risen from an estimated £1 million for the complete four sided redevelopment to £1.8 milion for just one stand.

Add to this relegation to the Second Division in 1978 and ever mounting debts and it appeared that once again St James' Park was destined to remain a half-finished ground for many years to come.

But then came a further blow.

Following another disaster, at Valley Parade in Bradford, in 1985, the old Main Stand at St James' Park was finally condemned.

In debt, and in a hurry, United forsook the Faulkner Brown masterplan and instead opted for a larger main stand supposedly using cheaper construction methods.

Opened in early 1988 and named after former United hero 'Wor Jackie' Milburn, the stand (*top, on the left*) was designed and built by Traer Clark Associates and Anglian Construction.

But far from being a cheap option it cost £5.5 million for only 6,600 seats, many of which were not sheltered by its shallow roof.

Too much, too little, the stand turned out to be one of the final acts of the old United regime.

Concrete and cobbles – two United fans inspect the rear of the new East Stand in 1973. Despite its bulk the architects' use of rippled concrete allowed it to blend in surprisingly well within its historic context.

St James' Park in 1995. This was the ultra-stylish concourse of the Sir John Hall Stand (*right*) – at that time unlike any football stand interior seen in Britain.

◀ If the Toon Army had grown understandably tired and cynical with all the many plans and promises they had seen and heard over the previous three decades, surely none of them could ever have imagined just how rapidly and comprehensively the new owners of **Newcastle United** – under the leadership of the Gateshead MetroCentre developer Sir John Hall – would transform **St James' Park** during the 1990s, not just once, but twice.

Or that after the embarrassment of missing out on the 1966 World Cup, St James' Park would be chosen to host three matches in the 1996 European Championships (matches that involved France, Romania and Bulgaria).

This aerial view from the south, with **Leazes Park** and the edge of the **Town Moor** in the distance, was taken following the first phase of the redevelopment, which took from March 1993 to August 1995 and cost £23.5 million, roughly half of which Hall himself funded.

Only two elements of the old ground were retained.

On the right the exposed roof steelwork belongs to the 1973 **East Stand**. The Grade I listed Leazes Terrace is to its right.

On the left, the ridged roof of the 1988 **Milburn Stand** can also be discerned, with an extension at the front to provide the extra cover that the original roof lacked.

In two respects the new St James' Park could be said to have been 'Taylor-made'.

Firstly, the architects responsible were a Gateshead firm called Taylor Tulip & Hunter (later to work for Sunderland, the Newcastle Falcons and most recently Gateshead FC). Also involved were the structural engineers Hutter, Jennings & Titchmarsh, and the contractors Ballast Wiltshier (who had worked on the MetroCentre, and whose Dutch parent, Ballast Nedam had recently completed the pioneering Amsterdam Arena).

In engineering terms the design team's greatest challenge was to build the South Stand up from the sloping ground at the Gallowgate End, and to marry up the corners with the existing side stands.

From the air these joins can be clearly seen. From inside, however, the roof appeared seamless.

But just as important was the style of architecture, inside and out.

Taylor Tulip & Hunter's choice of soft, sand coloured blockwork, combined with grey steel cladding and white tubular steel, created an almost Zen-like cool; not at all like the usual football stadium style of bright colours and corrugated metal (or 'crinkly tin' to its detractors).

Moreover, the interiors were a revelation (*see lower left*).

Instead of the usual cheap breeze blocks and clunky, industrial fixtures and fittings that so many clubs were content with for general fans' areas, the concourses in the Gallowgate and Sir John Hall stands were more like contemporary art centres or university buildings, thereby helping to set entirely new standards for what ordinary fans might expect.

Another aspect of the redevelopment that was 'Taylor made' concerned the spectator accommodation itself.

Three years before work started on the scheme, the publication of the Taylor Report kick-started a revolution in stadium design and management, simply by requiring that all terraces be phased out in the top two divisions by 1994.

Coincidentally, the report's author, Lord Justice Taylor, had been born on Westgate in the centre of Newcastle and had watched many a game at St James' Park in his youth.

Because one seat takes up roughly twice the space needed for two people standing on a terrace, the Taylor Report effectively meant that football grounds needed to double in bulk, simply to retain their existing capacities.

At St James' Park there was no going higher on the east side, because of Leazes Terrace, and no economic way (at that time) of enlarging the 1988 Milburn Stand, because it was a post-tensioned structure in which the roof and stand base were interdependent, and therefore expensive to extend.

On the eve of the Taylor Report St James' capacity had been around 37,703, of which 11,413 had been seats. When the 1993–95 redevelopment was complete, the all-seated total was 36,610.

When Hall first joined the board in 1990, Newcastle's average gate was around 21,500. By 1995, United were back in the top division, and already the new look stadium was too small. In fact there was now a waiting list of 20,000 names for season tickets.

Over the next few years 14 sites for a new stadium were considered, including one in Gateshead.

But the one that the club and the Council's ruling Labour group favoured, as did some of the Freemen, was a site only a few hundred yards north of St James'.

What happened next is a book in itself. United drew up plans for a 70,000 seat stadium on the Castle Leazes part of the Town Moor.

The southern half of the site of St James', meanwhile, was to be used for a 12,500 seat indoor arena, and the land between the two facilities landscaped to form an extension of Leazes Park.

The plans were well presented and in many respects made good sense. After widespread debate and consultation they also won a great deal of support. But they provoked massive opposition too, led by the indefatigable Chairwoman of the Friends of Leazes Park, Doris Potter.

Facing the likelihood of a long and expensive public enquiry, and with no certainty of success, in November 1997 United finally admitted defeat.

From that moment on, there were only three ways the club could expand St James' – westwards, northwards and upwards.

St James' Park in 2000 – a stadium of two halves, after Doris Potter and her allies had made sure that United left the rest of Castle Leazes to grass.

St James' Park in 2000. The new L-shaped roof is cantilevered to a dizzying depth of 65.5m, while at 60m tall at its highest point it is 1m taller than the Tyne Bridge.

▲ To employ a football cliché, the modern day **St James' Park** is 'a stadium of two halves' – to some an unbalanced and awkward mismatch, to others a remarkable feat of engineering that makes the best of a challenging site.

Once **Newcastle United** gave up on the Castle Leazes proposal, work on extending the north and west sides of the ground with an additional tier and new roofs started in June 1998, being completed in August 2000.

Remarkably, the contractors and engineers responsible for this

second phase, Ballast Wiltshier and WSP respectively, managed to keep the rest of the stadium operative throughout the building programme, even if at times fans had to sit out in the rain.

As a result of the extensions, the capacity rose from 36,834 to 52,339 (making St James' the third largest club stadium in England).

To achieve this cost United a further £46 million, although included within that sum was the provision of 1,100 spaces in a multi-storey car park integrated within the Sir John Hall Stand,

vast areas of hospitality and conference facilities in the newly extended Milburn Stand (including the largest banqueting room north of Birmingham), a restaurant, 90 executive boxes, and a media centre. In that sense, this is now a building that serves as a stadium only part of the time, and is otherwise used for a wide range of other activities 365 days a year.

St James' Park divides opinions as much today as it did a century ago. But there can be no denying that compared with most other large scale stadiums, thanks to

the measured approach of the architects Taylor Tulip & Hunter, St James' stands out for having its appreciable bulk tempered by the subtle use of materials, finishes and understated colour schemes; predominantly grey cladding, white steelwork and sand-toned blockwork. It is, furthermore, refreshingly free of the garish branding that scars and cheapens so many of our other stadiums.

To understand why the stadium is what it is today, one must understand its unique context, and therefore its unique developmental

history. It is a history peppered with 'what ifs'. What if the club had been able to buy the freehold? What if they had moved to Gosforth Park, or to Castle Leazes? What if the Leazes Terrace had not been such a crucial factor? What if the club had not been rescued by Sir John Hall?

Of course if United were not such a hugely popular club, none of this might matter. But they are, and therefore St James' Park is a building that virtually everyone in Newcastle knows, and on which they all have an opinion.

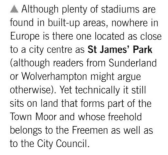

▲ Although plenty of stadiums are found in built-up areas, nowhere in Europe is there one located as close to a city centre as **St James' Park** (although readers from Sunderland or Wolverhampton might argue otherwise). Yet technically it still sits on land that forms part of the Town Moor and whose freehold belongs to the Freemen as well as to the City Council.

Even then, the stadium's reach, and that of United, extends well beyond its perimeter.

On the corner of Corporation Street and Bath Lane is Susanna Robinson's bronze sculpture of **'Wor Jackie' Milburn** (*top left*).

There is a second statue in Milburn's birthplace of Ashington and of course the West Stand at St James' is named after him too.

Also much loved was former manager **Bobby Robson** (*above left*) one of several Magpies who left their imprints in the floor at **St James Metro Station**, just south of the stadium (*above*).

Opened in 1982 on the site of St James' Hall boxing stadium (*see page 19*), the station is branded in United imagery and graphics to an extent seen at no other station

serving a football ground, not even Arsenal tube station in London.

On this page are views from around the stadium exterior. From **Leazes Terrace** (*top left*), it may be seen how the rippled concrete structure of Faulkner Brown's 1973 **East Stand** blends in subtly with the neighbouring Georgian terrace.

From the top of St Andrew's Street, looking through the Chinese Arch (*above*) the rear of the **Gallowgate Stand** looms above Strawberry Place, where on the corner is the **Strawberry Inn** (*top right*), a pub that was built in the mid 19th century to serve pleasure gardens in the vicinity and which as its sign suggests, has long been a meeting place for the Toon Army.

The big question is, can the stadium possibly grow any larger?

Very possibly. In April 2007 plans were announced to increase its capacity to 60,000, by extending the Gallowgate Stand.

Yet a month later new owners took over and as of 2010, the plans have not been aired since.

As ever, much depends on results on the pitch and the wider economy off it. But the St James' Park story is assuredly not over yet.

Chapter Three

Gosforth

Forming the core of Newcastle Racecourse is the Grade II* Gosforth House (now Brandling House), built for the colliery owner and Newcastle MP Charles Brandling in the mid 18th century. Since the estate's conversion into a racecourse in 1882 the house's west wing, dated 1757, has served as a hotel and bar, now called the Border Minstrel pub. Although greatly altered internally, the exterior, as shown opposite in 1895, remains relatively intact.

Sporting development in most British cities during the late 19th century was largely characterised by a flight to the suburbs; the principal factors being the loss of open space in inner city areas, combined with population growth.

In Newcastle, however, one of the major reasons for the spread of sporting facilities northwards, to Gosforth, was not so much a lack of space as the fact that the Town Moor, to which access was free for all, had become too popular.

Not only did this overuse bring conflict between sportsmen – not to mention non-sporting users wishing simply to enjoy the open space – but it also affected the quality of the turf.

So, for aspiring clubs seeking to improve their facilities and gain greater exclusivity, this meant leaving the Moor for pastures new.

That they headed to Gosforth was because, firstly, affordable land was available, in an area where two collieries, those at Coxlodge and Gosforth, were each reaching the end of their useful life in the 1880s.

One of several attractions introduced at High Gosforth Park was the exciting new sport of air racing. This image, from July 24 1911, shows part of the 40,000 crowd that paid to watch contestants in the *Daily Mail* £10,000 'Circuit of Britain Air Race' stop off en route from Harrogate to Edinburgh.

Secondly, the Great North Road offered convenient access, supplemented by the introduction of tram services to Gosforth in 1893, extending to the gates of High Gosforth Park by 1904.

Leading the shift northwards were Charles Perkins and Fife John Scott, members of Newcastle's Grand Stand Company, which promoted horse racing on the Town Moor. In 1880 they bought the 807 acre High Gosforth Park estate and shortly afterwards sold it on to the High Gosforth Park Company, set up to create a new racecourse and pleasure park where, at last, entry could be controlled.

Not everyone was happy, citing the loss of free admission and the extra distance from the city. Indeed, when the first races were held in 1882, the crowds were down. But they soon recovered, albeit changing subtly in character.

During the ensuing decades the Northumberland Golf Club formed at High Gosforth Park in

1898. Seven years later Gosforth Golf Club came into being, to be joined by the City of Newcastle Golf Club, who relocated from the Town Moor. Rugby appeared in 1912, on the site of what later became the County Ground and Gosforth greyhound stadium. Northern FC and Gosforth RFC settled in the area in 1937 and 1951 respectively.

But a 1939 proposal to build a substantial North East Ice Stadium, across the road from the dog track, was scuppered by the war. More recently, a late 1960s plan for Newcastle United to build a stadium just north of the racecourse also failed – an unusual case of a club staying on the Moor.

One significant change since then was Gosforth's absorption into Newcastle's political boundaries in 1974.

More recently, Gosforth RFC have left the area, and the County Ground and greyhound stadium has been replaced by a superstore.

▲ Nowadays a successful football team might expect a foreign holiday as an end-of-season bonus. In May 1895 **Sunderland**'s reward for winning their third League title in four seasons was a day out at **High Gosforth Park** racecourse and pleasure grounds.

The party left Sunderland in a pair of charabancs at 10.00am, lunched at Tynemouth before arriving at Gosforth Park to have two formal photographs taken by Charles Stabler of Sunderland.

This one, taken in front of Gosforth House's west wing – now the **Border Minstrel** pub (see *opposite*) – shows the entire party. The players then changed into their kit for a second photograph, in which the Championship trophy was proudly displayed.

There followed an afternoon of sports, including a 440 yards race, a sack race and an informal game of football. After a banquet in the hotel, the party rounded off the day by attending the theatre in Newcastle, where they gathered on stage to show off their trophy, receiving what was described, perhaps diplomatically, as a 'warm' reception. In fact the man chiefly responsible for assembling this famous 'team of all the talents', Heaton-born secretary-manager Tom Watson, had learnt his craft at both East End and West End football clubs in Newcastle.

Finally the party caught the train home, passing Watson's tobacconist shop opposite Monkwearmouth Station, and arriving around midnight.

This map shows sports-related sites in and around **Gosforth**, not all of which can be identified or dated accurately. Note: FC (Football Club), GC (Golf Club) RFC (Rugby Football Club).

1. **Northumberland GC** (1905-)
2. **High Gosforth Park Racecourse** (1882-)
3. **High Gosforth Park trotting track** (c.1885-1920s)
4. **Complete Football Centre** (2007-)
5. former **Squash Newcastle Club** (1972-87)
6. **Parklands GC,** formerly Wideopen GC (1971-)
7. site of **Scout Camp open air swimming pool** (1933-c.1970s) (*see page 188*)
8. probable site of **Northumberland GC** clubhouse (1898-1902)
9. probable site of **Northumberland GC** clubhouse (1902-5)
10. **Northern FC** (rugby), **McCracken Park** (1937-)
11. **Benson Park** (formerly Polwarth Park), **Garnett Bohemian FC** (1951-)
12. site of **Gosforth RFC, New Ground** (1955-89)
13. **City of Newcastle GC** (1907-)
14. **Newcastle City Cricket Club, Broadway West** (1985-)
15. **Red House Farm Junior FC** (2008-)
16. **Coxlodge Welfare Ground / Gosforth Empire Bowls Club** (1972-)
17. **Gosforth Pool** (1968-)
18. site of **Northumberland County rugby ground/County Athletic Ground/greyhound & speedway stadium** (1912-89) (*see page 115*)
19. **Gosforth GC** (1906-)
20. **Gosforth Garden Village Tennis Club** and **Bowls Club** (1928-)
21. **Hollywood Avenue pigeon crees** (*see page 154*)

▲ These early views of the racecourse at **Gosforth Park** show how a grandstand was grafted onto the south side of Gosforth House in time for the opening race on April 10 1882.

Built by John Waddell & Sons of Edinburgh (otherwise known for their work on railways, bridges and schools), the stand extended eastwards beyond the house

(*above*), although today only the western section, backing onto the house, survives.

The smaller detached stand (*top left*) had originally been designed by William Parnell for the Town Moor racecourse in 1867 (*see page 32*) and was re-erected at Gosforth Park at the rear of the house's west wing, where it remained in use until the Second World War.

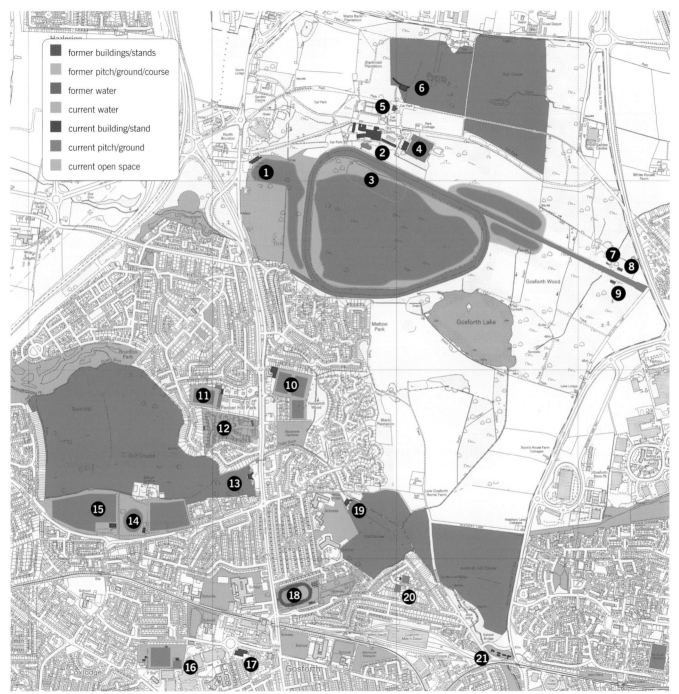

Legend:
- former buildings/stands
- former pitch/ground/course
- former water
- current water
- current building/stand
- current pitch/ground
- current open space

▲ Few artefacts associated with **High Gosforth Park**, as the racecourse was officially known, have survived. But small enamel **members' badges** do occasionally surface at various auctions.

Rarest of all are the early badges, bearing only lettering. This design, with a horse and rider, was used for most of the 20th century, the main differences being that the shape changed annually; for example, an elongated white diamond for 1930, a yellow oval in 1933, and a green and yellow rectangle in 1938. This 1960 badge is numbered on the rear, in contrast to modern badges which show their number on the face.

Forming the main entrance to Newcastle Racecourse is Gosforth, now Brandling House (*right*), designed by James Paine and built between 1755–64.

▲ Viewed from the south west, **Newcastle Racecourse** – as High Gosforth Park is now known – has courses for both flat racing and hurdles (or National Hunt). These are made up of an almost triangular circuit measuring one mile and six furlongs (c.2.8km), with a mile long straight extending eastwards.

Brandling House and its adjoining stands face the western end of the straight (*centre left*), with the **Parklands Golf Club** to the north (*top left*).

Also within the 812 acre park is the recently built **Complete**

Football Centre (to the immediate east of the racecourse stands) and, in the centre of the course, the **Northumberland Golf Club**, which moved here in 1898 and whose 1913 clubhouse (*lower left and page 60*) is on the western edge of the site, by the Great North Road.

But it was another sport that helped most to establish the park's viability in its early years. Within months of purchasing the site for £60,500, in March 1881 the High Gosforth Park Company opened the site for coursing – that is, the pursuit of hares by greyhounds

– within a specially enclosed 52 acre ground. Thirty kennels were built, and 200 hares brought in to add to the estate's existing natural stock. So popular was coursing, particularly amongst local gamblers, that for the first few years, before it ceased in around 1890, the dogs proved more profitable than the horses.

High Gosforth Park soon evolved into a typical pleasure ground, offering cycle racing (on a track laid in 1882), athletics, and skating and boating on the lake. Between c.1885 and the 1920s, trotting races were staged on a track laid in front of the main stand.

A fire at Brandling House badly damaged this stand in 1915, leading to the construction in c.1921 of a new brick-based stand (*right*) to the east of the house.

After another fire in 1962 two new stands, as seen above, were opened in April 1965, on either side of the surviving section of the main stand.

Newcastle thus appears typical amongst British racecourses; apparently unplanned, and yet characterful and thoroughly neat.

A red brick base set off by modern cladding makes for a pleasing combination in the racecourse's 1920s east stand (*left*).

▲ The combination of a Grade II* listed 18th century country house with an integral Grade II listed grandstand, complete with its original 1882 cast iron columns and awnings, is almost certainly unique in British racing.

For ticket holders, the Brandling Stand terrace provides splendid views across **High Gosforth Park**: of the parade ring (seen here and opposite, immediately in front of the stand), the main circuit of the racecourse, the golf course and, on a clear day, Newcastle city centre and St James' Park, five miles to the south.

In common with all big city racecourses, several of which, such as at Manchester and Birmingham, closed following reform of the betting laws in the early 1960s,

Newcastle Racecourse struggled to survive in the late 20th century, until in 1994 the estate was purchased by Northern Racing (currently owners of nine other British courses). Since then, corporate and exhibition facilities have been greatly enhanced at a cost of £11 million, while the number of race meetings has increased to some 30 per year.

Of these, the highlight is a three day festival in late June, known locally as Race Week, when the Town Moor Hoppings take place and the big race of the year, the **Northumberland Plate** – known traditionally as 'the Pitmen's Derby' – is staged.

Seen here is the early stage of the 2005 Plate, as the runners speed past the main stand.

First contested on the Town Moor course in 1833, switching to High Gosforth Park in 1882, the Plate is a flat race for three year olds and over, on a circuit just over two miles in length. The winning owner receives a silver salver specially commissioned each year, with the Percy lion, the emblem of the Duke of Northumberland, as its centrepiece.

The 2010 race, won by Overturn, was worth £175,000, and was watched by a capacity crowd of 25,000, with overall attendances during the festival totalling around 40,000.

According to one estimate, this yields at least £4 million for the local economy. Another more recent high point, for local fashion outlets in particular, is Ladies Day in July.

▲ Located by the main entrance to the racecourse is the clubhouse of **Northumberland Golf Club**.

Formed in 1898 as a golfer's haven away from the Town Moor, the club was first based in a wooden hut on the north side of the straight mile. This was replaced in 1902 by a prefabricated pavilion, supplied by Boulton & Paul of Norwich, on the south side of the straight. However, once trams began running to the west entrance of High Gosforth Park, the club relocated to the present site, opening a third clubhouse in 1905.

Still the golfers felt they needed something more substantial, so architects belonging to the club were invited to submit plans for a replacement. Seven responded, including CJ Marshall of Marshall & Tweedy, designers of several local pavilions. But the winner was Dennis Hill of Graham & Hill. His expansive Arts and Crafts style clubhouse opened in September 1913 and cost £5,000.

Despite many alterations since, it remains one of the best preserved historic sporting structures in Tyne and Wear, a worthy counterpart to the fine 18th and 19th century buildings it faces across the racecourse.

The golf course itself has a pedigree too. With 14 of its 18 holes placed within the racecourse, so that players must cross the track four times before returning to the clubhouse, its design was influenced by two of the leading golf architects of the early 20th century, Harry Colt and James Braid.

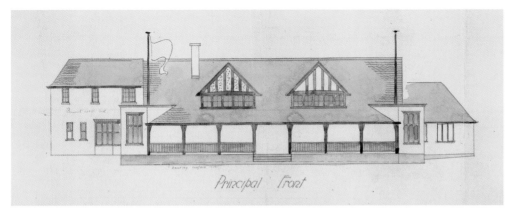

Principal Front

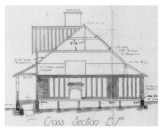

Cross Section E/F

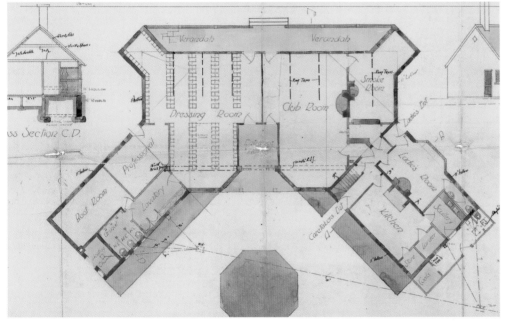

Cross Section C.D.

◄ A mile south of High Gosforth Park, down the Great North Road, lies the **City of Newcastle Golf Club**. Founded on the Town Moor in 1891 the club moved to its current Three Mile Bridge course, then in the countryside, in 1907.

Local architects Cackett & Burns Dick – better known for Newcastle's Laing Art Gallery (1904) and the domed Spanish City (1910) at Whitley Bay – designed the new clubhouse, based on a butterfly plan with a verandah looking out west over the course.

During the 1920s this feature was replaced by a sun lounge, the first of several alterations that – typical of so many golf clubhouses – have all but compromised the design's original charm, yet added greatly to the club's viability.

Inside the clubhouse is a curious reminder of the course's opening in August 1907. When the club secretary drove from the first tee his ball struck a crow in mid flight. Its stuffed remains have been on display ever since.

◄ Another intriguing set of plans from the archives show what would have replaced the 1907 clubhouse above, had the **City of Newcastle Golf Club** got its way in 1963.

Drawn up by Waring & Netts, a recently formed Gosforth practice (later to design Gosforth Pool, in 1968), the intention was to rescue the club's ailing finances by building a panoramic glass and steel clubhouse, topped by a ten storey block containing 60 flats.

To the committee's dismay, however, Gosforth Urban District Council deemed the plans to be an over-development, and so unlike two similar blocks of the period, overlooking the Town Moor's northern edge but coming under Newcastle's jurisdiction, these bold plans never left the drawing board.

▶ Completing the trio of historic golf clubs in the Gosforth area is **Gosforth Golf Club**, formed in 1905 and seen here in 1930 during the Northumberland County Championships.

Known as the Bridlepath, the club's course was opened in 1906, using as its first clubhouse a wooden hut bought for about £40 from the Newcastle and Gateshead Water Company. A ladies pavilion was added in 1909.

Within three years the members had outgrown both structures, and so turned to the club's vice president, FH Holford, to design a more substantial clubhouse.

For Holford, who was also Newcastle's City Surveyor, the commission no doubt offered a welcome change from his usual diet of housing and municipal buildings (one of which was Gibson Street Baths, *see pages 173-5*).

To meet the costs of £1,200, male members paid an annual levy of one guinea for five years. Lady members paid half that.

But other local women were clearly less impressed, for in July 1913, within weeks of the clubhouse's opening, an unexploded bomb was discovered nearby, its fuse burnt out.

The culprits were assumed to be suffragettes, whose organisation, the Women's Social and Political Union, had that same year adopted the tactic of attacking sports clubs, considered to be bastions of male domination. Indeed some golf clubs had the slogan 'No Votes, No Golf' burnt on their greens in acid, while in Heaton Park a bowls pavilion was torched in March 1913.

Since then, while surrounding trees have added much to the halcyon scene (*right*), alterations have rather diminished the impact of Holford's original design.

Still on the Great North Road, midway between Gosforth Golf Club and Northumberland Golf Club, is **McCracken Park**, home of Newcastle's oldest rugby club, **Northern Football Club** (formed originally as Elswick Football Club by two printers, William and Richard Cail, in September 1876).

Unusually, for the first six decades of Northern's existence they had no permanent base, playing initially at the Mill Inn, Westgate, followed by a number of pitches in and around the Town Moor, one of which was infamous for being laced with horse manure.

Only in 1937 did Northern head north to set up their current ground, named after a prominent player, club president and accountant, Angus McCracken.

Seen here in the 1980s is the original wooden stand, which faced one of four pitches and backed onto the Great North Road. Because of this ideal location, the adjoining clubhouse soon became a regular stopping off point for other rugby teams passing by on their journey home, leading to Northern's well deserved reputation as a focal point for late night revelries.

But for all Northern's early success at McCracken Park – at times they fielded eight teams and had to hire extra pitches at High Gosforth Park – amateur rugby's mounting financial problems in the late 20th century led them to follow a path familiar to many British sports clubs. One pitch was sold for housing development, with the proceeds going towards the construction of a £1.2 million ranch-style clubhouse, opened in December 1994.

Squash courts, originally introduced at McCracken Park in 1961, form an important source of revenue in the new clubhouse, which also provides a base for the **Gosforth Harriers & Athletic Club** (founded in 1927).

The rugby club itself, meanwhile, having decided to drop its brief dalliance with professionalism, still fields six teams, but has yet to replace its wooden grandstand.

▲ This is the **New Ground**, home from 1955–89 to the area's other historic rugby club, **Gosforth RFC**, and literally a few place kicks from McCracken Park, on the west side of the Great North Road.

Formed in 1877, like Northern Gosforth led a peripatetic life for many years, before raising £10,000 to purchase the 12 acre New Ground in 1951.

It was here that Gosforth achieved national prominence, before selling the ground for £1.7 million in 1989. The Greystoke Park estate now occupies the site.

Gosforth's next move was to the former Newcastle Chronicle and Journal sports ground at Kingston Park, purchased for only £55,000 and opened in 1990. The club's eventual transformation into Newcastle Falcons is explained further on page 113. But in 1996 the club's amateurs opted to recreate Gosforth as a separate entity, and since 2007 this has been based at Druid Park, Woolsington. The club have also reverted to their original green and white hoops, chosen because several of the founders in 1877 had played for Durham School.

Chapter Four

Hillheads

Five different clubs call Hillheads home: the Whitley Warriors ice hockey team, their immediate neighbours, Whitley Bay Football Club (the 'Seahorses'), Whitley Bay Cricket Club, Whitley Bay Boys Club and, the oldest of them all, Rockcliff Rugby Football Club, formed in 1887 and resident at Hillheads since 1907. During the summer of 1929 the rugby ground also played host to the newly imported Australian sport of dirt track racing. Shown right is the cover of one of the programmes. Dirt track soon evolved into what we now call speedway, staged on tracks surfaced with cinders.

Moving north into North Tyneside, and more specifically to Whitley Bay, the Hillheads cluster of sporting sites is centred upon a former 19th century brickworks, in an area once known as Whitley Hill Heads.

After the brickworks were exhausted in 1889, its owner landscaped the area, creating the basis of West Park (where the present cricket pitch lies), some 90 feet below road level and sheltered by steep banks.

Then in 1907 the cluster's first established club, Rockcliff Rugby Football Club, laid out a ground on a field just north east of the former brickworks.

For its part West Park was turned into a market garden in 1911, until in 1924 Whitley and Monkseaton Urban District Council bought the site and began to infill the old quarry.

The second sport to arrive at Hillheads, surprisingly, was dirt track racing, recently introduced from Australia. Organised by Tyneside Speedways Ltd., of Cross Street, Newcastle, and billed as the 'latest thrill in speed', the races

were staged on a 400 yard dirt track laid out around what is now the more southerly of Rockcliff's two rugby pitches. On its launch afternoon of April 20 1929 a crowd of 4,000 intrigued onlookers saw over 30 races and witnessed one of the motorbikes catching fire. Harry Whitfield of Middlesbrough won the Whitley Golden Helmet.

In total twelve such meetings were staged at Hillheads, but with public interest dropping off the meeting on June 26 1929 proved to be the last. (Speedway did catch on in Newcastle, however, as detailed in Chapter Nine.)

Hillheads as we know it today evolved mostly in the 1950s, although not quite in the way the authorities had intended.

In 1934 the Council announced plans for an ultra-modern stadium at West Park, which at the time was still being infilled by tipping.

Meanwhile, a local football club, Monkseaton FC, laid out a pitch to the immediate west. Their plans, however, and those for the much larger stadium, had to be shelved at the outbreak of war.

In 1950 Monkseaton FC became Whitley Bay FC, by which time the Council had revived its stadium plans, announcing in 1949 that it would turn West Park into a 25,000 capacity cycling and athletics stadium. The Council hoped that this venue, 'one of the most modern in the north-east', would be complete by 1951.

But, as would also be the fate of the proposed City Stadium in Newcastle (*see page 124*), and indeed of numerous other municipal stadium proposals around the nation, Hillheads' stadium remained a dream, as other priorities took precedence in the rebuilding of post war Britain.

Instead, in typical British style, Hillheads continued to develop piecemeal, providing Whitley Bay with a cluster of four quite different sporting venues, each adding their own distinct character to the area.

▲ Viewed from the east in 2009, the **Hillheads** area is dominated by the grey-clad hulk of the **Whitley Bay Ice Rink**, opened by Alderman Snowball, the mayor, in May 1955.

To the left of the rink is **Hillheads Park**, home of **Whitley Bay FC**, while to the right is **West Park**, the former brickworks site, now home to **Whitley Bay Cricket Club**.

To the left of West Park is the clubhouse of **Whitley Bay Young People's Club**, formed as a boys club in 1964. Below West Park are the two pitches of **Whitley Bay Rockcliff Rugby Football Club** (known more usually as Rockcliff).

The 1929 dirt track ran around the left of those pitches, and was overlooked by a stand put up in 1922 on the tree-lined south side, demolished in the 1950s.

A reminder of the area's industrial past can just be seen on the lower edge of the photograph. The lake is part of Marden Park, a former limestone quarry, landscaped to form a wildlife sanctuary in 1977.

Seen from above, the rink and three sports grounds appear to be the closest of neighbours. Yet although from each ground the roof of the ice rink is an ever present landmark, and Rockcliff's rugby posts just peep over the treetops, none of the cricketers, footballers or rugby players can actually see each other, being separated by allotments, banking and greenery.

As later chapters show, multi-sport clubs are still quite common in Tyne and Wear. At Hillheads each sport enjoys its own secluded existence.

▲ Although an earlier club bore the same name, today's **Rockcliff Rugby Football Club** was officially formed in 1887, the year that **John Baines** of **Bradford** also emerged as one of the earliest producers of sports-related collectables.

This Baines card, one of millions printed before the First World War depicting mostly rugby, football, cricket and golf clubs – and issued before Rockcliff dropped the final 'e' – carries the expression, 'O'ill show thee har ter tackle', which suggests that its creator hailed from Yorkshire rather than from the Northumbrian coast.

Rockcliff's first ground was a field on Grafton Road, Whitley Bay, above the Table Rocks swimming pool. Their nearest competitors were Percy Park RFC, founded 1872 and still going strong.

▲ In common with Northern RFC and many other rugby clubs now based in relatively anonymous modern surroundings, Rockcliff's heritage is mainly to be seen in the form of archive photographs and artefacts lining their clubhouse walls and filling glass cabinets.

This hand-tinted image from 1891 shows **Rockcliff** at their hilltop ground on **Grafton Road**, posing in front of an unusually ornate, oriental-style pavilion the club had bought on their formation in 1887. Prior to that it had served, most likely as a refreshment kiosk, at the first North East Coast Exhibition, held at the winter gardens in Tynemouth in 1882.

Rockcliff, their team including several Cullercoats fishermen, made an immediate impression.

Unbeaten in their first season they won the Northumberland Senior Cup in 1890. Two years later Ernest 'Little Billee' Taylor (second from right, standing) became the first of eight Rockcliff players to be capped, being appointed the England captain in 1894.

In 1901 housing developments forced Rockcliff to move to Whitley Park, a mile or so to the north, and in 1905 the club had to move again to make way for a funfair (later to become the Spanish City amusement park).

Two homeless and largely win-less seasons followed before Rockcliff made their final move to Hillheads in 1907, where within a year or two the final 'e' of their name was dropped (unlike at Rockcliffe Bowling Club, *page 139*).

Alas no photographs have been found of an impressive grandstand built at Hillheads in 1922. Costing £700 and holding 600 spectators, it was officially opened for a Northumberland County Rugby Union trial in October 1922.

After closing down during the Second World War Hillheads slipped into disrepair, leading to the stand and pavilion being demolished during the 1950s.

The current, rather utilitarian clubhouse then opened in 1964.

But if the building lacks character, Hillheads itself remains a vital social hub. Even better, during the 1984–85 season Rockcliff were able to buy the ground and its two pitches for a nominal fee, thereby offering a secure base for the future.

▲ Also on display in the **Rockcliff** clubhouse is this velvet and braid cap, supplied by athletic outfitters AF Donald of Newcastle and awarded in 1909 to **Joseph Brunton** (1888–1971).

The tradition of awarding caps began at Rugby School in 1839, originally as an aid to identifying fellow team members. But by 1909 they were purely decorative and were awarded on merit.

Brunton himself would win further caps for England, as a lock v. Scotland, Ireland and Wales in 1914 (although the official records erroneously named him as a player for North Durham RFC).

During the hostilities that followed he was honoured again, with both an MC and DSO for gallantry, before becoming an international referee in the 1920s.

Made a life member of Rockcliff, Brunton went on to be elected president of the Rugby Football Union in 1953. One of his official duties was to formally open Gosforth's New Ground in September 1955 (*see page 61*).

▶ Sporting their familiar strip of red and yellow, **Rockcliff** face their oldest rivals from Tynemouth, **Percy Park**, in the traditional Boxing Day derby of 2008. On the far touchline is the turf banking where the grandstand stood until the 1950s.

Unlike Northern RFC, whose modern clubhouse at McCracken Park in Gosforth offers squash and extensive hospitality suites, facilities at Hillheads are more basic, but no less welcoming and certainly well used by a wide range of teams at all levels, girls included.

To help fund this, like all community clubs run by volunteers Rockcliff have had to devise all manner of fund raising activities, the most notable of which is the annual **Super 10s** tournament.

Initiated in 2003, this sees clubs from all over Britain, and on occasions from as far afield as Holland, play a ten-a-side knockout tournament on a single afternoon in April. But while the rugby is taken reasonably seriously, the emphasis is on beer and boisterous abandon, as demonstrated by the contingent from Ellesmere Port (*right*), posing in their gladiatorial garb before the 2010 Super 10s. Note the ice rink, that ever present Hillheads landmark, in the background.

As might be imagined, numerous other images from the day were available, if not quite suitable for family viewing...

◀ Seen here in May 2010 during a 2nd XI match against Bates Cottages from Seaton Delaval, **Whitley Bay Cricket Club**, in common with Rockcliff on the other side of the fence, have no fine pavilions or stands at their disposal at **West Park**. And yet this sweeping, sunken expanse of green is an impressive sight.

The cricket club was formed in 1946 at the nearby Churchill Playing Fields, then moved to West Park in 1960. This being a former tip, players would often see specks of coal glinting through the surface of the newly rolled wicket.

The current, basic pavilion dates from 1967, the original having burnt down the year before.

Whitley Bay currently run four teams, playing in leagues on Saturdays, Sundays and midweek.

But with only 40 or so playing members, life at this level of club cricket remains a constant battle to find new players and sponsors. Their annual fund raising equivalent of Rockcliff's Super 10s is a popular community barbeque.

But West Park serves not only the cricketers. It is a haven for dog walkers and for the Whitley Bay Young People's Club, whose members use the outfield for games of mini-rugby league in winter.

A more constant presence is the looming form of the neighbouring ice rink (*left*), our next port of call.

▲ As an apprentice blacksmith in Barnard Castle, **John 'Icy' Smith** (1889–1965) loved to skate on the fishponds at Lartington. So much so that he went on to make his fortune from ice-making, becoming mayor of Darlington, as seen here in 1928, and later, uniquely, of Durham also.

As his profits started to be affected by the mass production of refrigerators, in 1939 Icy decided to diversify by creating an ice rink in Durham. Originally outdoors when opened in March 1940, it was then covered by a massive tarpaulin supported on timber posts, two of them in the centre of the ice (which made for some unusual tactics when the rink became a favourite with Canadian ice hockey players stationed at nearby RAF bases).

A permanent roof followed in 1946, with seating reportedly made from surplus war time coffins. Such was the rink's popularity that Icy and his son Tom, now a keen ice hockey player himself, looked for further sites.

Eventually they opted for Whitley Bay, leaving another son, John, to run Durham. (The family eventually sold the Durham rink in 1994, since when the building has been a bowling alley and fitness centre.)

▲ Opened in May 1955 and seen here six years later, the Smith family's second rink at **Hillheads, Whitley Bay,** dominates the local scene, in terms of its sheer bulk, but also as arguably the area's most celebrated building.

Built by Gunning & Co of Newcastle (the Gunnings had been schoolmates of Tom Smith), the rink was one of only three built in Britain during the 1950s, following the boom years of the 1930s, and predated a revival in interest from the 1960s onwards. (The Smiths also managed the rink opened at Billingham in 1967, for example.)

In Whitley Bay's early years several of the Smith clan even lived at the rink. Francis, the current manager, recalls growing up in the upstairs flat along with his father Tom, his four siblings and for a while, grandpa Icy himself.

In common with most ice rinks, Whitley Bay's survival has often depended on other events.

Between 1982–96 it hosted concerts by the likes of Sting, Status Quo, the Jam, Wham and Take That, plus several sell-out Torvill & Dean ice shows. The rink has also staged tennis in 1958, international netball in 1959, and a middleweight boxing bout between Chris Eubank and Jose Ignacio Barruetabena of Spain in 1995.

But in sporting terms Whitley Bay's most prominent contribution has been as a home to ice hockey (*see opposite*) and to the **Whitley Bay Ice Skating Club**, among whose alumni have been such figure skating champions as Lorna Brown, Joanne Conway and, most recently, Matthew Parr.

Following in their wake, hundreds of keen young skaters can be seen practising on the ice every day, some starting as early as 6.30am.

▲ The air is cold and the music extra loud as a few hundred fans urge on the **Whitley Warriors** (in white) against the Nottingham Lions, at Hillheads in April 2010.

Often called the fastest game on earth, ice hockey used also to be one of the most dangerous, at least before its players were properly padded and helmeted, and the fans protected from errant pucks by plexiglass screens. (Fighting amongst players still breaks out, but that is part of the appeal.)

But even harder to follow than the fast moving puck is the story of ice hockey in the north east overall.

Whitley Bay's original team in 1956 were the Wasps (who transferred from Durham). Then came the Bees in 1957, followed by the brief return of the Wasps in 1963. The Warriors then emerged in 1966, and for years local derbies against the Wasps, since returned to Durham, packed the venue's 3,200 seats. (There had been 3,500 until a tenpin bowling alley was added at the far end in 1966.)

In 1995 the Warriors moved to the new Metro Arena in Newcastle, but returned to Hillheads a year later when ousted by the Cobras (who were formerly the Wasps, albeit lately based in Sunderland).

After that, Sunderland's rink closed in 2000, while in April 2010 it was announced that another new team, the Newcastle Vipers, would leave the Metro Arena to play at... Whitley Bay.

Thus teams come and go, but Hillheads' ice age shows no sign of thawing.

▲ Immediately south of the ice rink, on an exposed, wind-buffeted plain, the fourth and final venue in this cluster is **Hillheads Park**, home of **Whitley Bay FC**, also known as the 'Seahorses'.

First laid out in the late 1930s – the club itself having formed in 1896 as Whitley and Monkseaton FC – the ground was developed mainly in the 1960s, when Whitley Bay were one of the top amateur outfits in England.

Seen here in 2010, the main stand was completed in 1963, despite a brief scare when the builders uncovered a mass grave.

Fortunately, the bones turned out to be of an equine nature.

The current Seahorse Social Club then opened in 1966, partly funded by a record gate of 7,301 for an Amateur Cup tie against Hendon, staged the previous year.

Floodlights were added in 1968.

There was, at that time, a roof over the south terrace (once known as the Creamery Side). But this was taken down for safety reasons in 1971, leaving no shelter other than the stand. But at least the terraces are in good order, having been concreted in 1989 for the visit of Preston in the FA Cup.

Today's Hillheads Park is limited to 4,500, more than enough for average gates of 4-500.

But above all, the ground is a community hub, used also by the club's various junior and women's teams, and much appreciated by those for whom watching football from the terraces is still considered the genuine article.

▲ Although the north east has long been famed as 'a hotbed' of football, and famous non-League clubs abound – the likes of Bishop Auckland, Crook Town and Blyth Spartans – relatively few historic grounds have survived the march of progress and rationalisation in the immediate Tyne and Wear area. (The same is also true in rugby.)

What Hillheads Park therefore lacks in structural finery it more than makes up for in terms of character and atmosphere.

Currently the Seahorses play in the Northern League, after various spells in more senior leagues.

But it is in knock-out competitions that the club have

achieved the greatest renown, and one which belies their modest and windswept surroundings.

During the 1960s they twice reached the semi-finals of the FA Amateur Cup. On twelve occasions since 1953 they have won the Northumberland Senior Cup.

However, it is in the successor competition to the Amateur Cup that they proved most successful, winning the FA Vase three times in eight years.

Their first triumph came in 2002, when the final was played at Villa Park. This they followed with two further winning final appearances in 2009 and 2010, both played at the new Wembley Stadium – a venue that, as their fans are quick to point out, their more illustrious neighbours at St James' Park had yet to experience.

Heritage takes many forms, but the memory of those 2009 and 2010 victories remain as important to Whitley Bay's collective psyche as any historic building or artefact. For weeks the entire town became bathed in blue and white. On the day of the finals themselves, the streets were deserted, as some 5,000 locals made their way south.

In 2009 the Seahorses beat Glossop North End 2-0. In 2010 they won 6-1 against Wroxham.

But more than that, their first goal that afternoon, scored by Paul Chow, was timed at just 21 seconds, making it the quickest goal ever scored at the new stadium. (It can even be viewed on the Football Association's website.)

On the left is one of the souvenir shirts created to commemorate the 2009 Vase final. Apparently the Seahorses' nickname was adopted in the mid 1960s after a competition. The winner was rewarded with a prize of £1 and season ticket.

Rusting in a corner of Hillheads Park is this Ellison's Patented Rush Preventive turnstile, one of thousands manufactured in Manchester between 1895–1963 and installed at stadiums, sports grounds, swimming pools, zoos and piers all over Britain. More on the development of Ellison's turnstiles can be found in *Played in Manchester* (see Links).

Chapter Five

Wearmouth

THE TOWN MOOR

Originally 80 acres was given to the Freemen of Weremouth by Hugh de Puisit, Bishop of Durham, in his charter of 1154. It was used for bull-baiting, horseracing, fairs and public meetings.

OLD SUNDERLAND HERITAGE TRAIL

Newcastle's may be larger and better known, but Sunderland has a Town Moor too. As this plaque on a wall facing The Quadrant relates, the 80 acre site was granted to the freemen of Weremouth in 1154 as part of the charter that gave Sunderland town status, and, like its Newcastle counterpart, became a cradle of sport in the area. Yet, located as it is on the eastern edge of Sunderland, flanked by the south bank of the mouth of the River Wear and by the North Sea, it is hardly noticed at all, even by many people living in Sunderland.

Our fourth sporting cluster takes us south into the coastal city of Sunderland, and more specifically into the area cleft 'asunder' by the River Wear.

In historical terms, and in terms of sporting governance, this part of Tyne and Wear is considered to lie within the county of Durham.

As such, it has an identity that it is quite distinct from its Northumbrian neighbours.

Topographically it differs too, in that the earliest settlements of Monkwearmouth on the north bank, and Bishopwearmouth on the south bank, faced each other across the deep gorge of the river valley, with the fishing village of Sunderland lying on the eastern mouth of the river, flanking the Town Moor and coastline.

Only with the construction of the first Wearmouth bridge in 1796 and the growth of such industries as glass making and ship building did Sunderland gain a more cohesive identity in the 19th century.

The earliest recorded organised sport was horse racing, which took place on the Town Moor from at least 1724 until the 1740s. But after that came a gap of almost a century until it restarted in 1835 at Tunstall Hope, a hilly area a mile and a half south of the town, owned by George Skipsey.

But the Sunderland Borough Races, as they were known, lasted only a decade before local opposition brought them to an end. Thereafter racing took place near Southwick, north of the Wear, during the 1850s, only to emerge again in 1898, south of the river at Grindon, on an oval grass track laid out on land owned by Colonel Vaux. The last steeplechase on this site was in 1906.

Sunderland's early cricketers also moved around a great deal.

The first known games took place on Monkwearmouth Shore in 1801. Others have been noted on Roker Beach. But the first proper grounds were all south of the river, starting in 1831 with one on Hendon Lane, roughly where Hendon Road and White House Road now meet.

Sunderland Cricket Club, as the town's club became known in 1850, then had three more grounds before settling in Ashbrooke, the subject of the following chapter, in 1887.

One of its grounds, known as the Blue House ground, would also be the first ground of Sunderland AFC, in 1879.

The football club led a peripatetic existence too, moving north of the Wear in 1883, where it would have three grounds before settling at Roker Park in 1898.

But it would be too simplistic to suggest that the south was cricket territory while the north was more amenable to football.

Instead, both sides of the Wear had their dense industrial areas and their leafier suburbs. Both were equally exploited for coal.

Sunderland's first colliery at Monkwearmouth (also called

simply Wearmouth) opened in 1835, joined by Boldon in 1869 and Hylton in 1900. South of the Wear, Ryhope opened in 1857 followed by Silksworth in 1869.

With most working men having little time or money to set up private clubs or secure grounds, this meant that during much of the 19th century the emphasis was on more impromptu sports such as quoits and potshare bowling, both heavily linked to gambling.

Countering this were the efforts of the town council to provide areas for more respectable recreation. Roker Park (the public park rather than the football ground of the same name) opened in 1880, and within three years had its first bowling club, still going strong today and seen opposite during a tournament in 1948.

A similar parks bowling club was set up at Mowbray Park, which had opened in 1857, in 1896.

To these and several other municipal sports facilities were added Colliery Welfare grounds in the 1920s. Of these, the most notable survivor is the Wearmouth Colliery Welfare Ground on Carley Hill, opened in 1928.

Also in the 1920s Sunderland witnessed a boom in boxing, as reported on page 19. Of many venues, only the Monkwearmouth Miners' Hall still stands.

Today's sporting map continues to have strong links with the past.

Wearmouth Colliery, which closed in 1993, became the site of the Stadium of Light, opened in 1997, and the Aquatic Centre, which followed in 2008.

And sport is still played on the site of the Blue House Ground. Exactly 150 years after cricket was first recorded on the site, the Raich Carter Sports Centre opened there in 2001.

▲ This map of Sunderland's **Town Moor** (with north pointing to the right) dates from 1750 and shows the roughly triangular layout of the **racecourse** in dotted lines, marked with the letter R. (For a clearer idea of the course layout see page 75.)

The earliest reference to racing on the Town Moor is in 1724. Race days were known as 'Horsecourse' days, and like their counterparts elsewhere in Britain attracted large crowds, not only for racing but also for cock fights, animal baiting and other gambling activities.

But by the time this map appeared the races had ended, probably during the 1740s, and other sports took root.

These included potshare bowling (see page 28), wrestling, archery and, in the 19th century, cricket. It is known that one early cricket club, called The Moor, sometimes had to complete its matches on the nearby beach when their pasture was otherwise occupied by potshare bowlers, or when they were driven off by freemen wanting to graze their cattle.

Encroachment on the Town Moor started with development of the Hudson docks between 1837–50, and the laying out of railway sidings on the eastern portion of the former racecourse. Although these sidings have since been cleared, much of that area, east of The Quadrant, is still walled off. But large tracts of the moor and parts of the former Coney Warren remain as accessible open ground, interspersed with modern housing and light industry.

The Holy Trinity Church, marked above, also still stands.

▲ Built in 1894 on Roker Avenue, the **Monkwearmouth Miners' Hall** – now part of an auto centre – was one of several boxing venues in Sunderland during the early 20th century. Holding around 500 spectators, it staged some top bouts, including those of the great Southwick-born Jack Casey, the 'Sunderland Assassin' (*see page 19*). Moreover, it is the only boxing related building from that era to have survived in the area.

In contrast, no trace at all remains of Sunderland's largest boxing arena, the Holmeside Stadium, known otherwise as 'the Palace of Punch' (*see opposite*).

This opened on Holmeside in May 1920, heralding a golden age of boxing on Wearside. Under a domed ceiling it held 3,000 people,

with no seat said to be more than 35 feet from the ropes. It was also claimed to be the first boxing venue in Britain to have water piped to each of the boxers' corners.

But come the Depression and Holmeside could not be sustained, and in 1930 it was replaced by a cinema and dance hall.

1. **Queen's Road pigeon crees** (*see page 153*)
2. **Wearmouth Colliery Welfare Ground** (1928-)
3. **Thompson Park BC** (1938-)
4. **Newcastle Road, Sunderland AFC** (1886-98)
5. **Newcastle Road Baths** (1936-2008)
6. **Binns Sports Ground** (c.1930s-1990s)
7. **Abbs Field, Sunderland AFC** (1884-6)
8. **TLF Recreation Ground** (1922-1960s)
9. **Roker Park, Sunderland AFC** (1898-1997)
10. **Roker Park BC** (1883-)
11. **Adventure Sunderland, Watersports Centre** (2003-)
12. **Sunderland Yacht Club** (1957-)
13. **Horatio Street, Sunderland AFC** (1883-4)
14. **Sunderland Bowl** (1964-)
15. **Monkwearmouth Miners' Hall** (1894-)
16. **Stadium of Light** (1997-)
17. **Aquatic Centre** (2008-) (*see pages 186-7*)
18. **Town Moor racecourse** (1724-1740s)
19. **Hendon Lane sports ground** (1831-50)
20. **Hendon Cricket Ground** (c.1888-1960s) / **Raich Carter Sports Centre** (2001-)
21. **Blue House grounds** (c.1845- c.1914)
22. **Mowbray Park BC** (1896-)
23. **Holmeside sports ground** (1864-76)
24. **Whitehall / Olympia Roller Skating Rink** (c.1890-1920), **Holmeside Boxing Stadium** (1920-30)
25. **Crowtree Leisure Centre** (1978-)
26. **High St Baths** (1858-1988)
27. **Chester Road sports ground** (1876-87)
28. **Ashbrooke Sports Ground** (1887-) (*see pages 90-95*)

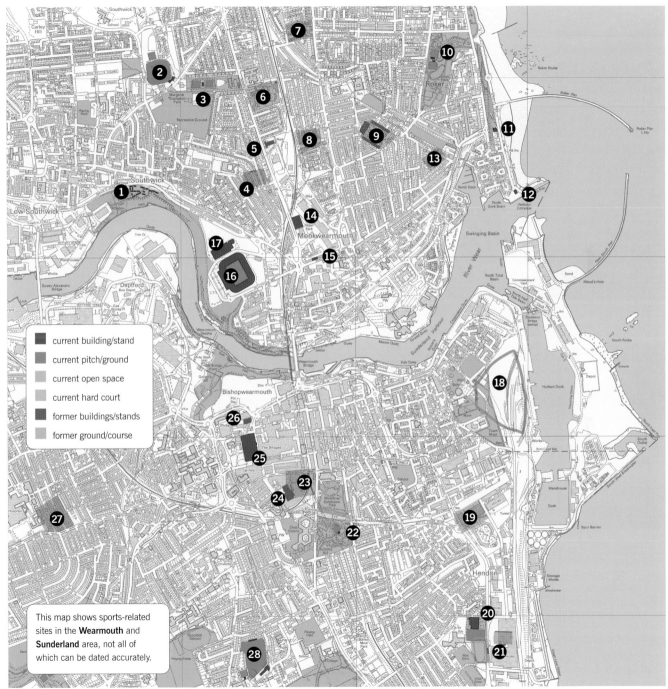

This map shows sports-related sites in the **Wearmouth** and **Sunderland** area, not all of which can be dated accurately.

current building/stand
current pitch/ground
current open space
current hard court
former buildings/stands
former ground/course

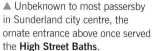
▲ Unbeknown to most passersby in Sunderland city centre, the ornate entrance above once served the **High Street Baths**.

Built in 1858 and remodelled and expanded in 1890, this public baths facility was the first of its kind in the north east to have been financed under the terms of the 1846 Baths and Wash Houses Act (*see Chapter Eighteen*).

The office block behind, Gilbridge House, was built after the baths building was demolished in 1988.

Barely a hundred yards away is the complex that replaced it, the **Crowtree Leisure Centre** (*above right*). Opened in 1978, the centre would have had an even more imposing presence had the planners allowed its Leeds-based architects, Gillinson Barnett & Partners, to proceed with the roof's original colour scheme of bright red.

Not that it needed to advertise itself. Dominating its surrounds, the £5 million 'municipal leisure palace' housed an ice rink, sports hall, indoor bowling green, squash courts and a leisure pool described as a 'south sea island dream world... just like the seaside', palm trees and all.

In common with so many 1970s leisure centres, Crowtree suffered from technical problems and high running costs. In 1999 its ice rink was closed, to be followed in 2008 by the pool, which was superceded by the new Aquatic Centre (*pages 186-87*). Nevertheless, it continues to be popular for various dry sports, and remains an iconic, if muted presence in the city centre.

▶ For residents of Sunderland living north of the Wear there were no local public baths until the completion of this splendid edifice in Monkwearmouth in 1936.

Designed by JE Lewis, the **Newcastle Road Baths** was a rather austere, institutional building on the outside.

But with a spectacular main pool hall spanned by tall reinforced concrete arches, and a pool measuring 100' x 39', flanked by raised seating on either side (*below right*), it was perfect for galas, and immediately became the home of the **Sunderland Amateur Swimming Club**, formed in 1889.

In more recent years it also hosted several annual Swimathons.

Thus when it emerged in 2006 that Newcastle Road would be replaced by the new Aquatic Centre there was considerable opposition, particularly amongst local residents who queried the relevance of an Olympic sized pool for everyday family users.

Another disgruntled group was the Friday Club. Formed in 1980, this was a club for naturists. They had swum at various pools around the north east and had only just settled at Newcastle Road when the axe fell. As one of its members pointed out, 'modern glass palaces' like the Aquatic Centre were not exactly suited to their needs.

Since the baths closed in April 2008 – the day before the Aquatic Centre opened – the building has been sealed up, and remains in good order (*far right*), albeit with the original arches concealed above a false ceiling, added in the late 20th century.

The current plan is to demolish the baths, however, and possibly to build a college on the site, as part of the wider redevelopment of the Sunderland North area.

▶ This photograph is one of a series recently discovered that appears to show the **Blue House Ground** in **Hendon**, or at least one of its adjoining pitches, in either the late 19th or early 20th century.

Named after the Blue House pub which served as its original dressing rooms – not the current pub of that name, further south on Corporation Road, but a building then located to the immediate south of the site – the Blue House ground was significant as the first home of **Sunderland AFC**.

As numerous histories of the club relate (*see Links*), the club was formed in 1879 by James Allan, a Scottish teacher at the Hendon Board School, part of which can be seen in the background.

In fact, unlike most other football clubs at the time its players were not manual workers but fellow teachers; hence the club's original name, Sunderland & District Teachers' Association Football Club.

Maps of the town in the 1890s show there to have been four fields in the Blue House area. The one shown here backed onto the school in Preston Road. North of this, on Robinson Terrace, was the ground of Hendon Cricket Club, thought to have opened in 1888.

To the immediate south was the main Blue House ground, which had a cycle track and a single stand on its east touchline.

(A third football pitch, which appears on 1919 maps, lay to the east of this, backing onto a series of oil tanks on Robinson Terrace.)

Football then being in its infancy in Durham, Allan's club struggled to gain a following, and so in 1881, unable to afford the Blue House annual rent of £10, it moved west to Groves Field, in the Ashbrooke area (*see Chapter Six*). At the same time non-teachers were admitted and the name Sunderland AFC adopted (this to distinguish it from a rugby club, Sunderland FC).

James Allan did play on the Blue House ground again, however. Disillusioned with how his old club was developing, in 1888 he set up a rival club called Sunderland Albion. They managed four seasons at the Blue House before finally disbanding in 1892. Sunderland also played on their original turf, the last recorded occasion being a reserve match in 1903.

Sport still dominates the Blue House area today. As noted earlier it is now the site of the **Raich Carter Sports Centre**, designed by Napper Architects and opened in 2001. Carter, who starred for Sunderland during the 1930s, had been educated at the Hendon Board School, the site of which is now the modern Valley Road primary school.

Reproduced from *The Golden Penny* weekly magazine of March 26 1898, this shows Sunderland's fifth ground, on Newcastle Road, shortly before the club moved to Roker Park. Of particular interest are the semi-circular markings defining the goalkeeper's area. The modern rectangular area did not come into being until 1902.

▲ A work familiar to all Sunderland supporters is this wonderfully detailed oil painting of the so-called 'Team of All Talents' playing the reigning League champions, Aston Villa, in a 4-4 draw at **Newcastle Road** on January 2 1895.

Believed to be the earliest painting of a professional football match, its artist was **Thomas Hemy**, who was best known for depicting maritime scenes (appropriately enough given that he had been born aboard a ship when his parents were emigrating from Newcastle to Australia).

Sunderland commissioned Hemy in order to celebrate winning the League in 1892 and 1893, to which they added a third title in April 1895 – a feat for which the team was rewarded with a day at High Gosforth Park (see page 51).

Although showing some artistic licence – for example the terraces were not that steep – the painting is of immense historic interest.

Note, for example, the pitch markings (as also seen opposite), and the straw piled up along the touchlines. This was commonly used at the time to protect pitches from frost. Also noteworthy is the discarded shin pad in the foreground, and the fact that all eleven Sunderland players are in view (and indeed are named on the painting's frame).

Goalkeepers, it should be added, were not required to wear shirts that differentiated them from their team-mates until 1909.

On the far touchline, the man seen holding a white flag is not the linesman but is instead thought to be Sunderland's manager Tom Watson, apparently added later once it was realised that he had been omitted from Hemy's original.

Newcastle Road's record gate at that time had been an estimated 21,000 in 1891. But still the ground was not large enough, and so in 1896 a limited company was formed to finance a move. Following this, the site was built over by housing on Netherburn Road and Newlington Court.

Recent research by Sunderland historian Paul Days has revealed that the club were not always so proud of Hemy's work.

Apparently in 1903 they offered the painting as a raffle prize in order to raise much needed funds, and when no-one claimed it – it does after all measure 12' x 8½' – put the painting into store, where it remained for many years until being re-hung at Roker Park.

Since restored, it is now proudly displayed at the Stadium of Light.

▶ Viewed from the west in 1976, **Roker Park** was home to **Sunderland AFC** for 99 years.

After the club had identified the site in 1897, in order to persuade the landowner to rent it to them, the club chairman JP Henderson had to agree to pay the ground rents of houses planned for the surrounding streets, at least until all were sold. It then took another decade before Sunderland could afford to buy the site, for £10,000.

In one respect Roker Park was ideally located, in the midst of a growing residential area, and close to the seafront at Roker, which had emerged as a favourite weekend retreat from the town's industrial quarters. Roker Park, the public park, lay a short distance to the east, as seen here at the top.

On the other hand, all those new houses and streets meant that any future development of the ground would always be constrained.

As was common at the time, Roker Park was opened, in August 1898, with a novelty sports event, grandly titled the 'Olympic Games' (this being two years after the first modern Olympiad in Athens).

The official inauguration then followed on September 10 with the first football match, a Division One game v. Liverpool, whose manager, coincidentally, was the former Sunderland boss, Tom Watson.

Also of note is that of the 22

players that day, 16 were Scottish, and not one hailed from Durham.

Another Scot destined to play a role at Roker was the engineer and ground designer Archibald Leitch.

Starting in 1913, Leitch designed a massive reinforced concrete terrace at the South or Roker End. This is the terrace on the right in the aerial view.

Leitch then designed a double decker main stand (top), in 1929, and, on the opposite side (nearer the camera) the simpler two tier Clock Stand, completed in 1936.

The final piece of major construction, this time not involving Leitch, was the roofing of the Fulwell End terrace (left), in 1964.

Roker Park's all time record attendance was 75,118 for an FA Cup replay v. Derby in 1933.

But as stricter safety regulations started to be enforced from the 1970s onwards, and more seats were installed, the capacity shrank to a mere 22,657 in its final years.

Roker Park staged three England internationals, in 1899, 1920 and 1950, and two Amateur Cup Finals, in 1926 and 1939. But undoubtedly the most high profile games were the four hosted during the 1966 World Cup. Seen here is action from the Soviet Union's 1–0 win over Italy. Also appearing at Roker were Chile and Hungary.

◄ Opened in September 1929 after seven years of planning and delays caused by the club's financial worries, Roker Park's **Main Stand** was a standard Archibald Leitch double decker, featuring the criss-cross latticework balcony truss that was to become his trademark.

With seats for 5,875 on its upper deck and room for 14,000 on the lower terrace, Roker's stand was a comparatively low budget structure, costing £25,000, a fraction of what other clubs paid for more lavishly fitted stands.

Nor was it always as colourful as seen here in 1982.

Until replaced by plastic seats in 1973, all the seats on the upper deck were wooden, as were those added to the rear portion of the lower deck in 1950. Also, the balcony steelwork was originally painted in green, rather than red.

Subsequent alterations included the insertion of a row of basic executive boxes in the central portion of the lower seating deck, and, during the 1980s, the complete recladding of the roof and the addition of external fire escapes at each end.

Even the balcony was covered with advertisments, so that in the final years the stand was barely recognisable as a Leitch design.

Seen on the left is the office and hospitality block that was added to the rear of the stand for the 1966 World Cup, facing Grantham Road.

To their credit, when Roker Park was demolished in 1997 Sunderland rescued two sections of Leitch's balcony truss, so that they could be displayed in the car park of the Stadium of Light (*page 88*).

Otherwise, as of 2010 only two examples of similar Leitch trusses survive in situ; at Ibrox Park in Glasgow and at Goodison Park in Liverpool.

▶ In the days before mass car ownership and motorway travel, 'football specials' on match days represented good business for Britain's railway companies, bearing not only thousands of supporters but in many cases the players and officials too.

One such company was the **London and North Eastern Railway**, which in 1936 decided to name a series of its new B17 locomotives – designed by Sir Nigel Gresley and built in Darlington – after those football clubs that patronised its services.

Seen here is the official naming ceremony of **loco number 2854**, with the Sunderland chairman, Sir Walter Raine in the centre (in the lighter overcoat), and manager Johnny Cochrane on his right.

Initially LNER hoped that supporters would be able to travel in trains hauled by their own club's named loco. In practice, however, logistics meant that this did not always work out.

For example, on the day of Sunderland's FA Cup Final against Preston in 1937, number 2854 was undergoing repairs, so the Sunderland nameplate was unscrewed and attached instead to the Derby County loco.

But the LNER still needed another 24 trains to accommodate all those thousands of Sunderland fans who were Wembley bound.

In total, 25 locos were named after football clubs served by the LNER, starting with Arsenal and ending with West Ham.

When all the engines were scrapped in the late 1950s British Rail handed each club one of the nameplates. But only a handful have remained in club hands, while the remainder have either disappeared or been sold into private hands. Extremely valuable they are too. In recent years the Liverpool nameplate was reportedly sold for £40,000.

Happily, as seen below, Sunderland's nameplate is one of the survivors, and can be enjoyed by all at the Sunderland Museum and Winter Gardens.

However, another Sunderland train is still in service. This is a modern diesel engine, number 66725, belonging to the railfreight group GBRf, which was unveiled by Sunderland chairman Niall Quinn in August 2007.

Newcastle United's nameplate, which is not on public view, is a replica. Apparently the original was mislaid by the LNER when the loco was rebadged for an exhibition in June 1936.

◀ Since the Hillsborough disaster of April 1989, and the implementation of the subsequent Taylor Report during the 1990s, nearly 40 senior football grounds in England and Wales have been demolished, together with a further nine in Scotland.

To the fans for whom these grounds, however basic or uncomfortable, represented a second home, an almost sacred place where they and their fathers and their fathers before them had attended, come rain or shine, thick and thin, the loss has been especially hard to bear.

Even harder if one of their loved ones had had their ashes scattered on the pitch.

In the past, whenever clubs vacated a ground it was common for them to sell off fixtures and fittings to other sports clubs, such as floodlights, or seats, or even, in rare cases, whole stand structures. The stand at Blaydon RFC, for example, originally stood at the Gateshead International Stadium (see page 111).

But in the 1990s a new phenomenon arose, and that was the public auction – usually for charitable purposes – of anything and everything that could be salvaged, so that the fans themselves could own a piece of their once beloved football ground.

In Sunderland the auction of bits and bobs from **Roker Park** took place in June 1997, six weeks after the final game on May 13 (a friendly against Liverpool, the club who had played in the first match, 99 years earlier).

For most fans attending the auction, a sign, or a piece of turf was sufficient. One of the penalty spots was sold for £120. (The other was replanted at the Stadium of Light).

But one fan, Bob Forster (*centre left*) went further, ending up on a whim spending £9,500 on 3,494 wooden bench seats taken from the 1936 Clock Stand.

It took Bob over two years to sell them all, having turned the benches into individual seats, restored them and added plaques bearing the motto 'A love supreme – the end of an era'.

Six were sold to exiled fans in Australia, three to New Zealand, plus others to South Africa, Norway, Turkey and Barbados. One was sold to the BBC journalist and Rokerite Kate Adie, another to former striker Ally McCoist. Forster had one order from an inmate at Durham prison.

Roker Park, meanwhile, was swiftly redeveloped as a housing estate (*below*), its roads suitably named with various footballing and Roker related themes.

Needless to add, many of the houses were snapped up by fans – perhaps the ultimate expression of a footballing home from home.

▲ When on the eve of its opening in July 1997, Sunderland chairman Bob Murray announced that the club's seventh home was to be called the **Stadium of Light**, there was widespread bafflement. After all, there already existed a famous Stadium of Light, in Lisbon.

This memorial outside the Sunderland version, designed by local artist Jim Roberts, helps to explain the choice. It represents a Davy Lamp, the simple invention that saved thousands of lives in coal mines, and which was first tested at Hebburn Colliery in 1816.

Further justification for the name was that the world's first incandescent electric light bulb was patented by a Sunderland scientist, Joseph Wilson, in 1878.

A number of other reasons were also cited; that the stadium would be a beacon to the area's regeneration, that it would be lit up at night and seen for miles around.

But it is the mining connection that retains the most powerful resonance. Added to which, despite fears to the contrary, the name has slipped comfortably into everyday usage and, just as importantly, into the nation's wider sporting consciousness.

▲ If the choice of the stadium's name was unexpected, so too was its location. When Sunderland decided in 1992 that they would leave Roker Park, their preferred site was a vast area on the A19, alongside the Nissan car factory.

Huge sums were expended on the plans, which entailed a 48,000 seat stadium as part of an entertainment and leisure complex, which would also include a 10,000 seat indoor arena.

But then Nissan decided to oppose the scheme, the arena was eventually built in Newcastle (*see page 24*), and Sunderland had to go back to the drawing board.

In the meantime, barely a mile from Roker Park, time was called on the **Monkwearmouth Colliery** on the northern bank of the Wear.

Seen here in 1990, three years before the colliery closed, the 41 acre site could hardly have been more central. Or more controversial.

The idea of stadiums acting as catalysts for urban regeneration was then in its infancy in Britain. Local opposition was intense. Traffic chaos was predicted, and the expected bill simply to reclaim the land was put at £8 million.

◀ Fast forward to 2009 and these images show how well suited the Monkwearmouth site was, after all, for a stadium – the **Stadium of Light** – and, let us not forget, for the north east's first 50m swimming pool, in the form of the adjoining **Aquatic Centre** (*see pages 186–87*).

In the end it took the Tyne and Wear Development Corporation three years to reclaim the site, and another 14 months for Ballast Wiltshier to construct the £17 million stadium, to the designs of a Gateshead practice, Taylor, Tulip and Hunter, who had also worked on St James' Park, and, in later years, at the Kingston Park rugby ground (*see page 113*).

Initially the club had planned to kick off with a capacity of 29,000.

But then Sunderland were promoted to the Premier League in 1996, and so this total was upped to 42,000. Yet by the time the stadium opened on July 30 1997, with a friendly v. Ajax of Amsterdam – preceded by a concert by Status Quo and a blessing by the Bishop of Durham – the team had been relegated again. Even so, in its first season average gates topped 34,000 and, once promotion was achieved in 1999, planning commenced for a further expansion to 49,000.

As a Hollywood sage once put it, 'Build it and they shall come...'

▶ Match day at the **Stadium of Light** is a sight to behold, unlike anything one might encounter at an out-of-town stadium planted in the middle of nowhere.

From all over Durham, from Boldon and Southwick, Fulwell and Roker, down the Newcastle Road and over the Wearmouth Bridge they flow, filling the Colliery Tavern and Joan's Café, next to the scrap yard; their red and white striped shirts bringing life and colour to a city that is in the midst of an almighty battle to reinvent itself in the post industrial 21st century.

And as they cross the railway bridge on **Millennium Way**, ahead lies the site where until 1993 2,000 miners had worked, while behind them tower the red brick and terracotta chimneys of the **Monkwearmouth Miners' Hall** (*see page 74*).

▲ Even if one never actually enters the **Stadium of Light**, a stroll around its perimeter is akin to visiting a sculpture park.

Over the last decade there has been a growing trend for statues and artworks in and around stadium complexes. But none can match Sunderland, where there are no fewer than eight memorials and pieces of public art, ranging from modern abstract forms to the traditional ironwork of the Murray Gates, dedicated to former chairman Bob Murray (and bearing the phrases 'Into the Light' and the more familiar 'Ha'way the Lads').

Above is a salvaged **Pit Wheel**, with a plaque recording the history of the Monkwearmouth Colliery. In the early 20th century, it is noted on the plaque, there were 304 pits in Durham, with a combined workforce of 165,000.

Opposite the main entrance is a bronze sculpture entitled **Fans, Past, Present and Future** (*above left*). Erected in November 2004 and crafted by a trio of artists known collectively as Artcyle, the work was unveiled in 2004 and has since become a favourite meeting place before games.

In complete contrast are the **Men of Steel** (*left*), by the Crook based artist Graeme Hopper. Installed in 2001, this has a group of figures hauling pieces of coal up the grassy slopes leading up from Wear, to symbolise man's struggle and will to survive... a theme all too familiar amongst Sunderland supporters.

▲ And still there are more. On the south side of the **Stadium of Light** this is **Bob Stokoe**, the manager who against all the odds led Sunderland to victory in the epic FA Cup Final of May 5 1973.

Sunderland, it will be recalled, were a Second Division side at the time, yet managed to beat the mighty Leeds United 1–0.

The statue, by Sean Hedges-Quinn, catches Stokoe in a famous moment, when, after the final whistle, he ran across the Wembley turf to embrace his heroic goalkeeper Jim Montgomery.

That Stokoe had spent most of his playing career in the black and white stripes of Newcastle is a mere detail.

On which note, a short distance away in the stadium car park are displayed two sections of the balcony truss that from 1929–97 formed such a distinctive element of the Main Stand at Roker Park, designed by **Archibald Leitch** (*above right and page 81*).

No doubt Archie would have been amazed that these mere details should be granted such iconic status, let alone preserved.

Yet when seen close up, the trusses, surprisingly tall and solid with their timber infills and bolted steel members, are as much a symbol of their time as are the tubular steel cantilevered structures that look down on the scene from the towering stadium above.

Definitely not an official artwork, this backstreet building off Millennium Way houses the headquarters of the Sunderland fanzine, *A Love Supreme*. Set up in 1989, the fanzine's credo states that 'We're all in it for the ride and not the destination, and we're all on the same side, however tortuous that journey becomes.' 'True supporters', it adds, 'care'.

▲ Finally, into the lair of the **'Black Cats'**, a nickname that harks back to the 'Black Cat' gun battery set up on the Wear during the Napoleonic Wars, and which is now enshrined within the club crest (*left*).

As noted earlier, the **Stadium of Light** originally held 42,000. But in 2002, thanks to its design, it proved straightforward to add an additional tier to the North Stand (at the far end), thereby increasing the total costs to £23 million and the capacity to 48,353. This made it the fourth largest club stadium in England. Should the extra tier be extended east and westwards, this total could reach 63,000.

But even as it is, the stadium is certain to be a venue in the 2018 World Cup should England's bid succeed. Indeed it has already staged two internationals, v. Belgium in 1999 and v. Turkey in 2003.

Maintaining such a colossal building, and also a place in the Premiership, is a costly business, and one that in 2006 resulted in a new owner seeking extra backing from Ireland and the United States.

In short, it may only be a mile or so from Roker Park, but in every other respect, it is a different world.

Chapter Six

Ashbrooke

Mixed doubles at the Ashbrooke Sports Club in the early 1900s. In the background is St John's Methodist Church, which opened in the same year as the club, 1887. Both were designed to serve the residents of Sunderland's newest middle class suburb. One of these residents, the daughter of a ship builder, was Ashbrooke regular Helen Aitchison, who won a silver medal in the mixed doubles at the 1912 Olympics in Stockholm.

Once it was known as 'the Lord's of the North'. Today they call it 'the home of sport in Sunderland'. And rightly so.

Covering nearly six acres of land in a quiet residential area of Sunderland, south of the city centre, the Ashbrooke Sports Club is that rare institution, a Victorian members' club that has steadfastly retained its multi-sport profile on a single site.

Such clubs are common in other parts of the world, and used to be common in Britain. But as the needs of individual sports started to become more specialised from the late 19th century onwards, most multi-sport clubs opted to focus on two or three sports at most.

Ashbrooke's founders set out as their objectives 'The practice of cricket, football, gymnastic and athletic exercises, lawn tennis and quoits, the physical training and development of the human frame' and 'the promotion of healthful exercises...'

Remarkably, six sports are still played at the club: cricket, rugby, bowls, tennis, squash and, from 2010, football.

In addition, a hockey club that played there until recently still has a base in the pavilion, as does a running club, so that overall, eight sports are represented (or nine if we include the snooker room).

Even Lord's, where in the 1830s some seven or eight sports were catered for, now hosts only three (cricket, real tennis and squash).

We therefore devote a single chapter to Ashbrooke because it offers a highly unusual bridge between the clusters featured in the previous four chapters, and the individual clubs and sports covered in the remaining chapters.

Moreover, Ashbrooke has an unusually comprehensive archive, which under its current club historian, Keith Gregson, has been admirably maintained.

These archives tell us that, as is the case with most multi-sport clubs, the Ashbrooke story starts with cricket, and more specifically with its cricket section, known as the Sunderland Cricket Club.

In Sunderland *per se* the first recorded match took place in July 1801, while the first mention of a Sunderland CC is in 1808. However, this club was only constituted in 1834, as Bishopwearmouth CC.

Its ground was at Hendon Lane until, following a merger with Hendon Terrace CC and a change of name to Sunderland CC, the club moved south to the Blue House field (*see page 78*), in 1850.

In 1864 there followed another move, to Holmeside, where in 1873 some of the cricketers formed a rugby club, calling it Sunderland Football Club.

(This form of title, it should be noted, was common in the days before rugby and soccer split irrevocably. Northern FC in Newcastle is another example.)

In 1876 railway developments forced the cricket and rugby clubs to move west to Chester Road. It was there in 1880 that a tennis section formed.

Sunderland Hockey Club's First XI of 1907–08. Their modern day counterparts are still based at Ashbrooke, but since the game's gradual switch to artificial pitches from the 1980s onwards, they play their home matches at the Raich Carter Sports Centre a mile or so to the east.

But the Chester Road ground was in a bleak setting and so the decision was made to acquire the more sheltered site at Ashbrooke.

(Ironically, Sunderland AFC had played four games on this site, known then as Groves Field, during 1882–83. How different the sporting map of Sunderland would have been had they settled there.)

The Ashbrooke Sports Ground as we know it today, with its entrance on the corner of Ashbrooke Road and West Lawn, opened in 1887 (*see right*).

Since then, as this chapter will show, a succession of sports has been staged. Some, such as athletics, cycling, baseball and boxing, made only fleeting appearances. But bowls, hockey and squash all took root.

Ashbrooke would also become a venue for sundry international matches, at times attracting crowds of over 20,000 spectators.

These red-letter days apart, Ashbrooke has endured some difficult spells. In the 1970s and 1980s, during the squash boom, membership levels topped 3,000.

But in 2010 the total was nearer 700, including juniors and social members. As a result, and as is typical of sports clubs all over urban Britain, on numerous occasions the holding company has had to sell assets in order to survive.

Most recently, in 2000 it sold a patch of land on its western edge for flats. On the other hand, the club has also bought extra land on Ryhope Road to provide more pitches for the rugby section.

Today the ground is run by a limited company with charitable status, and is run by a board of trustees, all of them voluntary.

To make ends meet a squash court has been converted into a fitness centre, an office into

a restaurant, and another area rented out to a physiotherapist.

The ground also now plays host to an annual firework display, attracting up to 7,000 visitors.

Alongside these commercial initiatives, the trustees must also try to meet the widely differing needs of all the various sporting sections, and of a membership that spans all ages and tastes.

It is a constant balancing act, and one that requires patience, ingenuity and absolute dedication (which is why so many clubs with grounds like Ashbrooke have chosen to narrow their ambitions and to specialise).

Here, then, is a special corner of Tyne and Wear; no longer the 'Lord's of the North' so much as a ground in a class of its own.

▲ Opening day at **Ashbrooke** on May 30 1887, viewed from the slopes at the Ashbrooke Road end of the ground, to which entry for this inaugural Whitsuntide Sports Meeting cost 6d. The markings of five tennis courts can just be seen at the near end, while on the left, or west side (behind the flagpole) is the original single storey pavilion.

This was replaced by a much grander two storey pavilion on the south east corner of the ground, shown left on its opening day on May 6 1899.

Costing some £600, it was designed by local architect James Henderson, who had also laid out the ground in 1887 and played in the first cricket match. He later went on to captain the first XI.

Although much altered, the pavilion remains in use today, and is the oldest sports-related structure in Sunderland. Indeed in the area covered by this book, only the pavilions at Gateshead Bowling Green Club (*page 97*) and Close House (*page 98*) are older.

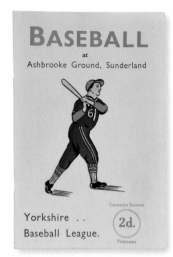

BASEBALL
at
Ashbrooke Ground, Sunderland

Yorkshire . .
Baseball League.

2d.

▲ Although **Ashbrooke** was seen for years as an exclusive club, it never shied away from fund-raising events, such as this exhibition match between a team of Canadians and representatives of the recently formed Yorkshire Baseball League.

The League was one of several set up in England during the 1930s in an unsuccessful attempt to popularise baseball. Ashbrooke lost £50 on the day.

Other more lucrative events included a military tattoo in 1951, boxing, displays of Cossack sword dancing and a two day cricket match, Durham v. Australia, in June 1926 (*above right*), which drew a packed house of 20,678 spectators on the first day, plus many more watching from neighbouring windows.

Also staged were international hockey matches, an England rugby trial, and in 1955 a men's county tennis championship between Sunderland and Durham (*right*).

From 1958–61 Ashbrooke's tennis section also staged several indoor tournaments featuring major stars, at the Whitley Bay Ice Rink.

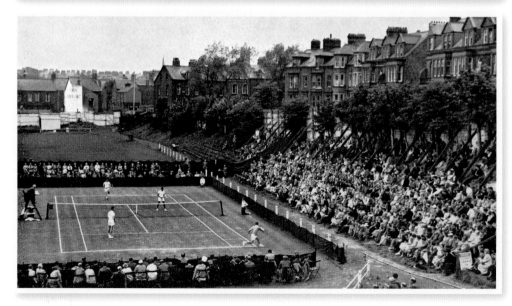

◀ Entered via its own sturdy gates alongside Ashbrooke's three tennis courts, yet almost totally hidden behind tall hedges in the south west corner of the ground, is the **Sunderland Bowling Club**.

Having a bowling green at a sports club is an important asset, for it helps to ensure that once their cricketing, rugby or tennis days are over, members have another reason to stay on, and play on.

Ashbrooke's green opened in 1889, two years after the ground's inauguration, and by 1905 had attracted enough support for the bowlers to club together to build the current pavilion.

Costing £267 and opened on May 18 1906, it was designed by architect Hugh Hedley, who lived close by, on The Grove, and who may well have been a member at Ashbrooke. (He is otherwise remembered as the architect of the Londonderry pub, built in 1901 on Sunderland's High Street West.)

Hedley's pavilion, barely altered since – despite being damaged during air raids in 1943 – with its wonderfully atmospheric wood panelled interior and a delightful elevation facing the green (*left*), is now the second oldest surviving bowls clubhouse in Tyne and Wear, and the sixth oldest sports related building of any type in the region.

It is also, assuredly, one of the most handsome.

▲ Pounding cross country during a winter's day meet of the North East Harrier League in 2009, Moyra Magowan may be a few miles south in Farringdon, but her club, the **Sunderland Strollers,** have been based at Ashbrooke for over two decades.

Formed in 1981, the Strollers number around 150 members, most aged 40 or over. Apart from regular Wednesday night meets at Ashbrooke, the club plays a lead role in the NEHL by co-hosting, with the South Shields Harriers, the annual Pier to Pier Run, staged along a scenic route from South Shields pier to Roker pier.

▲ The second oldest section at Ashbrooke is **Sunderland RFC**, seen here wearing their traditional red, gold and black hooped shirts in March 2010, in an under 17s match against Hartlepool Rovers.

As noted earlier, the rugby club formed in December 1873, and for many years was known as Sunderland FC, or, as sometimes referred to in Ashbrooke's archives, Sunderland Foot-Ball Club.

This is significant in historical terms because it required the local soccer team, formed six years later in 1879, to adopt the name Sunderland Association Football Club, in order to distinguish itself from the rugby club.

Even though the rugby players have since renamed their club RFC, the footballers have remained AFC ever since.

There was a time when the Ashbrooke club considered taking up the round ball themselves, 'with a view to increasing the income'. However this was rejected at the 1890 annual meeting.

Soon after matters improved on the pitch, and as crowds reached 2–3,000, it was felt necessary to install Ashbrooke's first turnstiles.

The club then enjoyed a successful spell during the early 1900s, when the First XV won the Durham County Cup and supplied several players to the equally

successful Durham County side. Four players from this period were also capped by England.

Throughout this time facilities for spectators were confined to uncovered terraces. Only in the early 1920s was a timber terrace built on the north touchline backing onto Tunstall Vale, with a roof being added in 1926 at a cost of £258.

As seen above, it is still standing today, characterful if somewhat rickety, with its boarding painted white in order to form a sightscreen for the cricketers.

One player from the 1920s who left his mark was Hartley Elliott, later to become an international rugby referee. It was Elliott who in 1953 designed the club crest (*left*). This depicts a lymphad, a single sail boat with oars used by the ancient Britons and thought to have been the first vessel used for trading purposes on the River Wear.

▲ Sunderland's oldest sporting structure has been subject to numerous additions since its opening in 1899 (*see page 91*).

These include the clock, added in 1913, and two wings, designed in 1930 by yet another architect to have been an Ashbrooke club member, Stanley Milburn, of the well known Sunderland practice of William and TR Milburn.

Since then, as is common at cricket grounds, the verandah has been glazed in to provide a sheltered viewing lounge. This and other additions have compromised the design, yet they provide facilities vital to the club's viability.

Until the 1970s Ashbrooke hosted regular matches involving Durham and visiting Australian XIs. Following Durham CCC's elevation to first class status in 1991 it has also staged occasional county matches.

Today, as seen here in 2009, the main fare consists of fixtures in the North East Premier League, a competition won by **Sunderland CC** in its inaugural season in 2000.

To accommodate these fixtures the rugby club has to play some of its own early season games at other venues. In 2010 soccer began on the area formerly used for hockey.

And so Ashbrooke continues as it set out in 1887, for 'the physical training and development of the human frame' and 'the promotion of healthful exercises'.

To which the current trustees might add, '...and the maintenance of tolerance and peaceful co-existence between all members'.

Chapter Seven

Clubhouses and pavilions

Stairway to heaven – this wrought iron balustrade is one of several original features in the pavilion of the Gateshead Bowling Green Club on Prince Consort Road, a building whose core dates back to the late 1860s or 1870s. (The club itself, formed in 1865, is the oldest bowls club in Tyne and Wear.) Maintaining historic buildings offers a considerable challenge to clubs like Gateshead, torn between a desire to preserve the past while ensuring that they remain viable in the present.

Forming the heart and soul of every community based sports club is its clubhouse or pavilion.

(The terms are actually interchangeable, but in practice the word clubhouse tends to be used more in golf circles.)

Providers of shelter, warmth, camaraderie and the occasional beer or three, clubhouses and pavilions are in most cases the most significant buildings a club possesses.

In this chapter – the first of three focusing on specific types of sports-related buildings – we have identified those clubhouses and pavilions in Tyne and Wear that, regardless of the club's size or sporting prowess, exemplify trends in architectural styles, from the Victorian era through to the present day.

As will be seen, in this part of Britain as in all others, from the mid 19th century until the First World War, the dominant style was a homely form of vernacular architecture, characterised by half-timbered detailing, pitched roofs, domestic-style windows and shallow verandahs.

In this respect, the buildings reflected the tastes of the club members, echoing even the homes in which they themselves lived, particularly in the newly settled middle class suburbs.

Undoubtedly the best preserved example of this generation is the cricket pavilion at Close House, built in 1894 (*see page 98*).

Between the wars the domestic style evolved to take on a more institutional appearance. But clubs still clung on to the pedimented gable, almost as if this were *de rigueur* in pavilion design.

It was not of course, as may be seen in a number of Art Deco and Modernist pavilions built during the 1930s (and illustrated in earlier books in the *Played in Britain* series).

But alas, apart from Gosforth Squash Club (*page 33*), no such designs emerged in Tyne and Wear.

But then came the 1960s, and a new generation of architects did their best to provide clubhouses and pavilions that at last genuinely reflected advances in design.

An outstanding example of this break with the past is the pavilion at Jesmond Cricket Ground in Newcastle, opened in 1963 (*see pages 102–03*).

Otherwise, in Tyne and Wear as in every area so far surveyed by *Played in Britain*, the one trait that so many sports clubs have proved unable to resist is the building of extensions, and the steady replacement of original features that, inevitably and irrevocably, have robbed many a handsome clubhouse and pavilion of its architectural quality.

Regrettable though this is, it is entirely understandable.

Clubs grow. They admit women and need extra changing rooms. They need more lounges to bring in income. They glaze in their balconies to extend those lounges. They seek to attract younger members with modern tastes.

All the more reason, therefore, to celebrate those buildings that do survive relatively intact in Tyne and Wear, and to understand the genuine problems that those clubs with historic buildings face on a day to day basis, as their members gather around the bar for that final thirst quencher before heading back to their other home.

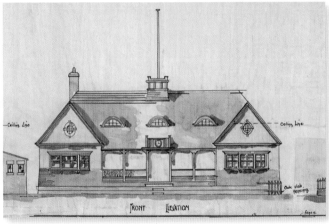

◄ Seen here during a women's cricket match at the **Jesmond Cricket Ground** on **Osborne Avenue** in the early 1900s, this rather wonderful timber pavilion started out life as one of three Swiss chalets erected for the 1887 Royal Jubilee Mining, Engineering and Industrial Exhibition, held on Newcastle's Town Moor.

In one of the chalets fancy goods were sold, in another jewellery, and in this one, sponsored by Nestlé, waitresses in Swiss costumes served light teas.

After the exhibition the chalet was re-erected at Osborne Avenue, which at that time was being used by the local police and was known as the Constabulary Ground.

In 1897 the ground was bought by Northumberland County Cricket Club, whose members nursed the chalet along until finally replacing it with an equally striking pavilion in 1963 (see pages 102–03).

Formed in 1847, **Tynemouth Cricket Club** moved to its current home off **Preston Avenue** (behind the ground of Percy Park RFC) in May 1885. By 1900 they had outgrown their original pavilion – transported from their previous ground on Preston Lane – and were therefore delighted to accept an offer to design a replacement from Tynemouth architect William Hope, of Hope & Maxwell, best known for their work on theatres.

According to the club's history Hope's designs had been based on another pavilion the committee had seen at Carlisle Cricket Club.

But if some members remained uncertain, the destruction of the old pavilion in a gale settled the matter, and so in January 1902 Hope's plans (centre) were submitted to Tynemouth Corporation.

Opened the following July, inside the pavilion was a central main hall with an impressive barrel vaulted roof. Off this, on either side, was a kitchen, a small visitors' dressing room and a larger members' room.

Regrettably Hope's pavilion did not stand the test of time and in 2005 it was almost completely rebuilt in simpler form by volunteers, keeping the twin gables but with a new central porch and extra wing. (Carlisle's pavilion has survived however, albeit also with an extension and later alterations).

Another pavilion that still stands but has been modernised and extended almost beyond recognition is that of the **Gateshead Bowling Green Club** on **Prince Consort Road**, seen here in the 1870s shortly after its opening (bottom left).

That the club was relatively wealthy may be seen not only from the attire of the members, but also from the solid brick construction and the ornate timberwork of the gable and porch.

▲ The original core of Gateshead Bowling Green's pavilion may be older (*see previous page*), but the building above, the **Close House cricket pavilion,** located in the middle of the **Close House Golf Course** near Heddon-on-the-Wall, is undoubtedly the oldest intact pavilion in the Tyne and Wear area.

Strictly speaking the pavilion lies within the jurisdiction of Northumberland County Council, being some 400 yards north of the Tyne, which forms the boundary with Gateshead. But we include it in this study, firstly because the golf course has such strong links with Newcastle, and secondly because the building itself is an outstanding and, externally at least, a finely preserved example of a late Victorian pavilion, clearly influenced by the Arts and Crafts movement.

Designed by the Newcastle architects Septimus Oswald & Son – known for their later work with Newcastle Breweries – the pavilion was built in 1894 for the Bewicke family within the grounds of their estate at Close House, a substantial Georgian mansion built in 1779.

Facing it across the former cricket pitch (now part of the golf course), and by the same architects, is an equally picturesque scoreboard building (*right*).

Over the years the two buildings and cricket pitch were used by a variety of clubs, including, between the wars, Close House CC and, during 1970s, by Wylam Cricket Club, who later returned to their original ground in the village of Wylam, a short distance west.

In 1961 the Close House estate was bought by King's College, the

forerunner of Newcastle University, who continued to use the pavilion for cricket, and in winter for hockey. It also served various other pitches laid out in the vicinity for football and rugby. In 1994 Close House itself was refurbished for use as a university conference and teaching centre.

Its present use as a private hotel and golf course dates from 2005 (*see page 22*).

When photographed here in 2010 the pavilion was serving as a temporary clubhouse for the golf club, while a new clubhouse neared completion next to Close House. Once this development is complete in 2011, however, the pavilion will be preserved, and hopefully given a new life, perhaps as residential or rented holiday accommodation.

▶ Crossing south over the Tyne and back into the Borough of Gateshead, and moving on into the Edwardian period, this is the clubhouse of **Tyneside Golf Club** on **Westfield Lane**, **Ryton**.

The club was formed in 1879 by a meeting of 25 gentlemen at the Douglas Hotel in Newcastle.

Their first course, designed by the Scottish golfer Mungo Park, was at Ryton Willows, a stretch of well drained land on the south bank of the Tyne.

Crucially it lay near a railway station, thereby providing good access for those Newcastle-based golfers fed up with conditions on the Town Moor course.

From Ryton Willows the club moved to a new course at nearby Western Falls in May 1903. It was here that ladies were first allowed to join, providing that they did not actually enter the clubhouse.

Tyneside's current home, known as the Ryton Falls course, dates from 1911, as does the clubhouse, seen here in 2009.

Opened in April 1911 and costing £720, it was designed and built by the Alnwick Foundry and Engineering Company.

Its unashamed domestic style, complete with an Arts and Crafts oriel window and timber weatherboarding, was something of a speciality for the company, which otherwise built 'artistic homes' for the new middle classes, as well as exporting a range of prefabricated buildings.

Despite inevitable alterations and extensions over the years – including, happily, the provision of facilities for female members – that 'artistic' quality remains very much to the fore, as a result of which the building was added to Gateshead Council's register of locally listed buildings in 2004.

Also listed locally by Gateshead Council is this neatly composed timber structure (*left*), the Avenue Green bowls pavilion, built in Saltwell Park in 1923 and used by nine clubs who play on the park's three greens. Saltwell Park is itself listed Grade II on English Heritage's Register of Historic Parks and Gardens, and in 2005 was voted Britain's best park.

▶ As noted earlier, the University of Newcastle emerged in 1963 from King's College, which was itself originally founded from a merger between **Armstrong College** and the **College of Medicine**.

This is the imposing pavilion of Armstrong College's sports ground, **Cochrane Park**, on **Etherstone Avenue**, **High Heaton**, now home of **Newcastle University RFC** and with facilities also for football, cricket, lacrosse and tennis.

As shown on the datestone above, the pavilion was built in 1922. The initials GEH stand for George Henderson, who funded its construction.

Henderson's initials are repeated on the pavilion's balcony, along with those of Cecil Cochrane, who gifted the ground. Mounted on the centre of the balcony is the Armstrong College crest.

The College of Medicine's rugby club, meanwhile – known officially as **Medical RFC**, but more commonly as 'the Medicals' – play in front of another solidly built, if somewhat functional inter war pavilion at **Cartington Terrace** in **Heaton** (*right*).

The ground dates back to the club's formation in 1898, but the pavilion was built in 1936, to the designs of a local firm, Newcombe & Newcombe.

◀ Staying in the inter war period, this is the pavilion at the **Wood Terrace** ground, Dean Road, South Shields, which hosts four sports: cricket, rugby, tennis and squash.

The ground was originally laid out in 1868 by **South Shields Cricket Club**, who had formed in 1850. They were joined in 1875 by the newly formed **Westoe Rugby Football Club** (Westoe being a village that has since been absorbed into South Shields).

The **Westoe Tennis Club** then formed on the site in 1880.

The current brick pavilion was designed by architect FW 'Wally' Newby, chair of the sports ground's governing board, and was opened in October 1934.

To its left can be seen a corner of the former Regent Cinema, which opened the following year, and is now a Mecca bingo hall.

Another relatively unspoilt inter war pavilion, but with a distinctly Italianate air, is that of **Novocastrians Rugby Football Club**, the 'Novos', at **Sutherland Park** in **Longbenton** (*left*), designed by local architects Marshall & Tweedy and built during season 1927–28.

Formed in 1898 by former pupils of Newcastle's Royal Grammar School, but now open to all, the 'Novos' ground is named after their benefactor, Sir Arthur Munro Sutherland.

▲ Such are changing tastes in architecture that the rectilinear brick and timber clad pavilion built by the **Northumberland County Cricket Club** at **Jesmond Cricket Ground** – to replace the Swiss chalet (*see page 97*) – might easily have been designed in recent years.

In fact it was opened in 1963. Its architects were L J Couves & Partners, a firm whose founder

played for Northumberland in the 1920s and which is perhaps best known for its early 1980s Metro stations in Newcastle city centre.

Costing £25,000, the pavilion represented the culmination of a major overhaul of the ground. This started in 1947 with the levelling of the pitch, followed by £7,000 spent on a viewing lounge next to the old pavilion, and on concreting

and seating the banks lining the perimeter, which are hemmed in tightly by Osborne Avenue and All Saints Cemetery.

Over the years a galaxy of stars has graced the ground, including Len Hutton, Gary Sobers, Ian Botham and Viv Richards. Yet in 2003 the ground's future appeared bleak. Unable to afford its upkeep Northumberland announced that

it would depart the following year. Fortunately, a campaign was launched, gathering support from as far afield as Dennis Lillee in Australia. In 2006 a newly formed club, **Newcastle Cricket Club**, established itself there, with the ground's lease being taken over by the Royal Grammar School.

Today the Jesmond Ground is a thriving community base which has twice been voted the North East Premier League's 'Ground of the Year'. And while for many years public opinion turned against the tower blocks and concrete mega-structures of the 1960s, a recent softening of attitudes has led to a much greater appreciation of the pavilion. As these images from 2010 show, like the ground, it too has stood the test of time.

More work for the scorer at Jesmond Cricket Ground, where the scoreboard, designed in 1977 by architect William Ainsworth – himself a cricketer and founder of the Ainsworth Spark practice – was adapted to house a digital display system in 2008.

A Tyneside sporting institution, the Wallsend Boys Club on Station Road has seen many a future footballing star enter through its distinctive 1960s entrance.

▲ Little changed since its opening in December 1966, apart from the addition of an artificial grass surface, this is the main sports hall at the **Wallsend Boys Club**.

Famous for nurturing a string of top-class footballers – including Steve Bruce, Peter Beardsley, Alan Shearer, Lee Clark and Michael Carrick – the club was set up in 1938 by directors and employees of the Swan Hunter shipyard. Indeed most of its early members were apprentices at Swan Hunter.

In common with other boys' or lads' clubs of the 19th and 20th centuries, Wallsend offered such sports as football, boxing, gymnastics, cross country running and snooker, not only as a means of recreation but to help instil discipline. Classes in woodwork were also offered, and for years the boys put on an annual pantomime.

In 1960 the club suffered a huge blow when the original wooden huts were destroyed in a fire.

It then had to wait six years before the current building was completed on the same site.

Since the mid 1970s football has dominated, although judo, martial arts and skateboarding also form part of the daily programme.

But whatever the sport, the club's values remain the same. Punctuality is paramount, swearing is banned, and much of the club's work is carried out by volunteers.

Most recently their efforts have concentrated on fund raising. This is to help further the construction of a new clubhouse and football pitches at Bigges Main, close to Wallsend Golf Club.

Thus in 2010 the club was preparing to bid farewell to a clubhouse that some have called 'a monstrous carbuncle' but which is fondly remembered by its old boys, many of whom have contributed to the funding of the new headquarters.

Wallsend is not the only such club in Tyne and Wear, however. Tyne Boys Club (founded 1949, now the Tyne Youth and Community Centre) began as a boxing club in the basement of Knott's Flats, Tynemouth. Grainger Park Boys Club (founded 1928) operates from Scotswood Sports Centre, and the Montagu & North Fenham Boys Club (founded 1948) has, like Wallsend, produced its share of professional footballers.

And of course, all these boys' clubs today cater for girls too.

▶ As we saw at Jesmond Cricket Ground, 1960s design lent itself well to pavilion architecture.

Another excellent example is this, the clubhouse of **Whitley Bay Golf Club**, completed in 1964.

Compared with pre war designs, its full width, wraparound balcony and picture windows contribute to a lighter, more sociable interplay between the interior and exterior, and of course provide much better views over the course.

On a practical level, an external staircase offers greater flexibility, while the flat roof obviates the need to heat large internal spaces, as was common in older pavilions (although such roofs have often added to maintenance costs).

Also notable for its flat roof, picture window and angular profile is the pavilion of the Durham Senior League's **Whitburn Cricket Club** (*right*). Designed by William Kirtley of SW Milburn & Partners, Sunderland, it was opened in 1961–62 during the centenary of the club (whose ground, laid out in the estate of Whitburn Hall, is Tyne and Wear's third oldest sports ground, after Whickham and Percy Main cricket clubs).

Just west of Whitburn is another admirable 1960s pavilion at Boldon, designed by an architect at SW Milburn's parent practice, W & TR Milburn, and shown on the inside of the back cover.

▶ We conclude this brief survey of pavilion architecture at one of the most historic grounds in Tyne and Wear, the **Roseworth Terrace** home of **South Northumberland Cricket Club**, immediately south of Gosforth Central Park.

South North, as they are generally known, formed in 1864 and settled at the ground in 1892. After buying the freehold in 1923 they built the current pavilion (seen on the left) in 1933. Its architects were Marshall & Tweedy, who were also responsible for the pavilion at Sutherland Park (*see page 101*).

However, it is its hi-tech neighbour that is of most interest in the context of this chapter.

Although not a pavilion or clubhouse, it is a fine example of an early 21st century building designed to help ensure that cricket grounds retain their focus as hubs of sporting life, seven days a week.

Costing £1.5 million and opened in 2003, this is the **Newcastle Cricket Centre**, an indoor coaching facility designed by the London-based David Morley Architects, a firm that has produced several outstanding buildings for a number of English grounds. Although used mostly by budding local players, it has also been used by the England squad. As they say at the Centre, 'It is always sunny inside!'

Another noteworthy modern building is the pavilion of **South Shields Golf Club** (*right*).

Designed by Fitz Architects of Sunderland and due to open in 2011, it features a 'living roof' and natural ventilation, with its balcony and terraces offering wonderful views over the surrounding countryside and coastline.

When it comes to any future survey of sporting heritage in Tyne and Wear, both these buildings will surely feature prominently.

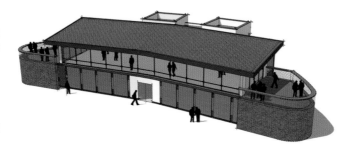

Chapter Eight

Grounds and grandstands

April 24 2010 was an historic day at the Dean Road sports ground in South Shields – the first time since South Shields Cricket Club had started sharing the ground with Westoe RFC in 1875 that the two clubs had played there on the same day, one after the other. Seen here on that day is action from the Wood Terrace side of the ground. Ground sharing between cricket and rugby or football clubs appears to be a distinct trait of sport in the north east.

One of the most powerful sentiments in the world of sport is the attachment felt by players and supporters to the ground on which their club plays.

The place they call 'home'.

In Tyne and Wear there are around a dozen grounds that have been home to the same club for over a century, and two that in 2010 celebrated their 150th anniversaries, the grounds of Whickham and of Percy Main cricket clubs.

Equally, there is a similar number of clubs which in recent years have had to bid farewell to their home grounds. Not only a high profile club like Sunderland AFC, leaving Roker Park, but the likes of North Shields FC and South Shields FC, who both, under financial pressure, lost substantial well appointed grounds and were forced to make new starts on council-owned pitches.

Tyne and Wear has a number of grounds that fall within two other categories.

First there are grounds that are shared by more than one sport, as we saw at Ashbrooke, with

the most common combination being cricket and rugby, as at South Shields and Westoe (*see left*), and Whickham. At Hebburn, the former works ground of the Reyrolle company is shared by four sports (*see page 110*).

Second are the grounds that were originally set up as part of Miners' Welfare schemes, as described in Chapter One.

Many of these grounds survive in various guises, particularly in the former Durham mining belt, from Wearmouth down to Eppleton, having been taken over by private or charitable organisations, or in some cases by local authorities.

A home ground does not have to be beautiful in order to be loved. In a similar vein, a grandstand does not have to be of any architectural quality to be cherished.

Thus in contrast to the pavilions in the previous chapter, most of the stand structures seen in this section are utilitarian, and in some cases, as below at Washington FC, positively makeshift.

At senior levels of football and rugby, Britain's grounds have

been transformed since the 1970s by three disasters: at Ibrox Park, Glasgow, in 1971 (which led to the Safety of Sports Grounds Act of 1975), at Valley Parade in Bradford in 1985 (which brought in tighter control of wooden stands), and in 1989 at Hillsborough, Sheffield (which led to the phasing out of terracing for standing spectators).

In truth, most of the community-based grounds in this chapter have not been directly affected by these measures.

Nevertheless, as standards at senior grounds improve – be it in stand design, floodlighting, turf management and so on – so too are expectations at all levels raised.

Moreover, if a small club now finds success on the field and wishes to rise up the ladder – to follow its dream, as it were – it has to match this achievement by meeting rigorous standards off the field. Kingston Park, the final ground in this chapter, exemplifies this imperative perfectly; from a works ground to a Premiership stadium in less than a decade.

Once a mere field. Now a stately home.

▲ It may not appear to be a structure of any great architectural merit, but timber grandstands of this type and vintage, once common across Britain, have become increasingly rare in recent years.

This is the stand at **Cartington Terrace**, the home of the **Medical Rugby Football Club** in Heaton, Newcastle (*see page 100*).

Built in 1933, after over a half century of service its days appeared to be numbered. Rather than take it down, however, the Medicals called in a structural engineer and, after raising the necessary funds, restored and reopened it in 1988.

As a result, apart from the stand at Newcastle Racecourse, (*pages 56-57*), which arguably falls into a separate category, it is now the second oldest stand in Tyne and Wear, after the 1920s stand at Ashbrooke (*page 94*).

Seen on the back of the stand is the club crest, a serpent entwined around a rod, a symbol representing the Greek god of medicine, Asclepius.

On the opposite page is the more modest, but still fairly typical stand of **Washington Football Club** at **Albany Park** on Spout Lane.

Originally called the Washington Mechanics, the Northern League club was formed in 1947 by miners at Washington's 'F' Pit, and moved to Albany Park in 1980.

They have a clubhouse on the south touchline, and on the opposite side this cover, erected for standing spectators in 1987 using a patchwork of materials, including a series of domestic panelled doors.

▶ The **Glebe Ground** on **Rose Avenue**, **Whickham**, is one of several cricket grounds in the north east that is shared by either a football or a rugby club.

Seen here during a game v. Chopwell, with the football stand in the background, it is also one of many grounds in Britain that, although lacking any buildings of architectural merit, is of genuine historical interest.

Representing as they did a rather affluent village, **Whickham Cricket Club** were known to their rivals as 'the Rose Growers'. They formed in 1860 and so in May 2010 celebrated the 150th anniversary of both club and ground.

As such the Glebe is the oldest sports ground in Tyne and Wear, along with St John's Green, North Shields, home of Percy Main CC, whom Whickham played in a joint 150th anniversary match at Beamish (*see pages 8 and 192*).

For years Whickham CC enjoyed sole rights to the Glebe, until in the 1950s the National Coal Board, which owned the site, insisted that the football team of the Watergate Colliery Welfare Fund play there too. As the cricket club's minutes testify, this caused considerable strain, especially when the two clubs' fixtures clashed.

Meanwhile, another football team were playing on the adjoining recreation ground. Formed in 1944

and consequently dubbed the 'Home Guard' team, **Whickham FC** also wished to play on the Glebe. But to do that they needed a colliery affiliation, so recast themselves as the welfare team of the nearby Axwell Park Colliery.

That mine closed in 1954, followed by Watergate ten years later. The NCB then sold the Glebe to Whickham Council, who leased it to a newly formed **Glebe Sports Club**, representing both the cricket

club and the football club.

The latter, having reverted to their original name of Whickham FC, achieved national fame in 1981 by winning the FA Vase at Wembley. Their semi-final against Windsor & Eton drew the Glebe's all time record crowd of 3,165.

Ground sharing does have its drawbacks. The football club must play their first 7-8 fixtures of the season away, and then, in order to comply with Northern

League ground regulations, erect a temporary barrier along the touchline that backs onto the cricket field.

It is the same at **Hebburn Town FC**, formed in 1912, whose pitch on **South Drive**, **Hebburn**, is overlooked by a rather quirky cricket pavilion, seen here in 1978 (*below left*). The factory to the rear – since replaced by a housing estate – belonged to the switchgear manufacturing company **Reyrolle**, now part of the Siemens group.

Reyrolle laid out the ground in 1928, charging employees a few pence per week for use of its facilities. In the late 1940s it was opened to the public, until in 1982 the ground was bought by South Tyneside Council. They in turn now lease it to the **Hebburn Sports and Social Club**, which apart from Hebburn Town consists of sections for cricket, tennis and bowls.

◄ This functional but tidy 250 seater stand is at **Filtrona Park**, the home of **South Shields FC** since 1992, and before that the works ground of the Filtrona company, manufacturers of cigarette filters.

The ground, which cost the club £400,000 to redevelop and now holds 2,000 overall, is on Shaftesbury Avenue, alongside the Metro line near Bede station.

South Shields are actually the third club to bear that name. The first, formed in 1899, were based at Horsley Hill (see page 116). The second played within the grounds of an 18th century mansion, Simonside Hall, from 1951–74. This ground held a record 18,500 crowd for a cup tie v. York in 1957, but is now a housing estate, just east of Filtrona Park.

The present day club, known as the Mariners, formed in 1974 but had to spend their next 18 seasons playing on a council pitch in Jack Clark Park.

Owning and maintaining a ground, even one as modern as Filtrona Park, is a major challenge. **Blaydon Rugby Football Club** – whose roots can be traced back to a club called Blaydon Star in 1888 and who have been based at **Crow Trees** in **Swalwell** since 1951 – raise funds by staging massive car boot sales every Sunday.

In the same spirit of self help, their 390 seater stand (left) was bought by the club from Gateshead International Stadium (see page 126) in 1980, and painstakingly re-erected over the course of the 1981-82 season.

The structure cost £3,000 to buy and, thanks to hours of voluntary labour and gifts of materials, another £1,500 to complete. The cost to the volunteers' marriages, as one of them recalls, was another matter altogether.

It may look relatively run down from these photographs taken during its twilight years in the 1980s, but at its peak Appleby Park, off Hawkeys Lane in North Shields, was one of the best non-League grounds in England. Its hodge-podge of stands and terraces reflected years of ups and downs, make do and mend, on a typically constrained urban site.

▲ Like several grounds in Tyne and Wear, **Appleby Park** started out as a cycling track in the late 19th century. North Shields Athletic FC took it over in 1900, and in the 1920s were succeeded by Preston Colliery FC, who adopted the name **North Shields FC** in 1928.

The ground's record gate was 12,800, for a local derby v. South Shields in 1936.

Despite winning the FA Amateur Cup in 1969, in common with many non-League clubs North Shields started to fall heavily in debt during the 1970s.

A further problem, caused by former colliery workings on the site, was subsidence; so bad, it is said, that on one occasion a player disappeared up to his waist in a hole that suddenly appeared.

Eventually the club had to admit defeat and the ground was sold in 1992, so that today the name Appleby Park appears only as a road name on the housing estate built on the site. The club itself, meanwhile, reformed and settled at the council-owned Ralph Gardner Park on Silkeys Lane, although in 2010 plans were announced for a more developed stadium elsewhere.

▶ St James' Park and the Stadium of Light apart, the most advanced ground in Tyne and Wear for field sports is **Kingston Park**, on the north western edge of Newcastle in **Brunton Lane**. Significantly, all three of these venues have involved the Gateshead based Taylor Tulip & Hunter Architects.

Originally the sports ground of the Newcastle Chronicle and Journal, the Kingston Park site was bought for £55,000 in 1989 by **Gosforth RFC**, who had sold their previous ground for £1.7m (*see page 61*). Renamed **Newcastle Gosforth**, they built a stand and clubhouse, opened in 1990.

For those members used to the relative simplicity and convenience of the old ground in Gosforth this out of town, greenfield site represented a mixed blessing.

Then in 1995 rugby union was itself completely transformed by a decision to allow clubs to adopt professionalism. It was at this point that Cameron Hall Developments, owned by Sir John Hall, chair of Newcastle United, took a 76 per cent share in the club.

Renamed **Newcastle Falcons**, the club won the Premiership in its first season of 1997–98.

Hall sold up the following year to former player Dave Thompson, who initiated a second phase of development, designed and built by TTH Architects and Metnor Construction. To add to the existing East Stand, terraces holding 2,500 were built at both ends, the south terrace being covered, together with a 4,000 seat West Stand, thereby creating a capacity of 10,000.

In its short life Kingston Park has seen many comings and goings. **Newcastle United** reserves played there during the 1990s, while from 2007–09 it was shared by **Newcastle Blue Star FC**.

Also in 2007 the actual ground was sold to the Gosforth-based Northern Rock bank (who were already sponsors of the Falcons).

Northern Rock then sold on the 23 acre site in 2008 to the University of Northumbria, owners of the adjoining Bullocksteads Sports Ground.

It is now the University's plan to establish a centre of sporting excellence at Kingston Park in conjunction with the Falcons and the Northumberland Rugby Union.

Meanwhile, another club to have entered the scene is the re-formed Gosforth RFC. Unhappy with the move to professionalism, a group of the original members broke away in 1996, set up a base at Bullocksteads, and adopted their old kit of green and white hoops.

Gosforth have since moved to

another ground in the vicinity – Druid Park at Woolsington – which, ironically, until 2007 had been the home of Newcastle Blue Star.

And so within just two decades this once distant outpost of Newcastle has been at the centre of a bewildering merry-go-round of clubs, grounds and owners; a story which may well entail more twists and turns in the years to come.

Newcastle Falcons play Leicester Tigers at Kingston Park, viewed from the East Stand on a wet afternoon in April 2010. In time it is hoped to build a roof over the north terrace, to complete what is already one of English rugby's finest club stadiums, and one with great potential, if only the heavy costs of professionalism can be sustained in the future.

Chapter Nine

Stadiums and tracks

Spectator sport has always been subject to fashion, and with the possible exception of ice hockey, there was no faster or sexier sight in 1930s Britain than that of dashing men in their leathers, roaring around a floodlit track on throbbing motorcycles. This 1938 programme is from Brough Park, where speedway made its debut under 'one hundred lamps' in 1929. It is now the only speedway venue left in Tyne and Wear.

When the White City Stadium opened at Blaydon in 1937 there were already five dog tracks in Tyne and Wear. True, the area could claim a long tradition of coursing and dog racing. But White City proved to be a speculation too far, surviving a mere fourteen years. This aerial view from 1946 is one of the very few images ever discovered of the venue.

We conclude this section on sports-related building types with a category whose definition has long been unclear.

By tradition, some of the largest spectator venues in Britain were always known as 'grounds'. An example is Roker Park in Sunderland. Yet its successor is patently a stadium, in both name and in concept.

From this we may deduce that a 'ground' is a venue that has been developed incrementally over the years, whereas a 'stadium' is one that has been designed and built to a pre-conceived masterplan.

But in popular usage, at least since the early 20th century, the word stadium has also been used to apply to a venue, however grand or basic, that has a track.

This was not always the case. Early Victorian track-based venues, designed to host professional running, were all called grounds. Probably the first in Tyne and Wear was the Victoria Running Ground in Low Elswick, opened in 1858, just west of the Wrestling Ground, which confusingly was also used for foot races (*see page 15*).

Located roughly on the site of the Metro Radio Arena, the Victoria Ground had a 444 yard track and a grandstand. A typical encounter there, such as the half mile race between two star pedestrians, Gateshead's James Rowan and his local rival Jack White, in 1861, would attract at least 5,000 spectators.

After the Victoria Ground was bought by the North Eastern Railway Company in 1863, the Fenham Park Grounds were then laid out on Ponteland Road. This had a track almost 600 yards long and, as was the norm at commercially run venues of the period, also offered dog racing, rabbit coursing, quoits and pigeon shooting. It closed in 1875.

Gateshead's Borough Gardens, meanwhile, opened in 1868 but had to move to a new site at Friar's Goose (roughly where the International Stadium now stands) in 1872 because of railway construction. Three years later a

police crackdown on betting led to the closure of all commercial grounds. But they soon reopened, more numerous than before.

In the 1880s running tracks could be found at Killingworth, Backworth, Gateshead, Walker and notably in Newcastle, where the Victoria Ground reopened on more or less its old site in 1881.

Although professional running remained popular, by 1935 only one track-based venue survived, Brough Park, in Byker, and that was because it was adapted to stage two of the latest crazes: greyhound racing, imported to Britain from the USA in 1926, and dirt track racing, an Australian sport which evolved into speedway.

However basic the venues built or adapted to host these new sports, they were always, and have always been referred to as 'stadiums'. And as this chapter shows, they have all had to offer as wide a range of sports as possible in order to survive.

▶ Enveloped in a swathe of corrugated sheeting, **Gosforth Stadium**, on the Great North Road, started out as the Gosforth Cycling Grounds in c.1900.

Rugby arrived in 1912, and in 1922 Northumberland County Rugby Union made it their **County Ground**. Two clubs also played there; **Northern**, until 1937, and **Gosforth**, until 1955 (*see page 61*).

Meanwhile, since amateur rugby hardly paid the bills, a 440 yard speedway track was inaugurated in June 1929. When this failed to take off a greyhound track took its place in May 1932, with stands and terraces being built for 18,000 spectators, under the aegis of Totalisator Holdings. This company sold up to Ladbrokes in 1976, but they could not arrest its decline either and the last dog race took place in August 1987.

An Asda superstore now occupies the site (*see page 53*).

As seen in these images from the 1980s, the actual greyhound track was completely sheltered by overhanging roofs, a feature known at only one other track, the White City in Liverpool.

Another **White City Stadium** was at Blaydon (*opposite*).

Costing £50,000 and holding 24,000, this opened in 1937 for greyhound racing, and like Gosforth staged rugby, when the shortlived **Newcastle Rugby League Club** played there from 1937–39.

Blaydon Harriers also trained at the stadium, and in June 1938 it staged a rare England v. Scotland women's football match.

But Tyneside was already over provided with tracks, and after the final greyhound meeting in May 1951 White City was demolished.

The site now lies beneath the modern road network, just south of the present day Scotswood Bridge.

▲ The stories of both the **South Shields Greyhound Stadium** at **Horsley Hill** (*above*), and the **Gateshead Greyhound Stadium** at **Redheugh Park** (*opposite*) were intertwined with that of a football club, known first as **South Shields FC** and later **Gateshead FC**.

Before football, the Horsley Hill site started out in 1900 as the ground of the **South Shields Rugby Union Club**. They converted to rugby league in 1901 but folded three years later. The ground was then taken over by **South Shields Adelaide AFC**, 'the Laides', whose first professional North Eastern League match in 1908 drew a 3,000 crowd. By 1910 the suffix 'Adelaide' (referring to a street in Laygate, South Shields) had been dropped, and in 1913 a stand and pavilion were added, both buildings having been bought from a defunct racecourse at Boldon.

South Shields' moment arrived with their election to the Football League's Second Division in 1919.

The early signs were positive, with a Horsley Hill record gate of 24,348 attending an FA Cup tie in February 1927, and some steady, mid-table ranking being achieved. But then relegation in 1928, followed by a huge drop in gates (exacerbated by the economic slump of the period), led to the decision in March 1930 to relocate to Redheugh Park, nearly nine miles to the west.

Gateshead Council welcomed them – an off-the-shelf League club in their midst! – though Newcastle United were much less pleased.

Horsley Hill, meanwhile, was converted into an impressive greyhound stadium, and from 1936–51 also played host to a newly formed South Shields FC.

Seen opposite is the stadium shortly after the original North Stand had been replaced in 1963 by viewing lounges backing onto a ten-pin bowling alley (aptly known as the Dog's Bowl).

But then in 1966 the greyhound racing authorities withdrew Horsley Hill's licence, and the following decade the site was redeveloped with housing (on streets inexplicably named after golf courses, such as Birkdale and Gleneagles).

The bowling greens seen behind the Tote board survive, however, as part of the South Shields Bowls Centre in Jack Clark Park.

Back at **Redheugh Park** (*above*), **Gateshead FC** endured a patchy response, and in 1937 were happy to welcome a greyhound company as co-tenants. That September the newly revamped stadium drew a record crowd of 20,752 for a Gateshead League match.

But by the late 1950s gates had plummeted, and on the fateful day of May 28 1960 – a day still remembered by many – Gateshead were voted out of the League.

Greyhound racing ended in 1966, and in 1971 the now struggling non-League football club moved to the Gateshead International Stadium (*see page 126*).

Two years later Redheugh Park was cleared, and today part of the site is occupied by a Powerleague five-a-side football centre.

▲ Once there were four greyhound stadiums in and around Newcastle. Today there is only one – the great survivor, **Brough Park**, **Byker**, seen here from the west, in 1971.

Brough Park is also currently the only speedway venue left in Tyne and Wear. (Speedway, incidentally, is staged on the stadium's inner circuit, surfaced with cinders, while the greyhounds run on the narrower outer track, covered with sand.)

In common with the stadiums at Gosforth and South Shields, Brough Park's origins go back to the early 20th century. It was first laid out in 1899 as a racecourse for trotting (a gambling related sport in which horse-drawn buggies raced around a track). But as was typical of such ventures around urban Britain, that alone could not pay the bills.

For two years before the First World War a football club called Newcastle City tried to establish an audience. In the tradition of 19th century pedestrianism, professional foot races were staged from 1917 onwards, continuing sporadically until 1951. From 1936–38 Brough Park also played host to Newcastle's rugby league team, before it decamped to White City.

▲ While speedway came and went over the years, following its debut at **Brough Park** in May 1929, greyhound racing, which started in June 1928, has continued uninterrupted to the present day.

As may be seen in this image from the late 1940s or early 1950s – showing what appears to be a donkey derby – the dog track at this time was turfed. Only in the 1960s did sand, which withstands more wear and tear, become the norm, after the government allowed more race meetings to take place following the legalisation of betting shops in 1961.

Other events at Brough Park during the post war boom in popular entertainment included show jumping, various stunt shows, and a curious series of races involving midget cars (an idea hatched in America in 1933). There was even an England v. Scotland midget car race at Brough Park on Easter Monday 1952.

During these boom years, when crowds of 5–10,000 were not uncommon, like most greyhound stadiums Brough Park had a main stand on the home straight and an assortment of terrace covers ranged around the bends and opposite straight, plus a Tote board at one end (see opposite).

Since then, as attendances have diminished, and again as is typical of tracks around Britain, spectators have been confined to the main stand and the paddock in front, leaving the remaining areas around the track out of bounds to the public.

▶ While the greyhounds hold sway at **Brough Park** on three nights and two afternoons a week, twelve months a year, Sunday nights are reserved for speedway, from March to October.

Like most British speedway teams, the **Newcastle Diamonds** – shown here in action against the Edinburgh Monarchs in May 2009 – have endured a patchy existence.

After a single season in 1929-30 they reappeared in 1938–39, again from 1945–51, then a third time from 1961–70. Three further spells followed between 1975 and 1994.

For one season in 1949, after the promoter relocated the franchise to Glasgow, a team represented Newcastle under the name 'Magpies'. The Diamonds moniker was restored the following year after a public protest.

The first meeting of the current Diamonds era was held in March 1997, thus beginning what has since become the team's longest unbroken run in Newcastle.

Brough Park is ideally located, being on the edge of an industrial and retail park, on Fossway.

The track itself is known for its fast straights and tight bends, which adds to the excitement but has also seen four riders suffer fatal accidents, the last in 1992.

Although the bikes themselves have developed considerably, speedway today remains a fast and furious sport competed under much

the same format as in its earliest years between the wars.

Two riders from each team complete four laps of the track, on 500cc bikes that can accelerate faster than a Formula One car (from 0–60mph in 3.5 seconds), and yet which have only one gear, one footrest, no rear suspension and, just to add to the thrill, no brakes.

Throttling and sliding round the bends are the essence of success. And of course speed. A typical race lasts less than a minute.

Add to this a pervading smell of grease, cinders, oil and methanol, laced with burning rubber, and it makes for quite a sensory experience; one that nowadays is enjoyed by an average of around 600 fans on bikers' night at Byker.

▲ Just yards across the Gateshead and Chester-le-Street border, with the East Coast Main Line running along its western flank, is the **Pelaw Grange Greyhound Stadium**.

Since 2005 this has staged licensed races under the auspices of the Greyhound Board of Great Britain. But before then it was what is known as a 'flapping track', of which there have been several in the north east, particularly popular amongst dog-owning pitmen.

Pelaw Grange began in this spirit, laid out almost single-handedly during the mid 1940s by a racing enthusiast, George Towers.

In order to keep the mechanical hare going during power cuts, Towers used to hitch up a bicycle to the motor and pedal furiously.

Today, Pelaw Grange may appear to be basic, with an assortment of lounges and a paddock on the east side. But under the McKenna family, who have run the track since 1965, it provides a friendly hub on three race nights a week.

The track measures 345m, with, as of 2010, the fastest performer recorded being a dog called Blue Genisis, who whipped round at nearly 39mph in 2007.

▶ Going to the dogs nowadays is for most punters a chance to dine out, have a drink and a flutter, all from within the comfort of a glass-fronted grandstand. Only a handful of hardier souls step outside onto the paddock (*above*), where the bookies have staked their pitches and where the dogs can be more closely observed as they parade before each race.

These views are from the **Sunderland Greyhound Stadium, East Boldon**, which like Pelaw Grange sits alongside a railway line, linking Sunderland and Newcastle.

Built at a cost of £60,000 and designed by architects Matkin & Hawkins, war had broken out by the time it opened in March 1940. By the 1960s it had lost its licence and reverted to a flapping track. But the first speedway meeting drew a crowd of 6,500 in 1964, and three teams would be based there, the Saints (in 1964), the Stars (1971–73) and the Gladiators (1974).

Interest in both the dogs and the bikes dwindled, and it was only after a major refurbishment of the main stand that greyhound racing returned in the 1990s.

▲ Since its refurbishment, **Sunderland Greyhound Stadium** has found itself as one of only 25 licensed tracks still operating in Britain (compared with 77 at the sport's peak in 1951).

That three of those 25 (all in this chapter) are in the north east, which also has three independent tracks (at Easington, Wheatley Hill and Cambois), suggests that the region's longstanding love of dog racing remains strong.

But there can be no denying that the sport faces a host of issues: tighter regulation, the lure of online betting, the cost of keeping dogs and the slim winnings to be made.

For the party-goers inside, racing provides a great night out. For the owners, trainers and bookies outside, a chill wind is in the air.

▶ From four legged to two legged runners, we now turn to athletics stadiums in Tyne and Wear.

During the immediate post war period, as part of their wider plans for urban reconstruction, and in the wake of the 1948 Olympics, numerous local authorities around Britain drew up ambitious schemes for large municipal sports stadiums, designed to widen sporting provision in areas of need.

Whitley Bay was one such authority (*see page 62*).

Another was Newcastle, which in March 1950 announced optimistic plans for a £250,000 **City Stadium** to be laid out on the former Ouseburn refuse tip on **Warwick Street**, near Byker Bridge.

Underneath the site flowed the Ouseburn itself, through a massive concrete culvert.

Initially the plans were to cover the area in soil and turf, so that a football pitch and both cycling and running tracks could be provided.

But long term the plan was to erect two huge seated stands on either side of the track, each seating 43,000 spectators and with three storey car parks underneath, plus a terrace holding 8,500 at the Warwick Street End.

(This total of 94,500 compared with St James' Park capacity at the time of around 70,000.)

Also on site there was to be an indoor sports centre containing badminton courts and an ice rink.

It took five years for the first stage to be realised, culminating in an opening event in June 1955.

At that stage there was a cinder track, a small wooden pavilion backing onto the terraced houses on Newington Road, and a modest, if attractive entrance block.

But as the years passed and other needs took precedence – at one stage an alternative site for a super stadium was considered on the Town Moor – plans for the City Stadium were abandoned, and as the photographs on this page show, from the *Evening Chronicle* in July 1967, the site fell into disrepair.

Today the area is open parkland, with a children's playground and artificial five-a-side pitch on the Newington Road site.

But in the midst of this can still be seen a narrow cinder running track, a ghostly reminder of a once grandiose post war dream.

▲ Another venue once with high hopes is **Gypsies Green Stadium** on **Sea Road, South Shields**. In the 1930s plans were drawn up for an indoor sportsdrome on the site. But all that emerged in the 1950s was a 400m asphalt cycle track.

A cinder athletics track was added in 1964 which, being inside the cycle track, measured only 352 yards, a fifth of a mile.

Despite its minimal facilities the stadium became a base for **South Shields Harriers**. Brendan Foster recorded a sub four minute mile there, and in 1977 it was the focal point of a visit by Muhammad Ali.

Today it is perhaps best known for its location next to the finishing line of the **Great North Run** (*see page 149*). But the cycle track is no longer in use, and in 2007

controversial plans were announced for a hotel on the site. These plans have since been shelved, and the South Shields Harriers, who train at the stadium twice a week, now hope that a modern 400m track will be laid at Gypsies Green as part of a proposed centre of sporting excellence.

Until that happens, the nearest competition-approved track and field facility in South Tyneside is **Monkton Stadium** on **Dene Terrace, Jarrow** (*above*).

This was originally laid out on an existing sports ground in 1937, as part of a work creation scheme financed by the Surrey Fund (itself set up, remarkably, by a Surrey MP in response to the previous year's Jarrow March to London).

The original cinder track is still in use, but next to it is an eight lane 400m synthetic track laid in 1988. Built at the same time, between the tracks and with a 60m indoor track of its own, is a 1,000 seat stand.

Monkton is the base of the **Jarrow and Hebburn Athletic Club**, the club where Jarrow born Olympic runner and holder of three world records, Steve Cram, first made his name in the late 1970s.

From the same period is the **Silksworth Sports Complex** in **Sunderland** (*below*), where the track, opened in August 1982, was laid out within a 167 acre site formerly occupied by Silksworth Colliery, which closed in 1971.

Based at the track is the **Sunderland Harriers and Athletic Club**, formed initially in 1897.

◀ Leading the field in Tyne and Wear, both in terms of athletics facilities and the sheer range of sports hosted, is the **Gateshead International Stadium**.

Built on a former industrial site, just south of the Tyne, the Gateshead Youth Stadium (as originally titled) was opened in August 1955 by the then world marathon record holder, Jim Peters.

At that time the £30,000 stadium had an asphalt cycle track and a cinder athletic track, until the latter was replaced by an artificial track in 1974. On its opening day, Gateshead Harrier Brendan Foster established a new world record for the 3,000 metres.

Seen here in 1978 is its original 400 seat grandstand, backing onto Neilsen Road.

The following year Gateshead Borough Council decided to press ahead with plans to transform the stadium into a venue capable of staging international meetings.

Over the next few years the stand was taken down and sold for £3,000 to Blaydon Rugby Football Club, where it remains to the present day (*see page 111*).

In its place rose an elegant 3,300 seat cantilevered stand, with a further 8,450 uncovered seats on banking around the three other sides. The first time all these seats were filled for a sports event was in August 1995, for a pre-season friendly between Gateshead FC and Newcastle United.

The stadium's prime location is shown left, in 2009, with the Millennium Bridge and The Sage Gateshead a mile to the north west.

Summing up all the stadium's many uses is no easy task.

Apart from rock concerts during the 1990s (including Tina Turner and Bon Jovi), first and foremost it has earned its reputation as the leading athletics stadium in the region. In fact in 2000 it became the first venue to have staged the European Cup twice, having hosted the same event the previous year.

It is also amongst a small elite of stadiums worldwide hosting annual Grand Prix meetings as part of the IAAF's Diamond League.

Football has been a staple too, if with mixed fortunes. The stadium's first tenant club was Gateshead FC, who moved there from Redheugh Park in 1971 (see page 117). After this club folded two years later a newly formed Gateshead Town took their place in 1974. They too were shortlived, however, and were replaced by South Shields FC (a club formed, ironically, when its precursor relocated to Redheugh Park in 1930). Under the new title of Gateshead United this club managed only three years.

Finally, in 1977, another new club, this time named after one of its predecessors, **Gateshead FC**, managed to establish itself; this despite the fact that watching football in an athletics stadium has never been popular. As a result, in 2009 the club unveiled plans for a stadium of their own on the former North Durham Cricket ground (see page 15).

Meanwhile, two other tenants at the International Stadium are an American football team, the **Gateshead Senators**, who have played there since 1988, and **Gateshead Thunder**, a rugby league club formed in 1998.

Last but not least, the most longstanding resident club of all, having moved to the stadium in 1956, is the **Gateshead Harriers**.

Formed in 1904 at St Mary's Church, Oakwellgate, the club meets twice a week and has nurtured the talents of a string of top athletes.

Athletics at the Gateshead International Stadium in 2002. For the Aviva British Grand Prix in July 2010 a new 4,000 seat East Stand was unveiled as part of a masterplan drawn up by S&P Architects. Built by Willmott Dixon the stand's 30m cantilevered roof was designed by Fabric Architects and is covered by a PVC coated polyester fabric held in tension across five barrel vaulted sections.

But still there is more, for in May 2006 Lord Coe opened the latest addition to the complex, a superb £9.5 million indoor athletics centre designed by the Newcastle based FaulknerBrowns Architects. This houses a hub for the **English Institute of Sport** (which offers training and backup for elite athletes) and also **Gateshead College's Academy of Sport**.

Add to this various fitness suites, three football pitches and sundry other outdoor training areas and a picture emerges of a stadium complex that clearly will have an immense bearing on any future study of sporting heritage in the north east.

At the last count over 200,000 people passed through the stadium's doors in a single year.

Chapter Ten

Cock fighting

Held in the collection of the Great North Museum in Newcastle, this stuffed gamecock is a reminder of a bloody sport once hugely popular across England and Wales, but especially so in the north east. Such cocks, at their peak between the ages of one and two years, were bred specifically for fighting. Often their comb and wattle would be removed, their wings and tail feathers trimmed, and their spurs cut off and replaced by lethal steel blades or, as seen here and below right, by sharpened metal spikes known as 'gaffs'. Other surviving examples of spurs and gaffs may be seen at Beamish and Sunderland Museums.

We begin this next section of our study, concerning individual sports, with an activity that according to modern sensibilities would not be regarded as a sport at all.

And yet until at least the mid 19th century, the word 'sport' referred almost exclusively to such pursuits; usually bloody in nature, and entirely rooted in gambling.

Although cock fighting was banned in 1849, its heritage is still with us, not only in the form of pubs called the Fighting Cocks, but even in the organisation of modern sport itself.

Support for cock fighting extended throughout the social hierarchy – it was often referred to as the 'royal sport' – bringing together aristocrats, merchants and agricultural labourers alike, often cheek-by-jowl in the intimate surrounds of a cockpit.

Particularly prominent were the second Duke of Northumberland, Charles Grey (1764-1845), who served as Prime Minister during the 1830s, and Sir Harry Vane-Tempest (1771–1813), holder of vast estates in County Durham and probably the north east's most enthusiastic 'cocker'.

All concerned paid close attention to the breeding of gamecocks, with certain feather colours becoming associated with specific places, such as 'Brandling Greys' and 'Felton Reds'.

As in horse racing, to which cock fighting was closely linked, the naming of birds also added colour, alluding to politics (such as 'Wilkes and Liberty'), to local affiliations ('King of the Lonnen'), or to everyday concerns ('The Weary Barnman').

Much of what we know of cock fighting in the north east derives from research published by George Jobey in the 1992 issue of *Archaeologia Aeliana* (*see Links*), the journal of the Society of Antiquaries of Newcastle upon Tyne, amongst whose early members were several cockers.

As early as 1712, Jobey noted, 'mains', or matches, were advertised on Newcastle's Westgate. Cock fighting could also be found on Dunston Bank.

Many of these mains took place in the open air, at locations known only to insiders. But as the 18th century wore on, purpose-built cockpits started to appear, either within existing buildings, usually inns, or in the form of free-standing buildings, with tiers of seating around a central pit.

The simplest form of contest was the 'common main', a series of individual fights.

More complex was the 'Welsh main', in which pairs of birds fought eliminating battles, until a single winner emerged.

There were separate mains for 'stags' – birds of less than a year old – older cocks, and 'blinkards' (one-eyed older birds).

In a Battle Royal or 'crowdie main' all the combatants entered the pit together, while a 'long main' was staged over successive

days, the result being determined by the number of overall winners.

Initially the cocking season ran from Christmas to July, but more important mains increasingly came to coincide with Newcastle's race week, when competition was often between birds owned by the 'Gentlemen' of Northumberland and their counterparts from Durham or other counties.

Even before cricket, cock fighting was thus the first sport to be organised along county lines, with prearranged fixtures and a predetermined set of laws in place.

The level of organisation required was considerable.

For example during a typical Newcastle race week a thousand birds might be pitched against each other, while prizes ranged from the odd sheep or pig up to 500 guineas for a main involving aristocratic cockers.

Inevitably there emerged considerable opposition to cock fighting, not only for its cruelty but because of its promotion of gambling and general immorality.

In Newcastle the last known advertisement for a cockfight during the races is dated 1821.

Even so, Pierce Egan's *Book of Sports* still felt able to claim in 1832 that Newcastle could 'challenge all the world for cocking'.

Three years later the sport was made a misdemeanour, before finally, in 1849, it was banned by the Cruelty to Animals Act.

But clandestine cock fighting persisted. The Gallowgate pit, said to have been the last active public pit in England, was closed only in 1874, following police raids and heavy fines. Even then, there is evidence that cockfighting carried on well into the 20th century, and that it continues to cause sporadic concern to the RSPCA even today.

THE

GENTLEMEN's SUBSCRIPTION MAINS,

At Mr Loftus's Pit, Bigg-Market, Newcastle,

On Thursday, February 9th, 1809,—50l.				Friday,—50l.				Saturday,—100l.			
16 Mr Hunter, red	3 10 0	Walton	13 Mr Maddison, red	4 0 0	Welsh	10 Mr Ridley, red span.			
2 Mr Story, red	3 10 0	Davidson	10 Mr Ridley, red dun	4 0 0	Davidson		4 4 0	Davidson
4 Mr Watson, red stag	3 10 0	Walton				6 Mr Dodd, dun	4 4 0	Walton
12 Mr Maddison, red dun	3 10 0	Welsh	8 Mr Wastell, bir.	4 0 0	Petree	3 Mr Watson, bir.	4 4 0	Walton
13 Mr Taylor, red	3 10 0	Walton	14 Mr Taylor, red	4 0 0	Walton	2 Mr Milburn, yel.	4 4 0	Dubmore
1 Mr Milburn, bir. pile	3 10 0	Dubmore	15 Mr J. Watson, red	4 0 0	Walton	9 Mr Hudson, yel.	4 4 0	Walton
7 Mr Heslop, yel. span.	3 10 0	Lockey	9 Mr Clark, red dun	4 0 0	Scott	4 Mr Mellish, bir. pile	4 4 0	Davidson
8 Mr Ridley, red span.	3 10 0	Davidson	11 Mr Hudson, black	4 0 0	Walton	13 Mr Maddison, yel.	4 4 0	Welsh
10 Mr Hudson, red	3 10 0	Walton	1 Mr Baker, red	4 0 0	Dubmore	14 Mr Taylor, red	4 4 0	Walton
14 Mr Clark, bir. dun stag	3 10 0	Scott	6 Mr Dodd, red dun	4 0 0	Walton	16 Mr Hunter, yel.	4 4 0	Walton
6 Mr Dodd, gin dun	3 10 0	Walton	5 Mr Mellish, red dun	3 15 3	Davidson	8 Mr Wastell, yel.	4 4 0	Petree
9 Mr Wastell, red span.	3 10 0	Petree	3 Mr Milburn, bir pile	3 15 2	Dubmore	15 Mr J. Watson, red	4 4 0	Walton
			12 Mr Johnson, red	3 15 2	Davidson	11 Mr Clark, bir. dun	4 4 0	Scott
15 Mr J. Watson, red	3 10 0	Walton	2 Mr Story, red	3 15 0	Davidson	12 Mr Johnson, bir. pile	4 3 0	Davidson
11 Mr Johnson, red	3 10 0	Davidson	16 Mr Hunter, red dun	3 15 0	Walton	5 Mr Baker, bir. dun	4 3 0	Dubmore
3 Mr Baker, red	3 10 0	Dubmore	7 Mr Heslop, red	3 14 2	Lockey	1 Mr Story, red	4 3 0	Davidson
5 Mr Mellish, red	3 10 0	Davidson	4 Mr Watson, red	3 14 0	Walton	7 Mr Heslop, red	4 2 0	Lockey

To begin precisely at Eleven o'Clock each Day.

S. Hodgson, Printer, Newcastle.

▲ This 1809 handbill for a Gentlemen's Subscription Mains at the **Turk's Head** pit in Newcastle's **Bigg Market** is exactly like the race cards sold at horse races, giving details of the combatants, their owners, trainers and weights.

The first, starting at 11.00am on Thursday February 9, featured the lightest birds, weighing in at three pounds and ten ounces (1.64kg).

Their numbers and owners (all gentlemen, and therefore Mr) are shown on the left of each column. Then comes the weight, and the surname of the feeders, who both fed and trained the birds for up to six weeks before the main.

Clearly the feeder named Walton

was the busiest, with six out of the 16 gentlemen subscribers using his services, for which he was doubtless well paid.

Not named on the handbill were the 'setters' or 'pitters', whose job it was to keep hold of the birds until the signal was given for battle to commence.

Both the Thursday and Friday mains offered prizes of £50. Saturday's main offered double that, being fought between the heavyweights, weighing up to four pounds and four ounces each.

The Turk's Head was one of eight cockpits in Newcastle to issue advertisements for mains during the 18th century. One, called

Henzell's pit in the 1770s, was in the Fleshmarket. There was also a Fighting Cocks Yard.

Elsewhere in Tyne and Wear, two cockpits are recorded in Gateshead in 1746, one being the New Cover'd Pit, which advertised fights with 'round pointed Silver Spurs'.

There was also a Fighting Cock Lane in Sunderland.

But George Jobey believes that there were probably many other cock pits that were never advertised or marked by place names; impromptu pits, sunk into the ground and surrounded by timber barriers, such as one thought to have been located at the west end of Barnes Park in Sunderland.

▲ Showing the often furtive nature of rural cock fights, usually staged in defiance of the local magistrates, this evocative moonlight scene was the work of the noted Northumbrian wood engraver **Thomas Bewick** (1753-1828).

The typical cockpit, whether impromptu or permanent, measured between eight to fifteen feet in diameter and was surrounded by wooden boards a few feet high, to prevent the cocks from retreating into the crowd.

Beyond the boards a second ring was kept clear for the setters, and beyond that, the spectators were able to gather.

No doubt in rural setttings, such as the one depicted by Bewick, access to the cockpit was free of charge, albeit confined to those in the know. After all, cocking was never strictly legal, and had many opponents.

But in commercially run, purpose-built cockpits, admission charges were the norm, set at a level to ensure that only genuine 'sportsmen' (that is, gamblers) would seek entry.

These charges ranged from a few pence up to five shillings for a gallery seat, an amount that only a wealthy patron could afford.

Shown on the left at their actual size, are the two faces of an undated brass token belonging to the Society of Antiquaries of Newcastle upon Tyne.

Presumably used to provide access to a cockpit owned by John Watling, one side shows a pair of gamecocks squaring up to each other on the 'sod' or matting of a cockpit floor.

Hence cockers were often known as 'gentlemen of the sod'.

▶ Identifying former cockpits is rarely straightforward. Local tradition is often wont to associate any circular building or sunken pit with cock fighting, while some that have been positively identified do not conform to a specific size or shape at all.

A good example of this ambiguity is a suspected former cockpit in the cellar of **74 Front Street, Tynemouth**, an early 19th century building that, until recently, was occupied by a Threshers off licence.

Although the basement is now accessible only from steps at the rear of the shop, a series of steps cut into the curved retaining walls (*below right*) suggests that entry was originally from above. (Clearly the upper section of timber stairs is modern, as is the ceiling).

The keyhole shaped pit area measures 11'6" in diameter, and is sunk 3'8" below the top of the retaining walls. Presumably barriers would have sealed off the open side, to form a complete circle.

Even with a higher ceiling, this must have been an exceptionally intimate place to gather. But then the clandestine nature of cocking meant that many pits were hidden away in confined quarters.

Conversely, its location on Front Street may well have been ideal in order to attract soldiers from the local garrison, and perhaps even day trippers to this most fashionable of seaside towns.

Two other suspected former cockpits in a form similar to that in Tynemouth are in the cellar of a house on the High Street in Totnes, Devon, and in the basement of a shop in Dorking, Surrey.

The Front Street pit is not listed. However, 28 other sites and structures that may reasonably be associated with cock fighting are listed by English Heritage, including

the Totnes building. Another site, actually called the Cock Pit, has turned out not to have any links with cocking – a familiar tale.

In Wales, meanwhile, one former cockpit has been positively identified – it has been rebuilt at the St Fagans National History Museum near Cardiff – and a further 26 sites identified that are suspected of having been cockpits, most of them in the form of earthworks in rural locations.

Interestingly, no similar sites have been identified in Scotland, where although cocks were routinely sported with by schoolboys on Shrove Tuesday, cock fighting was regarded as very much an English pursuit.

Chapter Eleven

Quoits

A miner from Houghton-le-Spring, near Sunderland, demonstrates the ancient sport of quoits for a local newspaper in 1957. Quoiting is one of the great forgotten subcultures of British sporting life, a muscular game once much favoured by miners, dockers and agricultural labourers. Today only a few pockets of the game survive in England, Scotland and Wales, with North Yorkshire and the north east being perhaps the strongest. And yet few people have even heard of it.

Another sport firmly rooted in the north east and once with strong links to gambling, quoits is one of the few quintessentially British games to have passed from the medieval to the industrial era with scarcely a change in its character or equipment.

It is, at first glance, a simple game. Iron or steel rings are tossed at a small post, or hob, embedded in a clay pit. But in truth it is far more subtle than that, requiring no little skill and cunning.

The earliest known reference to quoits is from a royal diktat in 1361, urging men not to play games that would distract them from archery practice.

But the game as we know it today first became organised in the late 18th century. Britain's oldest club, the Childwall Quoiting Club in Liverpool, probably dates from 1795, while the Darlington Quoit Club formed in 1846.

Both were, and remain gentlemen's clubs, with strict rules forbidding gambling (though certainly not drinking), in contrast to the many pubs where quoiting grounds, some of them covered, were established for their working class regulars.

By the 1870s some 52 pubs in 33 Northumberland villages are recorded as having quoits grounds, while in his 1873 treatise *Tyneside Celebrities*, William Lawson reported that quoits was 'more followed on Tyneside and in the pit villages of Northumberland and Durham, than in any other place in the United Kingdom'.

Anxious to emphasise their respectability, in 1881 Darlington joined clubs from Stockton, Durham, Middlesbrough, West Hartlepool, Guisborough and Whitby to form the Association of Amateur Quoit Clubs for the North of England. Its rules were published in *The Field*, a London journal, in June 1881.

It then transpired that clubs all over Britain were playing to diverging sets of rules, with varying throwing distances and differently weighted quoits.

The North of England rules specified an eleven yard throwing distance and a maximum quoit weight of 5¼lbs. This did not go down well in other areas, which retained much longer distances: 21 yards in Scotland and 18 yards in Wales and the rest of England.

Thus arose a distinction between the 'short game' of the north east and the 'long game' elsewhere.

Then, as now, the quoiting season ran from roughly May to October. The best players were virtually professionals, winning prize money and profiting from side bets. Inter-club competitions and leagues then formed from the early 1900s.

Yet despite the huge popularity of the game before the First World War, by the 1920s quoits was in serious decline, and by the 1970s had almost disappeared.

Today, the long game survives in Suffolk and Essex, in Wales (where eight clubs survive) and in Scotland, which has three clubs.

By comparison, the short game has fared much better. In 1986 its proponents formed the National Quoits Association, which currently embraces four leagues in Yorkshire, one each on Teesside and in County Durham, and two in Northumberland.

Readers wishing to learn more about the history and development of quoits are referred to Played at the Pub, *an earlier title in the* Played in Britain *series (see Links).*

Despite its steep decline after the First World War, quoits clung on in pockets of England, particularly amongst dockers in the east end of London, and amongst miners in the north east.

This group of quoiters, posing after a match in 1926, were in the mining village of **Chopwell**, while the image of players in **Gateshead** (*below*) was chosen by Tyneside Council of Social Service in 1937 to show how the unemployed could keep fit.

Thereafter quoits appeared to die away in almost exact parallel with the mining industry.

There was, it is true, a revival in May 1966, when a Northumberland Quoits League started up with teams from West Allotment, Forest Hall, Seaton Delaval, Blyth, Shiremoor and Killingworth. Meanwhile, by 1967 the Birtley Quoits League included teams from 26 clubs and pubs.

One club, Birtley Rex, fielded a player said to have been active in quoits for 56 years, thereby providing a crucial link with the pre war years.

Although this revival turned out to be short-lived, the game fought back yet again in the 1980s, when the North Tyneside Open Quoits Championship was staged annually at Seaton Burn's recreation ground.

According to one estimate in 1988, there were still more than a dozen leagues and some 7–800 pitches in the north east.

Since then, however, there has been yet another dramatic decline.

In fact only three quoits grounds are currently known in Tyne and Wear; those at the Lindisfarne Social Club and the Dorset Arms Hotel, both in Wallsend, and in Tynemouth, the venerable Hawkey's Hall Quoit Club, to where we shall now repair.

▶ Tucked away on an enclosed plot of land adjoining Tynemouth's golf and cricket clubs is the ground of the **Hawkey's Hall Quoit Club**, their home since 1906.

But the club are much older than that, for their first minute book dates from 1863, and there is good reason to believe that the club were actually formed three years prior to that. Accordingly they celebrated their centenary in 1960.

Hawkey's Hall were, like their counterparts in Darlington, a gentlemen's club. Their founder was Surtees Hope, a keen player who laid out several pitches for the club on his farmstead at Hawkey's Hall, at the north end of Hawkey's Lane, less than a mile west from the current ground.

Initially membership was restricted to just twelve gentlemen, a number which over the years has crept up to its current level of 28.

It remains men only, however, although guests are allowed, particularly on the club's Open Day, the annual Field Day in June.

Membership is not taken lightly. Gambling is forbidden, and a fine of one shilling (now 5p) – unchanged since the club's inception – is levied on members who are late, miss a meeting or do not wear the club tie.

Only 210 individuals have ever been members of Hawkey's Hall Quoit Club, which marks its 150th anniversary in 2010.

A fine achievement indeed.

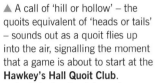

▲ A call of 'hill or hollow' – the quoits equivalent of 'heads or tails' – sounds out as a quoit flies up into the air, signalling the moment that a game is about to start at the **Hawkey's Hall Quoit Club**.

Such is the ritual that takes place every Wednesday evening from May until September.

'Hill' refers to the outer, sloping side of the quoit. 'Hollow' is the inner surface.

The order of play and the composition of each team of two players has already been determined in the clubhouse by the designated scorer, using tokens.

As seen on this page and opposite, there are four 'ends', each comprising two flat clay beds eleven yards apart. Before play and between ends these beds must be carefully prepared. Not enough water and the quoits will not stick. Too much and they will slide.

In the centre of each bed is the pin or 'hob', sticking out no more than three inches.

Each player has two quoits, marked in either red or blue.

Starting on the paved area the player may take two paces

before throwing overarm, or more frequently underarm, towards the clay bed at the far end.

The idea is to land one's quoit on, or as close to the hob as possible, or, as in bowls or curling, to displace the quoit of an opponent.

If more than one quoit rings the hob, then only the top one scores (for two points). In addition, a single point is scored for each of a

players' quoits that lands nearer the hob than that of his opponent.

Games may be played from scratch, or off a handicap, with the first team to reach 15 points winning the match.

Apparently simple. Yet once one sees the tactics and range of throws and handholds employed, quoits emerges as a game of tantalising subtlety and precision.

▲ Only on rare occasions are the callipers brought out to measure distances between quoits and the hob. Otherwise, another member is usually asked for his verdict, which of course is invariably accepted.

This is, after all, a gentlemen's club. Moreover, Hawkey's Hall never play against other clubs, so it is in everyone's interest to maintain a spirit of bonhomie (and avoid a fine for ungentlemanly conduct).

Staying clean is another matter, so buckets of cold water are always on hand.

Once the evening's play is over, players retire to the clubhouse, where, as a 150 year old tradition dictates, drinks are served by the newest members.

Chapter Twelve

Bowls

Behind an ordinary house front door, set into an anonymous stretch of wall on a roundabout passed by thousands of motorists every day, lies the home of the Gateshead Bowling Green Club. It is the oldest bowls club in Tyne and Wear, founded in 1865.

Numerous forms of bowls have been played in Britain since at least the 13th and 14th centuries.

In Chapter Two, for example, we featured Victorian potshare bowlers who threw small heavy bowls great distances.

In this chapter we focus on 'flat green' bowls, in which biased bowls are aimed at a target, or jack, on a rectangular area of flat turf.

Originally made possible by advances in turf management, flat green bowls was first codified in Scotland in the 1840s.

There is another variant called 'crown green', played mainly in Lancashire and Yorkshire, but this form of bowls never spread to Tyne and Wear.

Organised bowls goes further back than these two codes, however. Indeed, as previous *Played in Britain* studies have shown, in most towns and cities the earliest purpose-built sports grounds identified in any category have been bowling greens.

It is the same in Sunderland and Newcastle. According to bowls historian Albert Anderson (*see Links*), a bowling green is recorded next to 'Willie the King's' inn on Lombard Street in 17th century Sunderland, while on the corner of Sans Street stood a building known as Bowling Green House.

Newcastle's first recorded green was in the Forth pleasure grounds, just south west of the present railway station, as shown below on James Corbridge's map of 1723.

According to John Syke's *Historical Register of Remarkable Events*, this green was laid out in 1657 alongside a tavern built with a balcony and a parapet wall 'from whence the spectators could behold the bowlers'.

A later green lay on what is now the Eldon Square shopping centre, while another opened off Bath Lane in 1827, roughly where now there is a footbridge behind the Business School on Citygate.

Although this green closed in 1897, one of the gateways leading to it (since blocked up) can still be seen in the West Walls.

Of the clubs that have survived to the present day, as already noted, the oldest in Tyne and Wear is in Gateshead, formed in 1865.

Newcastle's oldest is the Portland Bowling Green Club formed in 1874 (*see opposite*).

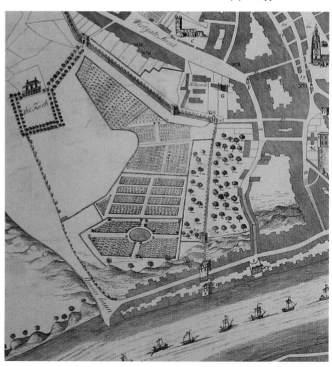

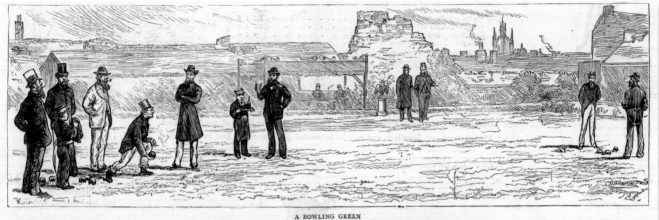

A BOWLING GREEN

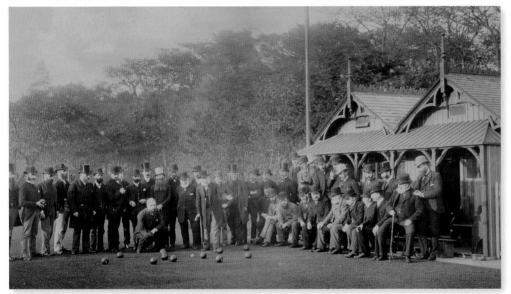

▲ Newcastle and Gateshead's celebrations to mark the centenary of the railway engineer George Stephenson's birth – in Wylam in 1781 – were deemed sufficiently newsworthy for a London magazine, *The Graphic*, to produce a special supplement in June 1881.

Here, the illustrator's eye is caught by a game of bowls which, judging by the distant flying buttresses of St Nicholas' Church, was taking place on the green situated by **Bath Lane,** just outside the West Walls.

Probably the most exclusive green in the city at this time lay in Jesmond (*left*). This was, and remains, the home of the **Portland Bowling Green Club,** on Hutton Terrace, shown here in 1887.

On Wearside the first to form was the Sunderland Bowling Club, on Thornhill Terrace in 1882, but this wound up in 1888 and was replaced by a club of the same name at Ashbrooke (*see page 93*).

Meanwhile in 1882 there began a trend that has characterised bowls in Tyne and Wear ever since. This was the laying out of the area's first green in a public park,

at Brandling Park in Newcastle (*see page 29*), followed in 1883 by one at Roker Park in Sunderland (*page 72*). Dozens more followed, and in 1892 it was four parks-based clubs in Newcastle who established the Northumberland and Durham Bowling Association, believed to have been the first county association in English bowls.

The predominance of parks

bowling continues. Whereas in most cities there is a fairly equal balance between private and public greens, in Tyne and Wear, as of 2010, there were ten private greens compared with 102 public ones.

Together, these greens amount to over 44 acres of neatly trimmed turf. That is, about one and a half times the area taken up by Newcastle's Town Moor Hoppings.

▲ No individual did more to popularise flat green bowling – south of the border at least – than **WG Grace**, seen here in action as England captain in a match against Scotland in 1907, at the **West End Bowling Green** on Summerhill Grove, Newcastle.

Grace had taken up bowls in London a few years earlier as his legendary cricket career drew to a close, and in 1903 played a key role in establishing the English Bowling Association.

The EBA (since renamed Bowls England) essentially adopted the rules of the Scottish game, so that with the exception of a handful of unaffiliated clubs, Britain's bowlers were now split between two codes, crown green in the north west of England, the Midlands and north Wales, and flat green everywhere else, the north east included.

◀ This is the quirky but immaculate clubhouse of the **Rockcliffe Bowling and Tennis Club**, **Victoria Park**, built onto the end of a row of terraced houses and facing the Promenade at Whitley Bay.

The view from its upper floor (*below left*) is one of the finest a bowler could wish for.

Founded in 1925, Rockcliffe is one of around one hundred clubs in Tyne and Wear which play on publicly owned greens, a reflection of the fact that the majority of working class bowlers could not afford to set up private clubs.

Some demand was met by the provision of colliery welfare grounds, such as at Backworth (*see page 23*). But in most cases local councils bore the costs.

Inevitably, this dependence on the public purse has led to closures when times have got tough, or demand has dipped.

Among several public greens to have gone to grass in recent years are two at **Hodgkin Park** in **Benwell** (*opposite, top*), where not even the pavilion survives.

As public spending gets further squeezed over the next few years, more closures seem inevitable, unless the clubs can recruit new and younger members and therefore yield more green fees.

But it is not just outdoor greens that are under threat.

In the late 20th century Tyne and Wear had a thriving network of indoor bowling facilities.

The earliest of these was the **Alexandra Bowling Centre** (*opposite, right*), in Sunderland's Grangetown, part of the still extant Alexandra Hotel, designed by local architects W & TR Milburn.

Vaux Breweries opened the indoor centre in 1937, but it closed in the late 1940s before becoming a dance hall.

HODGKIN PARK BENWELL 85

▲ Based in Souter Park North, Monkseaton, the **Forth Bowling Club** is one of many around Britain established as a works club, having been formed in the 1930s by railway workers at the LNER's Forth goods yard in Newcastle. Although the yard was not far from the 17th century bowling green featured earlier, other than the name there is no link between the two.

The club's timber pavilion, known affectionately by members as the 'Forth Hut', was put up by the LNER in 1936, but is likely to be replaced in the near future.

▶ One of the most intriguing public greens in Tyne and Wear is that of the **Byker Village Bowling Club**, part of **Headlam Green**.

Originally lying within Byker Park, the green was opened during the 1920s, with a pavilion on the north side.

Public demand ensured that the green was retained as part of the Byker Estate's redevelopment under architects Ralph Erskine and Vernon Gracie between 1970–81.

However, instead of building a new pavilion in a style that echoed that of Headlam Green's new sheltered housing, completed in 1976–78, the residents, with Erskine's blessing, went for a retro-styled pavilion, as seen here on the west side of the green.

Perhaps it was a straight copy of the original pavilion. But whatever, it is certainly a contrast, and even more noteworthy for being included within the Grade II* listing accorded to Headlam Green in 2007, if only for its group value.

No other 20th century bowls pavilion has been accorded such high status, which is ironic given its traditional styling.

In a very different setting is the **Summerhill Bowling Club** (*right*), on Winchester Terrace, Newcastle.

The club was founded in 1916 after the original owners, the West End Green Bowling Club, who had laid out the two greens in 1905, went into liquidation. But the clubhouse dates from 1937.

Today Summerhill finds itself in a not uncommon position, that of being in the centre of a conservation area, on a potentially valuable site, but with an ageing membership.

Not that many passers-by will notice, for unlike Byker's clubhouse this one is well hidden from view behind a sturdy stone wall.

▲ Similarly secluded, between Hutton Terrace and Jesmond Cemetery, and with the rear of a 1930s bus garage lining its north side, is the venerable **Portland Bowling Green Club**.

Not only is this the oldest green in Newcastle, but it is also a focal point for the dozen or so private bowling clubs still operating in Northumberland. For example Portland stages two annual county tournaments, the Bell Cup, dating from 1900, and the Oubridge Cup, held every September since 1910.

An even older competition, for Portland members only, is known as 'Spoons', for which the prize was for many years a silver spoon.

Several of the originals are still held by the club and, as seen on the right, give the club's foundation date as 1877.

And yet on the clubhouse on the south side of the green – designed by James Fatkin and built in 1938 as a replacement for the Victorian original *(see page 137)* – the club's foundation date is given as 1874.

This discrepancy is not uncommon in the world of bowls, for there was often a gap between the actually formation of a club and the date on which their green was ready for play.

It was the same at another of Newcastle's long established clubs.

The **Gosforth Recreation Company** was established in 1897 on West Avenue to create a private members' club with facilities for bowls, lawn tennis, croquet, quoits and even, when temperatures allowed, curling.

The whole scheme cost £2,600 and took five years to complete, with the green – which had been laid with the finest Solway turf – finally opened in May 1902, by the local MP.

Currently **Gosforth Bowling Club** has around 100 members, compared with around 60 at Portland. But Portland has one asset that is the envy of all private clubs in the area – a car park that yields vital extra income from local office workers.

Chapter Thirteen

Real Tennis

One of the great treasures of Newcastle's sporting heritage, Jesmond Dene Real Tennis Club is one of 23 real tennis clubs currently active in Britain, while its court is one of only 49 in the world. But why 'real tennis?' In truth, the name was adopted reluctantly by its Victorian and Edwardian adherents to distinguish it from that upstart game 'lawn tennis', which arrived on the scene in the 1870s. For centuries before it had simply been plain 'tennis'. The word tennis itself is thought to derive from the French *tenetz!* uttered by the server to his opponent and translated more or less as 'take this!'

For readers whose favoured sport is tennis, there is no better place to seek out the game than in the archetypal leafy suburb of Jesmond, in Newcastle.

Heading north from Jesmond Station there is the Jesmond Lawn Tennis Club, on Osborne Road, founded in 1883, the Northumberland Club on North Jesmond Avenue (1926), and, a few hundred yards to the north of that, on Castle Farm Road, the David Lloyd Centre, opened in 1996.

Admirable though these clubs are, however, like most tennis clubs in urban Britain their buildings are of little architectural or historic interest.

Fortunately, the real tennis club in their midst more than compensates for this.

Real tennis traces its origins to a medieval French game, *jeu de paume*, in which hands were used to propel a ball across a net on a paved court.

By the 15th century racquets had superceded the use of hands, and in 1541, James V of Scotland was able to play on his very own court, built at Falkland Palace, in Fife.

Over the next two centuries hundreds of courts were built, in Paris, London and elsewhere. Yet despite having no roof and being exposed to the elements, remarkably Falkland Palace has outlived them all and remains in regular use.

It is now the oldest tennis court in the world.

The second oldest, and the design on which all succeeding courts were based, is at Hampton Court Palace in London. Built on the site of an earlier structure played in by Henry VIII, it was completed in 1628.

One offshoot of real tennis was the game of 'rackets', a simpler but still indoor game which, as noted on page 16, is first recorded as being played in Newcastle at a court on Newgate Street in 1823.

Until the mid 19th century, all racquet sports were the preserve of the rich, if only because courts were expensive to build, and ball making and racquet maintenance required the retention of a full time professional.

Two developments were to turn this world upside down.

Firstly, the invention of the lawn mower in the 1830s allowed middle class people to maintain high quality turf without a team of gardeners. Secondly, the invention of vulcanised rubber in 1839 led to the development of air filled balls that, crucially, could bounce on grass, and therefore allowed the game to flourish outdoors.

Yet far from seeing the death of the old form of tennis, now renamed real tennis, the late 19th century actually witnessed a revival. Rather like a billiard room, a real tennis court now became the must-have status symbol of the Victorian era's new generation of super rich individuals.

Twenty real tennis courts opened between 1870-1914, most notably at the Queen's Club in 1888, where the sport's new governing body was set up in 1907.

But in the north there were only two, at Manchester, opened in 1880, and 14 years later, at Jesmond Dene.

At Jesmond Dene, as at all real tennis courts, crowns and sundry crests adorn the side walls to mark the series of lines used in the game's arcane scoring system. The game's popularity amongst members of the monarchy, from Henry VII to the present day Prince Edward, led to real tennis also being known as 'royal tennis'.

▲ Viewed from Matthew Bank, the **Jesmond Dene Real Tennis Club** is located in the former grounds of Jesmond Dene House, whose owner, the physicist and armaments expert Sir Andrew Noble (1831–1915), was a keen sportsman and popular socialite.

Designed for Noble by local architect Frank West Rich, in his trademark style of red brick and terracotta, the building opened in October 1894 and consists of three main elements.

At the near end, in the dip below Matthew Bank, is a house built for the resident tennis professional.

Behind this stands the court, with its buttressed sides, round upper floor windows and octagonal corner turrets.

At the far end, beyond the court, is a social area accessed via a porch (*top right*), formerly the building's main entrance.

Until the First World War and Noble's death the court was used only by Sir Andrew, his family and guests, of whom there were many.

For example the Liberal MP and future foreign secretary Sir Edward Grey, a former Oxford champion, played in the inaugural game. Other visitors included the MP and cricketer Alfred Lyttleton, the poet and all-round sportsman Alfred Cochrane (who worked for Noble's company, Armstrong Whitworth), and, in 1916, Rudyard Kipling.

Following the death of Lady Noble in 1931, Jesmond Dene House and the grounds were

bequeathed to the city. But family members and tennis enthusiasts saved the court by joining together to form the Jesmond Dene Real Tennis Club, in 1932.

For years the club shared the court's upkeep with the local badminton association. In fact only badminton was played between 1939 and 1981.

Fortunately however, that year Sir Andrew's grand-daughter helped orchestrate a revival of the club, since when it has enjoyed exclusive rights, at least to the building.

The surrounding grounds, on the other hand, are now dominated by a council-run nursery, which means that members enter via a door beside the caretaker's house, rather than through the original porch.

This splendid original cast iron radiator is one of two found in the club's changing rooms.

▲ Throughout its life, and more so since re-opening in 1981, **Jesmond Dene Real Tennis Club** has been much praised by visiting players, as much for the all important feel of the court as for its hammerbeam roof, fine brickwork and generous glazing.

No two real tennis courts are identical, but all measure within a few feet of the largest, at Hampton Court Palace. Jesmond Dene's measures around 113' x 40'.

But more important are its standard design features. On the left, for example, on either side of the net (which sags from 5' to 3' in the centre) is the gallery, a series of openings used for scoring as well as viewing, and topped by a sloping roof known as the penthouse.

On the far wall, the white square is the grille. To the right of this, just visible, is a protuding section of wall called the tambour.

Each feature plays a role in the strategy and tactics of the game.

Even more idiosyncratic is the scoring, similar to that of lawn tennis but with an added factor, the 'chase', playing a part when the ball bounces twice within certain grid lines marked across the court.

▲ One of the disadvantages of real tennis, but also part of its charm, is that apart from the side gallery, is that the only place to watch matches is through an opening at one end, known as the 'dedans'.

At most clubs the dedans is protected only by netting, requiring that spectators maintain a polite hush. At Jesmond Dene, however, there is an additional set of windows, which means that members and guests gathering in the club room behind the dedans can talk more freely (one of several reasons why Jesmond Dene enjoys a reputation as a friendly and sociable place to play).

The standing gentleman seen here is acting as 'marker' – that is, it is his job to call out the score.

Unlike in lawn tennis, in real tennis the score of the player winning the point is called first.

As to the racquets and balls, these too differ greatly.

The racquets, a selection of which lines the corridor outside the court (*above right*) are relatively small and heavy, made mostly from hickory or ash, with asymmetric heads to make it easier to 'cut' across the ball, or get close to the floor or walls. They are also strung tightly, in order to cope with striking the solid ball.

Real tennis balls, meanwhile, have remained virtually unchanged since the 16th century (although the use of human or dogs' hair as stuffing is no longer necessary).

Their inner core consists of

fragments of cork wrapped in rags, hammered and then wrapped again in used felt, and then tightly wound with cotton webbing and twine (*right*). After pressing this in a metal cup to round it off, a final layer of new Melton felt is sewn on, by hand.

This process, moreover, is completed on a workbench in a corner of the clubroom, by the court manager.

From scratch it takes at least 40 minutes to make a ball, or 20 minutes if recycling an old one. Each set of 70 balls used on court lasts around two to three weeks, which means that stocks have to be replenished continually.

It is an arduous task. But such is the price of tradition.

Chapter Fourteen

Running

For many years the Black Bull pub on Stanhope Street, opposite St James' Park and the entrance to Leazes Park, was the base of Tyne and Wear's oldest surviving running club, the Elswick Harriers, formed in 1889. This plaque commemorates the Newcastle-born Alex Burns, who represented Great Britain in both the 5,000m and 10,000m races at the 1932 Olympics in Los Angeles and the 1936 Games in Berlin. He trained from the pub between 1923 and the early 1950s, and died, aged 95, in 2003. Elswick Harriers, meanwhile, had several other headquarters before settling at the Newburn Leisure Centre in 1994.

Sporting heritage, as we hope to have demonstrated so far, is manifested in numerous diverse forms, primarily in the places of sport and in buildings, in the sports themselves – in their rules and traditions – in artefacts, in archive material and in the clubs; in their colours, badges, traditions and even in their rivalries.

But there is another form of sporting heritage that is much harder to pin down, and that is the heritage of those sports that crisscross the landscape in one fleeting moment and then move on, leaving little tangible evidence in their wake other than a set of results and a rich store of memories.

Road cycling is one such sport. Another is running.

In Chapter Nine we touched upon the stadiums and running tracks that have helped showcase and nurture athletes in Tyne and Wear, from the Victoria Running Grounds of the mid 19th century in Low Elswick, to the Gateshead International Stadium of today.

But these purpose-built tracks tell only a part of the story.

There is no single reason why the sportsmen and women of Tyne and Wear have embraced distance running so passionately, be it cross country or on roads.

Nor is it enough to say that the local landscape is uniquely suited to running, or to suggest that the people of this region are somehow hardier than their counterparts elsewhere in Britain (although it is easy to find individuals who will argue just that).

And yet, who would deny that distance running, as a sport, as a way of life, is deeply enmeshed in the culture of the north east?

Cross country and road running really took off in Britain as 'pedestrianism', that is, professional foot races staged mainly for the purpose of gambling. It started to lose favour in the 1880s (although lingered on in the north east until the 1930s).

The first of the amateur running clubs to form in Tyne and Wear were the Newcastle Harriers, whose inaugural run in October 1887 started at the Lord Hill Inn on Barrack Road, a pub well known for its football connections.

Following them in 1889 were Elswick Harriers and Tynemouth Harriers (the term 'harrier' deriving from an early Victorian brand of cross country running in which 'hares' would leave a paper trail for the 'hounds' to follow).

Of these three pioneers, only Elswick Harriers still meet.

Of the nine other current clubs that bear the title 'harriers', Saltwell and Heaton both formed in 1890, pursued by Sunderland (1897, but reformed 1905), South Shields (1900), Gateshead (1904), Blaydon (1908), Wallsend (1920, reformed 1975), Gosforth (1927) and Houghton (1958).

The list of great runners to have emerged from these clubs is a long one. At the very least most readers will know of Brendan Foster and Steve Cram.

But in heritage terms it is the races themselves that have had the most resonant effect on local life.

One of the best known of these was the Morpeth to Newcastle race. This started in 1891 when fifteen members of the Newcastle Harriers took a train to Morpeth one January evening and ran back in the dark, followed by a horse and cart carrying their overcoats.

'The Morpeth', as it became known, sponsored by the *Newcastle Journal*, then started officially in 1904, the same year that South Shields Harriers initiated the Sunderland to Westoe Road Race, claimed to be the world's first team-based road race.

This began at the Wheatsheaf in Monkwearmouth and ended at The County Hotel in Westoe, although in its present form it follows a loop course near Gypsies Green Stadium (*see page 125*).

Also legendary, for its hills as well as its longevity, is the Saltwell Road Race, run annually since 1911, excluding the war years.

It is now the oldest English race run solely on roads.

Seen top right is the start of a typical road race in the 1930s.

Since then, the kits might have changed and road surfaces improved, but the essential nature of the mass gathering has not.

On the right, seen in 2009, is the early stage of the Blaydon Race.

First run in 1981, on June 9 naturally (*see page 12*), this follows the route of Victorian racegoers from the Bigg Market to Blaydon, a distance of nearly six miles.

A total of 212 entered that first year. Now the field has had to be limited to 4,000, including entrants from all over the world.

Road racing's popularity has its downside. In 2006 the organisers of the Morpeth announced that the 2004 race, marking the event's centenary, would be the last, owing to a crippling rise in the costs of policing and traffic management.

On the other hand, that has not proved a stumbling block for another great road race, also born in 1981...

▲ Got the T-shirt? This is a memento of the very first **Great North Run** run on June 28 1981 (19 days after the first Blaydon Race), and handed out to every one of the 10,665 finishers that day.

It is a tradition that has continued ever since, so that early race T-shirts are now treasured items – no longer ephemera but sporting heritage in the making.

The idea for a half marathon on Tyneside was hatched by former Gateshead Harrier Brendan Foster, and appropriately enough, in its first two years was won by Elswick Harrier Mike McLeod, who went on to win silver at the 1984 Olympics.

The first women's winner in 1981 was also local, former South Shields Harrier Karen Goldhawk.

Since then the run has grown to its 2010 level of an astonishing 54,000 entries, of which barely a third now hail from the north east.

In fact entrants from various nations in Africa have won the men's race every year since 1991.

A more recent fixture at the race, initiated in 2002, is the fly past of the **Red Arrows**, pictured here in September 2009 (*right*) as the runners head south from Newcastle city centre over the Tyne Bridge.

▲ For every Olympic Games there is a cultural Olympiad. But in Britain at least the **Great North Run** is unique in organising its own annual cultural programme.

Since 2005, **GNR Culture** has commissioned a genuinely innovative range of running-related works using film, photography, dance and drama. Several of these can be viewed on the programme's website and offer worthwhile insights into the Great North Run itself, its participants and its impact on the local community.

This silhouetted figure is actually a still from a remarkable animated film, **About Running**, made by **Suky Best**, first shown at BALTIC Centre for Contemporary Art on Gateshead Quays in 2007.

▲ Runners in the October 1999 **Great North Run** head down Coast Road towards the finish by Gypsies Green Stadium in **South Shields**.

That was the year the race was switched permanently to a Sunday morning, to become the major televised event it has remained ever since. (It was also the day that the Stadium of Light staged an England v. Belgium friendly. Seldom has Tyne and Wear seen such a single day of sport.)

The race starts on the motorway at the southern edge of Newcastle's Town Moor (*see page 29*) with the elite wheelchair racers setting off first, followed by the elite able bodied runners and then the great mass of fun runners. It takes half an hour for everyone to pass through this starting line.

The route then heads across the Tyne Bridge, winding through Gateshead, skirting Heworth and Jarrow before hitting the coast at Marsden for the final approach.

But if the 13.1 mile route looks fairly straightforward on a road map, at ground level the route rises and falls with a series of punishing climbs at regular intervals.

One of the great wonders of any mass participation urban road race is how ordinary streetscapes are briefly transformed, turning streets into stadiums, bridges into grandstands, garden fences into prized vantage points. Imagine 54,000 runners passing by *your* front door.

Yet while the number of entrants may have increased, in essence both the Great North Run and the Blaydon Race are inextricably part of Tyne and Wear's sporting heritage, a heritage which took root not in 1981, but with the Harriers of the late Victorian era.

Chapter Fifteen

Pigeon racing

To some they are dismissed as 'rats with wings'. In days of old they were sources of meat, and of fertiliser. Before the age of telephones they offered a reliable means of sending messages, the so-called 'pigeon post'. But the sport of pigeon racing as we know it today is a relatively modern development, thought to have started in Belgium in the mid 19th century. Pictured here is a four year old Blue Hen, 'Jean H', winner of the North of England Homing Union's 2010 Bourges Classic, and owned by 73 year old Doug Henderson, a retired builder from Winlaton, Gateshead.

Among the many archetypes of northern working class men regularly paraded in the press, on film and in fiction, the pigeon fancier is a firm favourite.

Fag in mouth, face blackened from a shift down the mine, there he is in his humble loft, rough hands cradling a pure white bird, his racehorse of the sky, a delicate creature in the midst of his soot-covered world of grime and sweat.

And for sure, pigeon racing in the north east was most closely associated with miners.

But, unlike quoits, when the mines closed the men of Tyne and Wear did not forsake their birds.

In its early years in the mid 19th century pigeon racing took place on a purely local scale, with birds flying distances of less than ten miles. Then in the 1870s it started to become organised, with precise timing and record keeping systems introduced to ensure fairness, and respectability.

But there were soon splits.

In 1892 a Newcastle upon Tyne Homing Society was formed with the intention of running all races in Northumberland. This was countered by miners who set up the Northern Federation in 1900.

By 1904 five federations were in place in the north east alone.

Finally, in 1905 – largely in order to help negotiate cheaper terms for pigeon transportation on the railways – the different groupings came together to form the Up North Combine.

It still exists today, covering an area that includes Tyne and Wear, but ranging north to Berwick and south to Teesside.

Of the Combine's 142 clubs, about half are in Tyne and Wear, with a membership of around 1,000 individuals.

At the top of the sport is the Royal Pigeon Racing Association, founded in 1896. This now has a membership of around 50,000 nationwide, and there are similar organisations on the Continent, with the French, Belgians and Germans especially prominent.

Pigeon racing is a complex business, but a simple concept.

Because each race has one starting point but many finishing points – the owners' lofts (or 'crees' as they are known in north eastern dialect, meaning sheds) – the winner is determined by calculating the speed of each bird.

This is done by dividing the distance covered by the time taken, to arrive at a 'velocity' expressed in terms of yards per minute (ypm).

For example Jean H, winner of the 2010 classic race (left), which started in Bourges, France, covered 575 miles in just under 19 hours, at an average of 30 mph, or nearly 900 ypm. But with a good wind average speeds can reach 60 mph.

Perhaps the most extraordinary aspect of pigeon racing is that despite years of research, scientists are still not entirely sure how pigeons find their way home.

Theories include the possibility that they use the position of the sun, they are sensitive to the earth's magnetic field, they have an acute sense of smell, and that they also rely on visual cues, even following habitual routes such as motorways.

But as every fancier knows, it is the bird's sense of 'home' – and above all the place in which they reared their young – that is the most powerful instinct of all.

◀ Every stage of pigeon racing is precisely monitored, starting with the moment when each bird has a numbered rubber band or ring placed around one of its legs, as seen here at **Newcastle Central Station** in June 1950.

From there the birds were transported to Brussels for the start of the Newcastle Chronicle Cup.

The release of birds, known as a 'liberation', is a spectacle in itself, and one that in Tyne and Wear can be experienced only on occasional Saturdays in summer, at the **Brierdene Car Park** by **The Links** at **Whitley Bay**, one of 126 sites in Britain accredited by the Royal Pigeon Racing Association.

Thanks to women's liberation, you are no longer likely to see Miss North Tyneside performing the honours, as she did at Whitley Bay in August 1980 (*above*), when 4,000 birds were released to signal the start of the carnival race.

Moreover, you will need to arrive early, and be flexible, because the transporter may well have been travelling overnight, and its crew will only liberate its precious cargo when conditions suit.

When that moment comes, security seals on each pannier are cut, and with a single tug, bolts are released for the pannier fronts to drop down.

Out flap the birds – cocks and hens each from their segregated panniers – in a sudden, tremendous flourish of feathery release.

In seconds the truck is empty. Up rise the birds, initially in flocks, circling once, twice and maybe one last time before magically they find their bearings and head off across the skies towards home, which in the case of the liberation seen here meant Yorkshire, but could be anywhere in Britain or even further afield in Europe.

▶ In Tyne and Wear, as in so many other parts of post-industrial Britain, pigeon crees occupy the interstices of our urban landscape.

Backing onto **Dalton Street, Byker**, on an old wagonway, is this small cluster of crees, while on **Skinnerburn Road** (*below*), is a tight-knit group of around a dozen, overlooking the Tyne.

The contrast between these home-made lofts, built largely from salvaged materials, bits and bobs, and the refined, curvaceous modernity of both the neighbouring **Byker Wall** flats and the **Metro Radio Arena** appears stark.

And yet in their own fashion, pigeon crees are highly specialised building types.

Firstly they tend to face south or south-east. This orientation is favoured because birds from Tyne and Wear are normally released from southern locations and therefore must fly northwards to get home. If the cree faces another direction this forces the bird to circle round on its final approach, thereby wasting valuable seconds.

Secondly, their different colour schemes offer an all important visual aid to the birds. It is said by local fanciers that in the past the choice of colour often depended on the source of scrap material or paints used; for example British Rail green, National Coal Board yellow, or shipyard red.

◀ About 60 per cent of pigeon crees in the north east are located on council-owned allotments.

A good proportion are placed inside their owners' back gardens or yards.

But the ones that are most exposed to the public eye are those that sit on what is often called back-land; that is, those awkwardly shaped, brownfield sites that no-one else seemingly has any use for and which only their regulars even know how to access.

Here are two such sites. On the left is a cluster of brightly painted crees, most built on stilts, on the steeply sloping ground below **Queen's Road**, **Sunderland**, overlooking the Wear and just west of the Stadium of Light.

On the path along the riverside lies the Coast to Coast cycle route.

Below left are the crees at **Bensham**, **Gateshead**.

Located west of Elysium Lane, this pigeon paradise has sprung up on a tightly confined patch of back-land between the East Coast Main Line (in the background), a footbridge, and the line to Carlisle.

Follow this same line a mile or so to the west and yet more crees can be seen near Dunston Station, overlooking the A1.

But these are only a few of the many sites dotted around Tyne and Wear. Chances are that you pass by them all the time.

As with all good crees, Tony Carden's, on Hollywood Avenue, South Gosforth (right) is kept free from damp and predators, is not overcrowded with birds, and has good ventilation. On the outside, as seen above at Ryhope, many lofts also have 'spikes' lining the top of the walls. This is to deter birds from landing on the roof rather than heading straight inside.

◀ Nowadays self-assembly pigeon lofts can be bought from a catalogue, complete with ready-made nest boxes, perches and uPVC windows.

But none can compare with a home-made loft.

Seen here is probably the most celebrated pigeon loft in Britain.

Located on an allotment site behind the Blue Bell Inn, on **Back Ryhope Street**, **Ryhope**, Sunderland, the cree was built in 1955 by Maurice Surtees (*pictured left in 2008*) and his late brother William, using timber taken from colliery cottages that were being demolished nearby.

(Ryhope Colliery itself finally closed in 1966.)

The colours, says Maurice proudly, are those of the Union flag.

Apart from his successes as a pigeon racer, Maurice first made the news in March 1998 when his loft became the first, and so far the only one of its kind to be listed (at Grade II), an extraordinary accolade and public acknowledgement of the importance of this popular working class pursuit.

However Maurice's return to the limelight in December 2007 was rather less welcome.

Just as his lease and that of his 21 fellow allotment holders was coming to an end, a Newcastle-based developer tried to buy the site for housing.

Yet not even an offer of £250,000 compensation could persuade them to move, and after a drawn out battle, lapped up by the press and debated in the House of Commons, the developer finally backed down in 2008.

It is a story that might so easily have come from Ealing Studios.

Indeed it has been told in a 2008 film, *The Homing Instinct*, produced by Meerkat Films.

▶ On this page we see three aspects of what goes on inside a loft before and after a race.

As noted earlier, prior to each race, the bird is 'marked' by having a numbered rubber band placed around its leg using a small spring mechanism (*right*).

Each owner then sets, seals and synchronises their timing clock before the bird is transported to the liberation point.

A key feature of loft design is the entry point for the returning birds. This can be in the form of sliding doors, as at Ryhope opposite, or protruding landing boards, as seen on the far right at a loft in Coxhoe.

At this loft, as is common, a web of plastic coated 'bob wires' is strung inside the landing board so that the pigeon, once landed and with his or her wings folded, may enter easily. But because of the wires it cannot then exit, as with no board on the other side it would have to extend its wings.

On the right is a typical Toulet 'lock in the box' clock, dating from the late 1940s or 1950s.

After the race, the rubber band is hastily removed from the bird and inserted into a small slot in the top of the clock. By pressing together the two side levers the clock then records the exact time by punching a hole in the paper dial on the clock face. Thus the bird's velocity can be calculated and verified by race officials.

Although still in use, such clocks are increasingly becoming collector's items. Instead, the modern way is for each bird to carry on its rubber tag a tiny RFID (or radio frequency identification chip), which is automatically scanned as the bird re-enters the loft. Not only is this accurate, but it means the owner no longer has to be present at the time of arrival.

Chapter Sixteen

Rowing

The next time you see a rowing race, watch how the rowers slide back and forth within the boat as their oars dip in and out of the water. Without sliding seats the sport would be even more punishing than it already is. This is the first sliding seat ever seen on the Tyne, used by Robert Bagnall in a four oared race in November 1871. With its help, Bagnall, who had seen similar seats in America a few months earlier, and his fellow oarsmen, pocketed £400 for winning the race. The seat is now displayed at the Discovery Museum in Newcastle.

In a part of the country defined by water – by the Rivers Tyne and Wear, by the Derwent and of course by the North Sea – boat racing, or 'aquatics' as the Victorians called it, and rowing in particular, claims a special place in the area's sporting heritage.

But only recently has that heritage come to be appreciated.

Partly this is owing to the researches of local historians, notably Ian Whitehead (*see Links*).

Tyne & Wear Museums and the River and Rowing Museum at Henley, opened in 1998, have also done much to highlight the contribution made by Tyneside rowers and boatbuilders.

A further factor in reviving interest has been the instigation of the University Boat Race on the Tyne in 1997.

For in truth, large crowds on the riverbanks are nothing new.

As a spectator sport and as a focus for gambling, rowing was as popular in Newcastle, if not more popular, than distance running during the mid 19th century.

Races featuring professional oarsmen such as Harry Clasper

and the two world champion scullers, Robert Chambers and James Renforth, attracted 'seething masses of humanity' on to the High Level Bridge.

The Tyne's first known official boat race took place in 1821, with the first Ascension Day regatta being staged in 1830. Other regattas soon followed, including the Tyne Regatta (held at the mouth of the Tyne) and the Wear Regatta, starting in 1834.

Just like modern regattas, these were great social events, the result being that rowing, once the province of working rivermen, eventually came to be seen as a suitable pastime for gentlemen.

There are currently seven rowing clubs based in Tyne and Wear (plus another 20 or so on the Wear in Durham).

The oldest of these, and indeed the oldest sports club of any ilk in Newcastle today, is the Tyne

Amateur Rowing Club, founded by 'upwards of sixty gentlemen' in December 1852. The clubhouse they built in Scotswood in 1893 is shown on the front cover.

Tynemouth RC, based at Prior's Haven, dates from 1867, while Sunderland City RC, based at South Hylton, formed in 1898.

All these clubs were and remain strictly amateur. But it was the professionals who led the way.

Driven by an intense rivalry with their counterparts on the Thames, and later from America, Canada and Australia, Tyneside's rowers and boatmakers were at the forefront of innovation in rowing techniques and in boat design.

They were largely uneducated, from poor backgrounds, and toughened by years of working in heavy industry and on the river.

But for a golden period from the 1840s to the 1880s, they were genuine world beaters.

This photograph records the ceremonial opening of the Elswick Works' Amateur Rowing Club boathouse in 1886. Many of these men may well have spent their working hours building, rather than rowing boats, battleships included.

A BOAT RACE—THE START

Harry Clasper, for example, stung by defeat by a London crew in a race on the Tyne in 1842, was one of a coterie of Tyneside boatbuilders, including Matthew Taylor and Robert Jewitt, who helped advance the design of such key elements as outriggers, inboard keels and of lightweight, narrow racing shells.

Clasper also developed a sliding style of rowing, known as the 'traditional Tyne stroke', which ultimately led to the Americans inventing sliding seats (*see opposite*).

These and other technical innovations were to have lasting consequences for boat design.

Cruelly, Clasper and his proteges, Bob Chambers and Jim Renforth, were to die within just over three years of each other, after which rowing on the Tyne slipped steadily out of the limelight.

A further blow came in 1882 when the southern-based Amateur Rowing Association banned all professionals from their events; not merely working rivermen but any men who earned a living from any form of manual labour.

This left Tyneside's professional rowers with one main annual competition, a half mile Christmas Handicap last contested for a cash prize in 1938.

▲ Two scullers prepare to race what was known on Tyneside as the **Championship Course**, starting from the High Level Bridge on the left (opened 1849) and continuing towards the Scotswood Suspension Bridge, some 3.5 miles upstream.

Viewed from the north bank of the Tyne (where now stands the Quayside pub, on The Close), this etching from *The Graphic* in June 1881 depicts a scene that had become commonplace during the 19th century, yet was coming under increasing threat.

Courtesy of the new Swing Bridge, built to the east of the High Level Bridge in 1876, steamships

were able to ply the upper reaches of the Tyne, turning this once rural stretch of river into a polluted commercial highway.

Dredging operations carried out by the Tyne Improvement Commission also removed two islands that punctuated the course between Elswick and Dunston (one of which, called King's Meadows, was home to a pub popular amongst rowers).

Equally damaging would be the imminent rise of Britain's next great sporting fad, Association football.

Rowing on the Tyne never stopped however. It was just that the crowds grew steadily smaller.

Next, in 1870, came Clasper. 'In this sacred spot,' reads the inscription on his grave (*left*), 'commanding a full view of that noble river, the well loved scene of former triumphs, rest the mortal remains of Henry (Harry) Clasper, the accomplished oarsman and boat builder of Derwenthaugh.'

Today, there is no longer a 'full view' of the Tyne from the churchyard of **St Mary's Church, Whickham**. Tall trees and modern buildings have put paid to that.

Interestingly, Burn depicted Clasper not in his rowing kit, as he did Chambers, but holding what appear to be the plans of a boat, suggesting that his reputation as a craftsman ranked as highly as his prowess as a sportsman.

That said, Clasper was indubitably a man of the people.

Born in 1812, he grew up, illiterate, in Jarrow, worked in collieries, as a carpenter, as a coke burner and as a ferryman, before finding fame on the water.

According to his biographer (*see Links*), Clasper assumed that his own funeral would be a much more modest affair than that of his young friend Chambers, and that his career would soon be forgotten.

Instead, an estimated 100-130,000 turned out.

Over a century later, in 1985, both his memorial and that of his family members (*above right*), were listed Grade II.

There is also a Clasper Way near to the Metrocentre, down in the valley of 'that noble river'.

Neither Chambers nor Clasper were what we might think of as model Victorians. Both gambled, and both tried and failed to make a living as publicans in their later years. But as their memorials testify, they were as revered as any modern day sporting celebrity.

Robert Chambers' memorial in the graveyard of Christ Church, Walker (*top*), has 'Honest Bob' reclining in his rowing kit. Above is the curious gravestone of Harry Clasper's mother, father and two brothers, erected by him in 1849 and standing, like the upturned prow of a skiff, close to Clasper's own memorial in Whickham.

▲ For some historians, tracking down the grave of a sporting hero is a necessary quest, if only in the hope that the headstone or memorial will bear some form of sporting reference or motif.

In Tyne and Wear there are three of the best.

As already noted, **Harry Clasper**, **Bob Chambers** and **Jim Renforth** died within just over three years.

All three were given lavish send-offs. And as these pages show, all three were commemorated by memorials carved by George Burn, a Newcastle sculptor who was much in demand at the time.

Chambers, the youngest of the trio, died from tuberculosis at the age of 37 in 1868 (*top right*). His funeral procession drew reported crowds of 50-60,000.

▶ Unquestionably the most moving of George Burn's three memorials is his last one, to **James Renforth**.

Carved in Prudham sandstone and originally positioned over Renforth's grave in Gateshead East Cemetery, in 1992 it was restored by Gateshead Council and now sits outside the Shipley Art Gallery, Prince Consort Road.

Some may consider the memorial as overly sentimental.

Yet as Ian Whitehead has written (*see Links*), Renforth's was no ordinary death, or life.

Born in Newcastle in 1842, but raised in Gateshead, Renforth worked in an iron foundry and was a strong swimmer, winning a medal in the Northumberland Baths.

But rowers earned more than swimmers, and having married young and learnt to row as a ferryman during the demolition of the Old Tyne Bridge, Renforth won his first race in 1866.

From that moment on he hardly lost. Within two years he was world champion, and a cult hero to boot.

Renforth was no angel. He was fined for assault. He deserted the Durham militia and, like Chambers and Clasper, became a publican. He also suffered from epilepsy, and had to train hard to compensate for his love of the good life.

In September 1870, months after he had been a pall bearer at Clasper's funeral, Renforth was one of a four man crew to win a challenge race in Canada that attracted bets of $40,000. The following August he returned for an even more hotly backed rematch.

Shortly into the race, on the Kennebecassis River, the English boat suddenly veered inshore.

'Harry, Harry,' called out a clearly ailing Renforth to his crewmate, the Cockney Harry Kelley, 'I have had something'.

WE ARE IN DEATH

In death as in life James Renforth represented good business. This etching from *The Graphic*, published two weeks after his death (*top*) was frequently reproduced, while St Peter's pottery in Newcastle rushed out the commemorative jug above. One priceless relic is the flannel shirt Renforth took off shortly before his last race, now held by the Beamish Museum.

As Renforth staggered ashore, the crowd suspected a fix. Some assumed he'd had an epileptic fit.

'What will they say at home?' moaned Renforth. Soon after he died in Kelley's arms.

Rumours spread that he had been poisoned. But a post mortem and all subsequent enquiries showed that he had in fact died from natural causes.

And so, for the third time, the streets of Tyneside filled for another massive outpouring of grief.

Apart from Burn's memorial, there is a marble plaque in St Mary's Church, Gateshead, a Renforth Street in Dunston, a Renforth Close in Gateshead and a town named after him in New Brunswick, on the lakeside close to where he died. He was just 29.

▲ Neptune looks down from the boathouse of the **Tyne Rowing Club**, just west of Newburn Bridge, and appears to like what he sees.

For although rowing may never regain the following that it enjoyed on Tyneside during the 19th century – a following that was in any case driven by gambling interests – as a participation sport it has enjoyed an encouraging revival in recent years.

Not least because rowing finally opened its doors to women at the Montreal Olympics in 1976, followed by the first women's regatta at Henley in 1988.

Today, approaching its 160th anniversary in 2012, the Tyne RC has around 200 members, of which 40 per cent are female.

Their boathouse, opened in 1957, is also said to be busier than ever within living memory.

Among its regulars are the **Northumbria University Boat Club**, formed in 1994. Seen above, four of its members take out a coxed four carbon fibre boat, complete with sliding seats and outriggers; design features that are now standard, but of course owe much to the Tyne's pioneering boatbuilders of the 19th century.

▲ Boathouses are seldom of much architectural interest, but there is a certain practical elegance to this trio of lightweight steel sheds, located across the river from Tyne RC. This is the base of **Tyne United RC**, founded in 2007, but named after an earlier club formed from the merger of five clubs; Gateshead & District, Empire, Hawthorn, Walker and Wallsend, in 1946.

The boathouses also host the **Gateshead Rowing Development Partnership**, an initiative supported by Gateshead Council and eight other partners, to encourage young people to take to the water.

A fine stretch of water it is too. Some 1,800m in length and known as the **Newburn Straight**, this part of the Tyne is said to offer the best conditions for racing in the region.

▲ In a thrilling climax to the **Northumbrian Water University Boat Race** in May 2010, Durham's senior men's eight, on the left, beat Newcastle to the line by inches, watched from above by crowds gathered on the Gateshead Millennium Bridge.

It is a scene that would have been unthinkable before the recent transformation of both banks of the Tyne, and yet, like most rowing along this stretch of the river, it is rooted in history.

Inter-collegiate racing between teams from Durham and Newcastle started between the wars, when King's College (formerly Armstrong College), in Newcastle, was still part of Durham University. In 1963 it became independent.

The Tyne in those days was hardly inviting. Since then, however, rather as has happened on the Thames, the Clyde and the Trent, cleaner water and the switch from industrial to leisure usage along the banks, has brought rowing back into the public realm.

Fittingly, the inaugural Newcastle v. Durham boat race, in May 1997, was started by David Clasper, the great great nephew of Harry.

Chapter Seventeen

Model boating

Given the north east's shipbuilding heritage, it should be no surprise that model boating is so deeply rooted, or rather firmly anchored, in Tyne and Wear. Or that the area has three long established clubs, more than any other part of Britain. South Shields Model Yacht Club, formed by local aldermen in 1886 at the newly created South Marine Park, claims to be the oldest in the country. However, the Model Yacht Sailing Association, founded in 1876 at the Round Pond in London's Kensington Gardens, claims otherwise. Whatever, South Shields MYC are certainly the oldest existing in the north east.

After the big boats we now turn our attention to the even more arcane world of 'straight running', 'fast electrics' and 'marbleheads'.

To casual observers model boat racing may appear as little more than a hobby for overgrown schoolboys. In the 1880s, for instance, a retired sea captain, the son of a shipbuilder, recalled how as a child in the 1820s he had played with a boat on the pond on Sunderland Town Moor.

Yet by the end of the 19th century numerous clubs had formed around Britain, turning model boating into an organised sport with rules and regulations no less strict than those applying to full-size craft.

Not least, competitive racing galvanised efforts to improve upon model boat design and engine technology, both areas in which the ship builders of the north east shared an obvious interest.

As noted on the left, claims as to which model boat club is the oldest can be hard to verify, particularly as clubs have tended to split up, reform, or relocate to different ponds.

Like their full scale counterparts, model boats are raced against each other at regattas, in this case, from the 1950s, at the North East Coast Regatta, staged at Roker Park. Entrants that year came from South Shields, Sunderland, Tynemouth and Heaton. One stated advantage of powered boats over yachts was that they were easier to transport on a bus.

But it appears probable that the first to form in Tyne and Wear was the Newcastle Model Yacht Club, at Exhibition Park in 1882. However, although its 1894 boathouse survives in the park (*see page 29*), the club itself ceased to function in 2007, sailing having become impossible due to a build up of weed and silt in the pond (a recurring problem that Victorian clubs complained of equally).

Gateshead Model Yacht Club, formed in 1886 at Saltwell Park, is also now defunct, leaving the South Shields Model Yacht Club, as the oldest functioning club at the same site. (Even this title is contested however, as the club may have gone into abeyance during both world wars.)

Two other historic clubs are Tynemouth Model Boat Club, founded in 1893 at Tynemouth Park, and Heaton & District Model Power Boat Club, formally inaugurated in 1910, although boats had certainly been sailed on the lake at Paddy Freeman's Park as early as the 1880s.

In national terms, the survival of these three historic clubs is especially noteworthy, since the vast majority of the hundreds of other clubs dotted around Britain are much younger. Most, in fact, date from the introduction of cheap and efficient radio control kits in the 1970s, and the much wider availability of kit-form or even readymade boats.

Local clubs of a more recent vintage include Wearside MBC, formed in 1982 and based at Ryhope Pumping Station (now the Ryhope Engines Museum), Saltwell Park MBC (2002), Roker Park MBC (2005), and Herrington MBC (2008), whose base is a lake created from a former open cast mining area, overlooked by Penshaw Monument.

◄ Early model boat clubs in Tyne and Wear tended to have informal links to particular shipyards, with membership spread amongst white collar workers, artisans and engineers, and those workmen who could afford the sport. Some gentlemen members even hired professional sailing masters to sail their craft, which entailed wading into the water to trim the sails.

Shown here in c.1910 are the founding members of **Heaton & District Model Power Boat Club**, with their collection of scale models, mostly naval craft. Note how their headgear – from flat caps to peaked yachting caps, the latter being part of the official sailing uniform – reflected the hierarchy within the membership.

At the **1929 North East Coast Exhibition** (*below*), the 'straight running' competition was a popular spectator event. Powered boats were set off, one at a time, to sail towards a target, gaining points for accuracy over several runs. Once released – in what was judged to be the correct direction – their owners could exercise no further control over the boat.

Although modern clubs still hold straight running contests, the advent of radio control has allowed a totally different type of competition; for instance navigating around a course formed by a series of hazards.

▲ As seen at **Heaton & District Model Power Boat Club** (*above and top right*) the model boathouse interior is a shipshape environment in which club members store their models and kit in personal lockers. Some clubhouses have workshops and most, such as at **Tynemouth Park** (*above right*), have a worktable for ongoing repairs and last-minute, pre-race adjustments.

The models themselves have evolved considerably. In the late 19th century factory-made tinplate boats, mostly made in Germany, fed a rising demand for toys amongst the middle classes. British-made boats became popular in the first half of the 20th century, with well known names such as Meccano of Liverpool and Bassett-Lowke of Northampton to the fore.

Bassett-Lowke was, however, careful to advertise its products as models rather than toys.

In the 1950s the sport was transformed by the introduction of radio control technology. This, combined with the availablility of cheap plastics, has since made model boating more affordable, albeit rendering handmade traditional designs less common.

▲ Heaton & District's boathouse in **Paddy Freeman's Park** was built in 1923, and is now on Newcastle City Council's list of local buildings of special architectural interest, while Tynemouth MBC's boathouse at **Tynemouth Park** (*top right*) is even older, dating from 1893.

Built at a cost of £102 12s, it was doubled to its present size during the 1930s.

One of the club's most influential supporters was the Duke of Northumberland (on whose land Tynemouth Park and boating pond was laid out in 1893). It was thanks to the Duke's agent that in 1908 the club was able to secure longer hours on the pond, after rowing boats threatened to take over. Nowadays it is 'the old enemy' they must confront, weeds.

As can be seen, some model boats are still powered by tiny petrol or diesel driven engines, or even by steam. (Cheaper forms of propulsion used clockwork or even twisted rubber bands.)

Not all are designed to race, but are judged according to their minute detail and accuracy. Some, dating back to the 1930s, are rarely risked in the water at all.

▲ Remote controls have totally changed model boat racing.

Before it became affordable in the 1970s, the direction a boat could take was controlled only by setting the rudder, or the sails, at a specific angle, either for straight running, or to sail in a circle, which required a large area of clear water.

With modern day remote controls each boat operator is allocated a specific radio frequency – marked up on a pegboard in the clubhouse – so that several boats can now be out on the water at the same time without fear of interference, and more intricate obstacle courses can be set. (Some radio controls have additional functions, for example for sounding fog horns.)

Even so, straight running competitions between a course marked by flags are still held, as at **Paddy Freeman's Park, Heaton** (*right*). Bisecting the centre pair of flags gains most points.

Perhaps the most difficult task is that of the catcher, whose job it is to stand in the water and collect the fast-moving boat before it rams the pond wall, then turn off its engine.

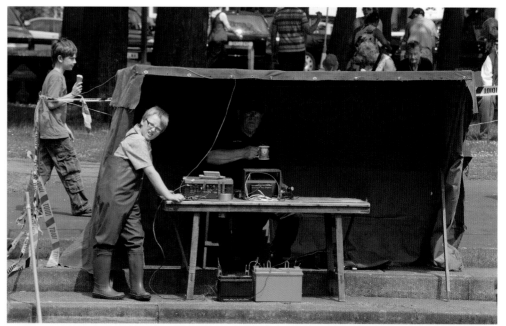

◄ Sometimes, as demonstrated here at **Paddy Freeman's Park**, the greatest pleasure to be gained from model boating is the simple mastery of one's craft from shore to ship.

An ideal place to see such skills in practice is at **South Marine Park** (*below*), where, swans permitting, members of **South Shields Model Yacht Club** use radio transmitter handsets to navigate their elegant boats deftly around a set course defined by buoys. No easy task.

Each yacht is controlled using two separate radio channels on a single frequency. The boat's receiver is connected to two battery-powered motors, one which operates the rudder, the other a winch, which adjusts the sails.

The rules governing model yacht racing are more or less the same as those for full-size crewed boats, and are governed by the Model Yacht Association, which in 2010 had 111 affiliated clubs, from Aberdeen down to Yeovil.

Seen here is the most popular One Metre class, with a maximum hull length of a metre.

A more hi-tech class of model yacht is the Marblehead, named after the Massachusetts port. This measures 50 inches long, the length deemed ideal to fit onto the rear seat of a typical American car.

Not so easy for taking on the bus though.

Chapter Eighteen

Swimming

In towns and cities all over Britain there are Bath Lanes and Bath Streets, marking the location at one time or another of public baths and wash houses. Most date from the period after the passing of the 1846 Baths and Wash Houses Act, which heralded a new era of affordable bathing and laundry provision for the general public. Newcastle's Bath Lane, off Westgate Road in the city centre, was however named after one of Britain's earliest known privately funded baths, opened in 1781 (*see opposite*). For a more detailed history of indoor swimming pools, readers are referred to an earlier *Played in Britain* publication, *Great Lengths* (*see Links*).

Our final chapter concerns, according to numerous surveys, the nation's most popular physical recreation apart from walking.

We leave it to the end partly because the structures designed for swimming form a quite distinct building type, unlike any of the other buildings so far featured in this book. The story of their development also strays into hitherto unexamined areas such as public health and hygiene.

After all, it is only in recent years that we have started to call them swimming 'pools', rather than swimming 'baths'.

The earliest known baths in Tyne and Wear were at the Segedunum Roman Fort, at the eastern end of Hadrian's Wall, in what is now Wallsend. This was occupied for nearly 300 years, starting in c.120 AD.

What we do not know is if the bath house, which stood outside the fort's south-western defences, above the river Tyne, contained plunge baths, as did many Roman baths, and if so, whether they were large enough to swim in.

However we can safely assume that even without man-made baths, the people of our region have always swum in the North Sea, the Tyne and the Wear, and indeed in any other available natural body of water. Certainly sea bathing is recorded in Sunderland in the 18th century.

In post Roman times, purpose-built baths designed for washing and for their health-promoting qualities first appeared in London in the late 17th century.

Newcastle's earliest baths, seen opposite, opened in 1781.

When the first Baths and Wash Houses Act was passed in 1846, its prime concern was to give local authorities the powers to provide 'slipper' baths (that is, individual baths) and laundries, in order to combat disease in overcrowded urban areas. Swimming was not mentioned at all.

In Tyne and Wear, Sunderland was the first local authority to adopt the Act, building the High Street Baths in 1858. Newcastle waited longer, building its first public baths in 1886, in Byker, Arthur's Hill and Elswick.

Thereafter, as detailed in this chapter, a succession of baths appeared throughout the region, with the provision for swimming becoming ever more important as the 20th century wore on, while the need for public washing and laundry facilities diminished.

That said, a public laundry was still deemed necessary in Newcastle's Montagu Baths, completed in 1964.

More recently we have seen the emergence of leisure pools, with Whitley Bay leading the way in 1974, and in the last decade, a return to the focus on competitive swimming, with the construction of several 25m pools and, in Sunderland, of the region's first 50m pool.

Currently there are 22 public pools in Tyne and Wear, including two community-run pools in Jesmond and Fenham that are of special relevance in today's challenging economic circumstances.

The newest is the Hadrian Leisure Centre in Wallsend, which opened in July 2010, although by the end of 2010 two more should

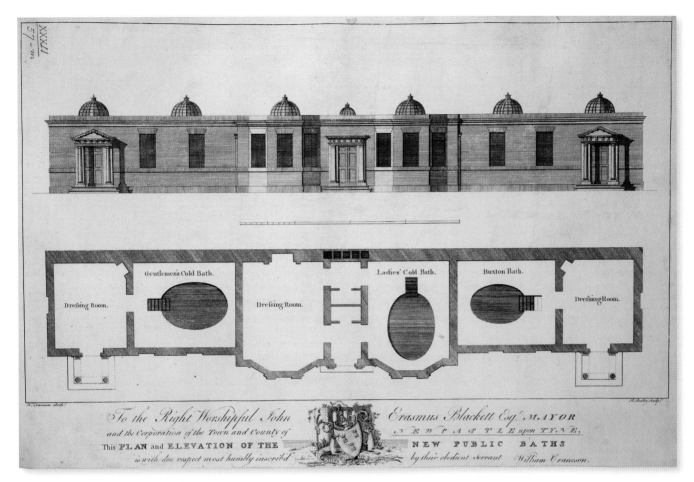

Gentlemen's Cold Bath.

Ladies' Cold Bath.

Buxton Bath.

Dreſsing Room.

Dreſsing Room.

Dreſsing Room.

To the Right Worshipful John Erasmus Blackett Esq. MAYOR
and the Corporation of the Town and County of NEWCASTLE upon TYNE.
This PLAN and ELEVATION OF THE NEW PUBLIC BATHS
is with due respect most humbly inscrib'd by their obedient Servant William Craneson.

be opened in Gateshead, together with Northumbria University's publicly accessible Sport Central, in Newcastle. A new pool for the sea front at South Shields is also planned for completion in 2012.

From a heritage angle, the issue of which historic baths should be retained, and which jettisoned, is one of the toughest questions facing planners and conservationists today.

All the more reason, therefore, to place those buildings that do survive into their correct historical and architectural context.

▲ These plans, held by the British Library, show one of the earliest subscription baths to have been built in Britain, Newcastle's **New Public Baths**, opened on May 1 1781 on what would become Bath Lane, opposite the Town Wall.

The only earlier known examples were built in Birmingham, London, Liverpool and Bristol between the 1730s and 1760s.

Subscription baths gained their name because although nominally titled as 'public baths', entry was usually only for subscribers, with a single entry typically priced at a minimum of one shilling, well beyond the means of the majority.

Newcastle's baths, designed by William Craneson (who presented these plans to the Mayor), were commissioned by a Dr Hall and two surgeons, Henry Gibson and R Bryan Abbs, at a time when the benefits of hygiene and full immersion in water were starting to be recognised in medical circles.

'Elegantly and completely fitted up', the building comprised two strictly segregated cold plunge baths for ladies and gentlemen – neither large enough for serious swimming – and a separate mineral water 'Buxton bath'.

Outside, in a garden setting, was 'a large open or swimming bath', where, as one observer noted in 1800, 'young gentlemen acquire this necessary and useful art, free from the danger of those fatal accidents which too frequently happen in large rivers or deep ponds'.

Craneson's baths functioned until around the 1820s when their water supply was cut off by the sinking of a new pit shaft. By 1860 the building had been demolished.

▲ After the closure of William Craneson's baths, in 1836 the Town Council recommended that a private company, the Newcastle upon Tyne Public Baths Company, be set up to build a replacement.

The result, the **Northumberland Baths**, was a neo-classical building designed by the town's most celebrated architect, John Dobson, on the site of the present day City Pool, on Northumberland Road.

Opened in 1839 at a cost of £7,300, with an oval pool measuring 104' x 52', annual subscriptions were set at two guineas, with an individual swim costing 6d.

But although the fees were similar to those in other towns, the baths were not successful.

Firstly, contrary to Dobson's original plans drawn up in 1837, there was no roof over the pool.

Secondly, there was no immediate supply of fresh water (whereas most other baths of the period were sited close to natural springs or sources of seawater).

In September 1842 the company's directors were still hopeful that the townspeople might 'ere long become more sensible of the luxury of Bathing'. But they were soon forced to convert part of the building into an inn, while the east side, with its impressive arcaded entrance, became the clubhouse of the Northumberland Cricket Club (*as depicted on the inside of the front cover flap*).

In 1856 the Baths Company was wound up, and in 1860, 14 years after the 1846 Act had given them the powers to provide baths, the Town Council bought the building for £2,000. After protests from the newly formed Newcastle Swimming Club in 1863, the Council then provided a roof, in 1868.

Yet still the Council preferred not to run the building, leasing it out to a private operator called Hastie, who in 1869 installed a suite of the newly fashionable Turkish Baths. Entry to the swimming pool, meanwhile, was set at 7d.

Finally, in 1888, the baths were placed under Council management, and, as seen here in 1898, the earlier roof and its stone pillars were replaced by a much lighter and intricately engineered glazed canopy supported on slender cast iron columns.

Note also the wooden diving stage at the deep end (a mere 6' 3" in depth) and the gas lamps suspended over the pool.

Single sex sessions were the rule, with women allowed in to swim only for limited periods.

◀ By the time this photograph was taken at the **Northumberland Baths** in the early years of the 20th century, two higher diving boards had been installed, despite the maximum depth being reduced by four inches (Boards of a similar height today would require a depth of 12' 6", or 3.8m, by comparison.)

Not that this would have deterred local swimmers. By 1913 the city had six registered swimming clubs, and local authorities all over Britain were now well aware that for all their provision of 'slipper' or individual baths for washing, and wash houses for laundry – as specified by the 1846 Act and its 1878 successor – no public baths could remain viable without catering for the needs of swimmers.

Even catering for spectators became essential, as interest grew in swimming club galas and the newly popular sport of water polo.

Lacking these facilities, and being without a modern water filtration system (introduced elsewhere from 1904 onwards), the Northumberland Baths fell far behind the city's other more modern establishments.

Even so, and despite a report in 1919 that the building's fabric was now in a parlous state, planning for a replacement commenced only in 1921. It was, by then, the oldest public baths in Britain.

▲ A party of schoolboys line the poolside at the **Victoria Sea Water Swimming Baths** on **Pier Parade**, **South Shields**, in 1913.

Opened by a private company in July 1885 and designed by local architect Joseph Morton at a cost of £6,000, the baths were among several private salt water baths – supplied directly from the sea at high tide – built during this period to capitalise on the growing popularity of swimming.

Yet, only 16 months later, the baths were sold on for just £2,710. The new owners were then wound up in 1902, and although as we see here the pool remained in use after that, swimming ceased around 1916.

In 1921 the building became the Marina Theatre, then the Majestic Ballroom with a new 1930s frontage, then an amusement arcade. Most recently, it was occupied by a Quasar Centre. The pool itself had long since been infilled, but as seen right, the original timber-framed roof structure remained intact.

Not for much longer, however. In 2010 South Tyneside Council announced plans to build a new £15 million, 25m public pool on the site, this time using mains rather than seawater.

▲ The two largest surviving baths buildings in Tyne and Wear, both Edwardian and Grade II listed, are **Lawson Street Baths** in **Wallsend**, by the Newcastle architects Edwin FW Liddle and Percy L Browne, opened in 1912, and **Gibson Street Baths**, **Newcastle** (*above right*), by the City Surveyor, FH Holford.

Lawson Street, forming part of a group with the adjoining fire station and town hall, was closed in 1989 and has lain disused since.

The latter remains in use for badminton, after swimming ceased in around 1965.

Gibson Street was the fourth public baths built in Newcastle under the Baths and Wash Houses Act (after Byker, Westgate and Elswick, all 1886). Planning started in 1903, but negotiations to buy the site proved tortuous, as did attempts to raise the funds.

Holford's original plans in 1904 also came in for scathing criticism from the Local Government Board in London, and had to be redrawn.

Finally, the building was opened in April 1907, the Lady Mayoress and guests being treated to a display of 'fancy swimming' by the renowned Arthur 'Jack' Jarvis from Leicester, who had five Olympic medals and numerous world records to his name.

Costing £28,000, Gibson Street was lavishly fitted out, with separate entrances for men and women decorated with stained glass windows (*below right*) and green glazed brick walls at ground level. There were 23 slipper baths (only four of them for women), and a pool measuring 75' x 28'.

Gibson Street was technically advanced too, being the first baths in Newcastle to incorporate electricity and water filtration, whereas all the earlier baths operated on the 'fill and empty' system, whereby the water was changed only once or twice a week, growing progressively dirtier as the days went by.

As the interior view from c.1908 shows (*above right*), Gibson Street also featured the latest form of arched and plastered ceiling – designed for improved acoustics – plus amphitheatre seating on both sides, lined at the rear by demountable wooden changing cubicles, to allow for greater flexibility when the pool was boarded over for winter use.

PLUNGE BATH.

▲ Inside the former men's entrance hall of **Gibson Street Baths**, still with its original turnstile and ticket windows, lie these quite unexpected and wonderful treasures.

Mermaids cavort upon rocks whilst the men play a hard fought game of water polo. A swimmer in a striped costume dives headlong into the water as red-sailed yachts drift towards a golden horizon.

For sure, Victorian and Edwardian baths were often adorned with patterned tilework and beautifully crafted fixtures and fittings. But these four wall panels, each around four feet by two feet, are without parallel, even in the nation's most palatial historic baths such as in Manchester, Birmingham and Hull.

(Only a pair of tiled panels depicting seaside and lakeside scenes, originally at Longton Baths in Stoke-on-Trent, dating from c.1880 and now on display at the Potteries Museum and Art Gallery, are remotely comparable.)

As to their creators, the two mermaid panels at Gibson Street bear the signature of Carter & Co., tile and pottery manufacturers from Poole in Dorset, who supplied many an Edwardian public house,

butcher's shop and fishmonger with similar sorts of painted tiled scenes.

Yet oddly, the two other panels (*above*) are unsigned.

Just as intriguing is why the panels are at Gibson Street at all, especially in a building whose costs were so scrupulously monitored.

Certainly neither the minutes of the Baths & Wash Houses Committee, nor Carter's archives make any mention of the tiles. Nor do two otherwise fulsome reports on the baths in the *Newcastle Daily Journal* and *The Builder*.

A clue may lie in the fifth panel of the set, not shown here, which, beneath the city's coat of arms, lists the 15 members of the Baths & Wash Houses Committee, and both the architect and builders.

Such rolls of honour, usually in the form of brass plaques, were common in public baths.

So could it be that the Committee decided retrospectively to commission and pay for the tiles themselves, perhaps to highlight their own commitment to an often controversial project, at a time when so many local authorities were vying with each other to deliver lavish public works?

Or were they simply added later in an attempt to lure more men into the building?

Whatever, sadly, these unique tiled panels now sit in shadowy isolation in an unused part of a building that is nowadays used only for badminton.

Better hidden than lost, but nevertheless, worthy of a wider audience.

▲ Built to replace John Dobson's original Northumberland Baths, Newcastle's **City Pool** is one of the few city centre swimming facilities, historic or otherwise, to have survived in a northern provincial city, those in Liverpool, Leeds and Bradford having been closed over the past half century.

The City Pool has survived for two main reasons.

Despite the lack of any immediate local community, the facilities are highly prized by those city centre workers, students and swimming club members who use them on a regular basis.

But just as importantly, the building houses not only two pools, a fitness centre and Turkish baths, but also Newcastle's prime concert venue, the City Hall.

The idea to combine sport and the performing arts within one building was originally conceived after a deputation from the city's Baths and Wash Houses Committee went to visit Bradford's Central Baths in November 1921.

Seen above is the main entrance block on **Northumberland Road**, designed to offer entry during the swimming season to the women's pool, which lies directly behind in the central axis of the building, and to the men's pool on the west side (flanking the aptly named John Dobson Street).

Then in winter, when the pools were boarded over to save fuel costs and allow other uses, separate entrances were opened on either side, through the colonnades.

The entrance on the east side leads to **City Hall**, which now seats 2,135 (reduced from its original, somewhat cramped capacity of 2,518) and which has played host to a variety of performers, including concert orchestras, Yehudi Menuhin, The Beatles, Bruce Springsteen and Billy Connolly.

The need for all three spaces to be used independently and flexibly, while sharing heating, lighting and ventilation systems, required careful planning to a strict brief.

The Corporation thus launched a design competition in 1923, with the experienced baths architect Alfred Cross appointed as assessor.

Forty one submissions were received, the winning entry being that of the London practice of C Nicholas and JE Dixon-Spain.

In particular they were deemed to have provided a sufficiently grand neo-classical frontage, whilst also providing a coherent plan based around shared circulation spaces and service corridors. No easy task at a time when both pools had to be segregated for swimming, yet free flow was

required at all other times.

Costing around £160,000 – a considerable investment at a time of great economic hardship – the new Northumberland Baths and City Hall officially opened on November 7 1928.

Reflecting the changing times and its city centre location, only nine slipper baths were provided (six male, three female). Nor was a wash house deemed necessary.

As always, the men's pool, also used for galas, was the largest, at 100' x 37', while the women's pool measured 75' x 32'.

Being located next door to the City Hall has had its drawbacks. In the days before the Sage concert hall was opened in Gateshead, for example, swimmers using the former ladies pool, directly next to the City Hall, recall having to desist from whistling, cheering or even, it is said, using fins, to avoid loud splashing whenever an orchestral concert was in progress.

▲ With its curved ceiling, recessed rooflights and gallery seating, the gala pool at the Grade II listed **City Pool** (formerly the Northumberland Baths) is a classic inter-war design.

Along with the smaller training pool next door (the former women's pool) it is also the oldest pool in use within Tyne and Wear.

As seen here in 2007, the pool tank has been boomed to create one section measuring 25m, with a children's pool at the near end. The original changing cubicles, which were demountable for when the pool was boarded over during the winter (for use at one time as a cinema), have also been removed.

At the time of going to press the future of the building's second pool remained uncertain, following an announcement in 2009 of plans to convert it into a dry area for multi-functional usage.

To compensate for this loss of a valued training facility, the Council negotiated for public access to be available at a new 25m pool being opened in Northumbria University's Sport Central complex in September 2010, a few hundred yards to the east along Northumberland Road.

◀ Having invested so heavily in the new Northumberland Baths during the 1920s, Newcastle Corporation built a further five public baths during the period 1925–38.

Not only did this construction programme allow more people to swim, particularly schoolchildren, it also provided much needed work at a time of mass unemployment.

Of the five new baths, those at Heaton, Scotswood and Walker have since been demolished, leaving two, at **St George's Terrace, Jesmond** (*left*) and **Fenham Hall Drive, Fenham** (*below*).

The pair share numerous characteristics. Both were designed by the Newcastle practice of Hetherington & Wilson and opened in 1938. Both had single storey brick entrance blocks in front of a top-lit pool shed containing a pool measuring 75' x 35'. Both, reflecting changing social patterns, catered for mixed swimming sessions, with changing rooms set apart from the poolside and only limited numbers of slipper baths.

But it is in recent years that comparisons between the two have grown even stronger.

Starting in the 1980s, the City Council began a programme of cutbacks at local pools, leading to reduced opening hours and a mass protest of swimmers in 1986.

Fearing even more stringent cuts, the Friends of Jesmond Pool was formed in 1989.

Finally, in February 1991 the Council announced that Jesmond would indeed close, a scenario that was echoed all over Britain.

Of the nation's sportsmen and women, swimmers have always been amongst the most vociferous, and sure enough within weeks of the announcement campaigners formed the **Jesmond Swimming Project**, a not for profit company.

Despite an all night sit-in – a form of protest that would be repeated at several threatened pools – Jesmond was shut on March 29 1991. Yet within days the JSP struck back, launching plans to take over the pool under community management.

Their first victory was to gain an award of £50,000 from the newly formed Foundation for Sport and the Arts. This led to the pool re-opening on April 11 1992, with longer hours, a range of new activities and, crucially, tighter control of running costs. No doubt to the Council's surprise, the pool's income rose rapidly.

It took another five years for the JSP to secure extra funding from the National Lottery, culminating in a £1.5 million refurbishment completed in February 2003.

The JSP's lease from the Council was also extended at this time.

Over in the west end, a similar tale of protest and triumph ensued at Fenham. There, despite lengthy protests, the pool was closed on June 28 2003.

Emulating their Jesmond counterparts, pool users then formed the **Fenham Swimming Project** as a charitable company limited by guarantee. This too was able to raise funds, totalling £200,000, leading to the pool's re-opening under the FSP's management on July 28 2005.

Since then the FSP has managed to oversee various improvements, financed by a £80,000 grant from the Big Lottery Fund in 2007.

Further modernisation followed in 2009-10 after another major effort raised £400,000 from an array of charities and trust funds.

Not surprisingly, Jesmond and Fenham's achievements have brought with them a string of accolades, firstly as social

enterprises that have responded brilliantly to local needs – largely because they have been carried out by committed local residents – and secondly for their determination to maintain historic pools in a sustainable manner.

No-one pretends the process is easy. It cannot happen without a council's full co-operation and ongoing support. It requires huge dedication, imagination and regular fund-raising.

And yet the results speak for themselves. At Fenham, for example, annual losses have been slashed to a fifth of their previous levels, whilst annual usage of the pool has more than doubled, to reach 72,000 in 2010.

In the harsh economic times of today, Jesmond and Fenham can no doubt expect even more visitors. That is from swimmers all over

Britain, seeking to learn how they too might take control of their own much loved but threatened pools.

Nor are they alone. Similar groups at Chester's City Baths and Birkenhead's Byrne Avenue Baths, plus a handful of community groups now running outdoor pools, have shown that community management can succeed, if all else fails.

Jesmond Pool is a superb example of how a 1930s facility can benefit from modern technology and sensitive refurbishment. Particularly appreciated is that its water is now treated using an ultra violet system rather than the usual chlorine-based agents. Note, however, the survival of its 'scum trough' (*left*), a system introduced in the early 1900s to channel pollution from the water's surface.

Foundation stones are rarely given a second glance, though most pre war baths have them. This one, however, laid by Alderman Norman McGretton, chairman of Gateshead's Parks and Baths Committee, at Shipcote Baths, is especially poignant, given the thoughts of most of those present. It is dated July 24 1939. Six weeks later, war was declared.

◀ Moving south of the Tyne, to the corner of Alexandra Road and Shipcote Lane, **Shipcote Baths**, now part of the **Gateshead Leisure Centre** – seen here shortly after it opened – is another example of an historic pool building recently brought back to life.

It is also an interesting example of the transitional phase baths architecture entered in the late 1930s, as local authorities finally embraced modernism, only for the outbreak of war to lead to an almost complete dearth of new baths in Britain until the 1960s.

Gateshead had two early public baths. The first, on Oakwellgate, opened in 1855, had only slipper baths and a wash house, but no pool. The second, on Mulgrave Terrace, dating from 1890, had a single pool and 23 slipper baths.

But a more modern pool had been under consideration by the Borough Council since before 1914.

Not until 1931 did serious planning start however.

The first scheme, costed at £90,000 and drawn up by the Council's architect H Cook, allowed for two pools, one of which, at 100' x 40', would have been 'just bigger than Newcastle's largest in Northumberland Road', as one local newspaper gleefully reported.

Rejecting a modernist approach, these new baths were to be built in Renaissance style, with a domed portico 32 feet in diameter.

Site works on Shipcote Lane began in late 1931, but were soon halted as the town's economy slumped ever further into recession.

By the time building restarted seven years later, the plans had altered considerably, as had the cost, dropping to £35,000. Now only one pool was planned, albeit still at 100' x 40'.

As noted left, the timing was

unfortunate. Once war broke out the government withheld its grant, and only after repeated lobbying did the Ministry of Health finally relent. Shipcote Baths thus became the only baths in England to open during the war, on April 29 1942.

In one sense, however, the delays proved a blessing in disguise. For instead of the ornate, fussy building planned in 1931, the completed design, drawn up by Borough Surveyor Fred Patterson, was a strikingly modern composition in brick, stripped of detail and with a single storey, flat-roofed entrance block offset in front of the dominant pool hall.

Had it been built in a larger city, in peacetime, this was a design that might well have been hailed as a modern triumph.

Certainly it proved popular, attracting local swimmers and visiting teams, particularly water polo players. In the 1950s the French and Swedish water polo club champions took on the Northumberland and Durham team.

Three Gateshead swimmers – Jennifer Bradford, Dorinda Fraser and Neil Nicholson – became national champions, Nicholson going on to swim in the 1964 Olympic Games in Tokyo.

By this time a new generation of concrete, glass and steel pools, such as in nearby Felling (*see overleaf*), made Shipcote look prematurely outdated. In 1971 the Council therefore agreed to a modernisation programme and the addition of a learner pool, completed in 1976.

This was followed shortly afterwards by the construction of a substantial dry sport centre on the adjoining site in 1981, designed in matching brick by the Borough Architect and opened by the Queen.

Together, the two facilities were merged under the title of Gateshead Leisure Centre.

Again though, fashions quickly caught up with the Centre, and in 2009 the whole building closed for twelve months to undergo a complete £8 million overhaul, as part of a £36 million investment in sporting facilities across Gateshead.

Ironically it was the 1980s areas that required the most radical treatment, with internal walls taken out, natural lighting introduced, and a third pool added, along with a new 650 square metre gym, sauna and steam rooms, three fitness studios, new changing areas, a new entrance and reception atrium and café.

Overseeing the revamp were S&P Architects with contractors Willmott Dixon, a pairing also responsible for two other new Gateshead leisure centres, at Blaydon and Heworth.

But for the purposes of this book it is the refurbishment of the original main pool on Shipcote Lane (*above and right*) that really captures the eye.

Re-opened in April 2010, the pool now looks fresher and lighter than ever, yet another example of how an historic pool has proved timeless in its appeal.

Gateshead Council has recognised this by placing the pool on its list of buildings of special local architectural and historic interest.

The spruced up exterior of the 1981 Leisure Centre (*above*) now sits more comfortably with its elegant 1930s vintage neighbour, to create a complex which is considered a potential pre-Olympic training camp for 2012.

▲ In a scene that captures so well the spirit of post war urban planning, **Felling Pool**, a concrete and glass icon built to serve the new Leam Lane Estate, looks down over the recently completed shopping parade of Fewster Square.

Like so many post war pools, planning for this behemoth had started in the early 1950s, only to be held up by financial constraints and political wrangling. Its architects, clearly influenced by the 1956 Melbourne Olympic Pool, were JH Napper and Partners.

As was the trend at this time, the main pool measured 110' x 42'. But a gross over provision of seats (1,000 in total) and the sheer scale of the structure, combined with subsidence problems, sent the costs rocketing to over £234,000.

And yet it proved hugely popular, attracting 107,500 users in its first three months in 1963, more than had been expected in a single year.

Alas its glamour was not to last. In common with so many 1960s pools – designed by a generation of architects robbed of experience by the war and its aftermath, and yet keen to make a splash with bold use of materials – Felling would prove less enduring than even its Victorian and Edwardian predecessors.

Gobbling energy, difficult to maintain and with entrance being via stairs leading up to the first floor – making access problematic – Gateshead Council decided to replace Felling Pool with a modern leisure centre at Heworth, due to open in late 2010.

▶ By the mid 1960s over one million swimmers were using Newcastle's facilities each year, putting ever greater pressure on the existing stock of ageing pools.

This is **Montagu Baths**, on **Harehills Avenue**, **Cowgate**, the city's first post war swimming pool, designed by the Newcastle practice of Cackett, Burns Dick & Mackellar, together with City Architect George Kenyon, and opened in May 1964.

As at Felling (*see opposite*), a pool measuring 110' x 42' was overlooked by a generous bank of seating, with glazed screen ends and side windows, supplemented by overhead lighting recessed in a false ceiling.

Note also the Pop Art inspired tiling in a 'pleasing pattern' (as the official brochure put it) surrounding the pool, and the cantilevered reinforced concrete five metre diving board at the deep end.

Reflecting the needs of the residents for whom the pool was built, there was a public laundry in the basement.

Newcastle would gain two more new pools as a result of local government reorganisation in 1974: Gosforth Pool, built in 1968 by Gosforth Urban District Council, and **Newburn Pool** (*right*), built by Newburn Urban District Council.

Opened in January 1970, Newburn cost £278,000 and was designed by the infamous John Poulson, jailed for corruption three years later. It was also Newcastle's first metric pool, being built to the new standard length of 33.3m (just short of the previous norm of 110').

Since renamed **Outer West Pool**, with an extra 25m training pool and fitness centre added in 2009, it is home to Newburn Amateur Swimming Club, which originated as the Arthur's Hill Club at the end of the 19th century.

Newburn Pool's former entrance (*left*) has been sacrificed to make way for the centre's expansion, but the 33.3m pool remains the longest competition pool in Newcastle. Montagu (*above*), in contrast, was demolished in 2009.

▲ If the 1960s proved to be a problematic era in pool design, the 1970s were characterised by two trends. Firstly, more pools were built in Britain during this decade than any other since the 1846 Act.

Secondly, there occurred a revolution in design, in which the north east was to play a key role.

This is the **Whitley Bay Pool**, designed by Gillinson Barnett and Partners and opened in March 1974. Costing £500,000, it was only the second freeform leisure pool built in Britain, the first having opened weeks earlier in Bletchley.

Bletchley came about after its architects, the Newcastle firm of Faulkner-Brown Hendy Watkinson Stonor (now FaulknerBrowns), visited the Royal Commonwealth Pool in Edinburgh, opened in 1970, and noticed how few people swam, compared with those simply splashing around for fun.

Peter Sargent of Gillinson Barnett reached a similar conclusion after being commissioned to design a

new leisure centre at Herringthorpe in Rotherham, which was a twin to Whitley Bay.

The result was a new generation of pools based on curvilinear forms, slides, flumes and lagoons, very much aimed at families and children. At Whitley Bay, for example, a £15,000 wave machine sent waves nearly a metre high rolling from the deep end towards a simulated shore area.

Serious swimmers were understandably shocked. But the Whitley Bay Pool attracted so many users that initially numbers had to be carefully monitored to prevent overcrowding. Meanwhile, legions of local authority representatives visited, keen to see how they too could capitalise on the new trend.

After three decades of intense use, the structure at Whitley Bay started to suffer, leading eventually to the failure of its roof.

But North Tyneside remained committed to the concept, and in 2007 began constructing in effect a completely new structure (*left*) over the top of the existing pool area, as part of a £6 million refurbishment.

Reopened in March 2009 and renamed **Waves** (as suggested by a local schoolboy), the revamped pool, complete with a new spa, slides, and play area featuring a replica pirate ship, attracted 405,000 visitors over the next year.

Clearly, the leisure pool is no passing fad.

◀ Back in Newcastle but continuing the theme of leisure pools, **Elswick Pool** sits on rising ground in the midst of Elswick Park, looking down over the parish church on Westmorland Road and the north bank of the River Tyne.

Elswick Park had been gifted to the city in 1881, but by the 1970s was in poor state, as was the original Elswick Baths, down on Scotswood Road, and the nearby Westgate Baths in Arthur's Hill (both dating from 1886).

Also reaching the end of its useful life was Scotswood Baths on Armstrong Road, dating from 1933.

Thus arose a £1.8 million plan to revive the 15 acre park, with the new leisure pool forming a hub for other outdoor sports activities, to create what was called a 'leisure centre without a roof'.

The pool itself was designed by the Napper Collerton Partnership (who, having started with Felling now had several pools to their name), and combines a free form pool with a four lane section for serious swimmers, a combination that has since become a popular compromise.

Meanwhile, on Hadrian Square, Byker, Newcastle's newest pool is the **East End Pool** (*left*) opened in conjunction with a library and gym in September 2000. This also replaced three earlier baths: nearby Shipley Street in Byker (closed in 1992 and now a climbing centre, *see page 193*); Heaton Baths (1925) and Walker Baths (1930s).

The presence of a 50m flume in one of East End's three pools, seen here protruding from the main core, helped increase user numbers to four or five times those recorded at Heaton and Walker.

A second flume has therefore since been added.

▲ Leisure pools may be popular amongst the general public, but for competitive swimmers only pools that measure 25m or 50m are acceptable. In the former category most towns and cities are well served. But in the latter, Britain has for many years lagged far behind.

Depending on the criteria applied, as of 2007, there were some 20–22 indoor public 50m pools in Britain, whereas in Germany, Berlin alone had 19.

Hence in the mid 1990s when Sunderland City Council started to clear the 30 hectare site of the former Monkwearmouth Colliery for the Stadium of Light (*see pages 84–5*), the site adjacent to the stadium was an obvious candidate for the north east's first 50m pool, and indeed the only such facility between Leeds and Edinburgh.

As noted earlier (*pages 76–77*), Sunderland was the first local authority in the north east to build public baths under the terms of the 1846 Act, completing the High Street Baths in 1858. This facility, rebuilt in 1890, was supplemented by the Newcastle Road Baths in 1936 and Crowtree Leisure Centre in 1978.

But the £20 million **Sunderland Aquatic Centre**, opened to the public in April 2008, and officially by the Princess Royal in January 2009, is a rather more ambitious building.

Designed by the Newcastle firm Redbox Architecture and built by Balfour Beatty, not only is its pool 50m in length, but its width extends to 25m; that is, able to accommodate ten lanes, as is the Olympic requirement.

Only four other British pools meet this standard, the others being in Sheffield, Leeds, Glasgow and Cardiff (although of course the 2012 Aquatic Centre in London will soon join this elite group).

As is also now standard at modern competition pools, each pool floor is moveable so that the depths can be adjusted to cater for different users, even those in wheelchairs.

The main pool, which is now home to the **City of Sunderland Amateur Swimming Club**, can also be divided into sections by a moveable boom, to allow maximum flexibility of use.

Sunderland's reward for this striking building was to be chosen as the host for the ASA National Championships in August 2010, for the first time in the city's history. The Centre will also become a pre-Olympic training centre for 2012.

The hope is to develop the remainder of what is now being called the Stadium Village regeneration site, perhaps with an indoor ski slope, a hotel and other sports and leisure facilities.

▲ The combination of heat, water and chemical agents used for water treatment has long conspired to make the environment of swimming pools extremely corrosive. Vast pool halls have also, historically, been expensive to heat and maintain.

To counter these effects, the **Sunderland Aquatic Centre** – seen here looking towards the separate diving pool at the far end – has been designed to meet the highest possible levels of sustainability.

Indeed it has attained a rating of nearly 73% (deemed 'excellent') from the Building Research Establishment, the highest so far awarded for a building of this type.

Most noticeable are the eleven curved glulam roof beams, each spanning 52m across the pool. This form of glued, laminated beam, sourced from managed sources in Austria, is regarded by many as far more suited for swimming pools than concrete or steel, as well as being more sustainable.

Moreover, every drop of rain that falls on the roof is collected and recycled for use within the Centre.

The building's fabric is also super-insulated, using a combined heat and power unit to maximise energy usage, and make viewing as comfortable as possible for those watching from its 500 seats.

Elegant, uncluttered and bathed in natural light, the Aquatic Centre represents over a century of accumulated experience.

It will now be fascinating to monitor how it performs, both as a building and as a nursery for future aquatic champions.

▲ Between the wars, five public outdoor swimming pools were in operation in Tyne and Wear.

Today there are none.

Above is **Hawkey's Lane Salt Water Swimming Bath** in **North Shields**. Originally a reservoir in which members of **Tynemouth Amateur Swimming Club** (founded 1875) were allowed to swim from 1907 onwards, Tynemouth Corporation used unemployed men to build the pool there during 1908–9, leaving its upkeep to the club. Eventually rising costs forced them to leave in 1969, and soon after the pool was demolished.

The pool on the **North Foreshore** at **South Shields** (*above right*), had a much briefer life. Opened in 1923, it closed in 1939.

Two other public open air pools were at Birtley (1937–c.1970), on the site of the fire station on Durham Road, and at Ryton, in Ferndene Park (1958–c.1990s).

Alongside the racecourse in **Gosforth Park** a private pool was built in 1933 as part of a **Scout Camp** (*right*). Described as 'a perfect paradise for boys', the pool was infilled during the 1970s.

BATHING POOL, SOUTH SHIELDS.

SWIMMING BATH, GOSFORTH PARK.

The most substantial of Tyne and Wear's outdoor swimming facilities was the **Tynemouth Open Air Pool**, built after a campaign to provide a safe bathing spot at Long Sands.

Designed by the Deputy Borough Surveyor, a Mr Forrest, this robust, stone lined and concrete tidal pool, with terraces for up to 2,000 sunbathers, opened during a Whitsun heat wave in May 1925.

So popular was it that two years later the Council added a cliffside pavilion with changing rooms and a turnstile to control entry.

The impressive building seen overlooking the beach, beyond the pool, is the **Aquarium and Winter Gardens**, opened in 1878 and later renamed the **Plaza**. This was used for a variety of entertainments, but in later years fell into disrepair, and in 1996 was destroyed by a fire.

The single storey building to its right was a short-lived roller skating rink, opened in connection with the winter gardens scheme in 1876. It survives today as shops.

In its heyday during the 1930s and 1950s, Tynemouth's Open Air Pool was often packed. But despite claims that its presence helped deter casual and inexperienced swimmers from risking the treacherous currents of the North Sea, it was closed in around 1990.

An attempt in 1996 to create a rock pool in its midst, as seen here, still leaves visitors baffled.

Readers interested in more detail on the history of outdoor pools and lidos are referred to an earlier study in the Played in Britain *series,* Liquid Assets *(see Links).*

▶ Now that so many of Britain's seaside lidos and open air pools have been closed or abandoned, as at Tynemouth (*see previous page*), a welcome alternative is the tidal pool, of which many still survive and are well catalogued by various publications and websites.

Less costly to create and maintain, but still offering a degree of safety compared with the open sea, tidal pools, as the name suggests, fill with the tide, allowing the trapped seawater to warm during the day.

Overlooked by Windsor Crescent, at the southern end of the promenade at **Whitley Bay**, **Table Rocks** was initially a naturally enclosed pool some 20' x 11'.

It was first developed as a pool in 1894 by Mr W. Scott, who then extended its length to 70' in 1896.

In July 1910 a group of early morning bathers decided to form the **Whitley and Monkseaton Bathing Club**. Each member was given a gold-painted winkle shell, hence the custom of local ladies and gentlemen showing each other their winkles whenever they met.

The winkle motif also adorned the club's official red and black swimming costumes.

As membership reached 200, in September 1910, separate changing pavilions were opened for ladies and gents, designed by a Newcastle architect and club member, WN Scaife.

Both pavilions remained in use, it is thought, until the 1950s.

Neither survives today, although the Table Rocks pool can still be seen, as can some ageing graffiti around its edges.

But given the renewed interest in tidal pools shown elsewhere along Britain's shorelines, we must ask, is it time to get our winkles out again in Whitley Bay?

BATHING POOL TABLE ROCKS, WHITLEY BAY.

◀ To prove that not all of Tyne and Wear's swimmers refuse to leave the cosseted climes of their heated indoor pools, we devote this final page to the hardy souls of the **Panama Swimming Club**.

Formed in the early 1900s, around the same time as the neighbouring club at Table Rocks, a mile or so further south, the club was named after Panama House, a café built on the Whitley Bay promenade in 1895 but burnt down in 1945. Its owner, Stephen Fry, was said to have worked on the construction of the Panama Canal.

There are also the Panama Gardens opposite the club's early 1950s headquarters.

From its homely clubroom, every single week of the year, whatever the weather, members emerge to take a dip in the North Sea.

Mostly their outings go unnoticed. But not on New Year's Day, as here in 2010, when even snow failed to deter them or the watching crowds.

Here, truly, is one of the great annual traditions of sporting and recreational life in Tyne and Wear, and a suitably bracing, and even humbling note on which to draw our journey to an end.

Chapter Nineteen

Conclusions

A knock-up on the village green in May 2010 as Whickham and Percy Main cricket clubs celebrate their 150th anniversaries with a game played to the 1860 rules at Beamish Museum. There are seven clubs in Tyne and Wear that are at least 150 years old, with three more due to reach that landmark by 2015. But can historic clubs do more to tell their story?

Sporting heritage, we hope readers will agree, is a precious asset in the cultural and social life of the people of Tyne and Wear.

But if this book is to fulfil its wider aims, it should not be viewed as an end in itself.

For this reason, we conclude with a few ideas that might help to safeguard this valuable heritage.

Heritage Open Days
One of the most common responses from readers of *Played in Britain* titles is that they simply had no idea that the club on their doorstep, or the one that they pass every day on their way to work, was of such historic interest.

Our first recommendation therefore is that more clubs follow the example of Jesmond Dene Real Tennis Club and Backworth Hall by allowing the public entry to their premises during Heritage Open Days.

Not only do many of these clubs have a fascinating story to tell, but by welcoming a new audience they can do much to promote their own sports and even recruit new members.

Built in 1886 but closed in 1992, Shipley Street Baths in Byker is now the home of Climb Newcastle. Conceived and funded entirely by local climber Andy Earl and two colleagues, since opening in 2008 the Centre has welcomed over 50,000 climbers per year. It is a fine example of how an historic building can be given new life in a sporting context.

Heritage Open Days also offer an opportunity to stage re-enactments of historic sports, as was seen with the 1860s game at Beamish in 2010 (*see left*).

Quoits, once such a vibrant feature of north east life, is one such game that, with the help of the area's remaining clubs, could be demonstrated and enjoyed by a wider audience.

Similarly, it would be fascinating to gather a group of experts and suitably muscled individuals to re-enact the lost game of potshare bowling, perhaps on a Heritage Open Day at a cricket or rugby ground, or even at Newcastle Racecourse.

Finally, we believe that in conjunction with Heritage Open Days there is scope for sporting heritage trails in areas such as Gosforth, Jesmond, Tynemouth, Gateshead and Sunderland.

Commemorations
Several sites featured in this book might be considered worth commemorating with perhaps a plaque or a piece of public art.

St James Metro Station in Newcastle, for example, though strongly identified with Newcastle United, actually sits on the site of one of Britain's foremost boxing stadiums, St James' Hall.

Other candidates might include the site of Newcastle's first public baths, on Bath Lane, the site of Appleby Park in North Shields, and the surviving entranceway of the High Street Public Baths in Sunderland.

Historic sports buildings
Buildings for sport are of course already eligible for protection under the current system of listing.

In 2010 there were seven listed buildings in Tyne and Wear either

purpose-built for sporting use or subsequently adapted for sport, all of which are featured in this book.

Arising from our research, further candidates that merit consideration for some level of protection include the Sunderland Bowling Club pavilion at Ashbrooke, Close House cricket pavilion, the pavilion at Jesmond Cricket Ground, the Tynemouth cockpit and the monument to James Renforth outside the Shipley Art Gallery in Gateshead.

It will be interesting to see if readers have other suggestions.

Another historic building that merits attention, if not actual listing, is the disused Tynemouth Open Air Pool, a structure that is highly visible and which might well lend itself to imaginative use, perhaps as an enclosure for public art installations (along the lines of the fourth plinth in Trafalgar Square, for example).

Collections and archives

Sports historians in Tyne and Wear have good reason to thank private collectors for their efforts to gather and preserve a wealth of artefacts and ephemera, and, in many cases, to share their collections online.

But sports clubs themselves bear an equal responsibility to safeguard and make public their own historic assets.

For this reason, we recommend that clubs looking for advice on conserving their historic artefacts should contact professional organisations such as the Institute of Conservation.

Clubs should also consider making their collections more widely available for historical research in the public realm, the most popular option being to publish them online.

Oral histories

Much excellent work has already been done by both Beamish Museum and the Northumberland Collections Service to record the oral histories of local people, some of whom have alluded in passing to the place of sport in their lives and communities.

However we suggest that a programme be initiated to record the oral histories of people involved in three specific areas of sporting life; boxing, quoits and pigeon racing, activities that have few written archives and which are best explained to future generations by personal testimony.

Further research

Many areas of sporting life in Tyne and Wear have been well documented. However there remain certain areas that we feel deserve further research; for example, the history of women's sport in the north east and the role of gambling in local sporting life.

We further suggest that research be carried out into the history, sporting and otherwise, of the High Gosforth Park estate.

Outreach and education

Finally, Tyne and Wear's museums and libraries have a commendable record of staging exhibitions and publishing material on the area's sporting history.

Indeed, this book is part of a year long series of events designed to broaden awareness of sporting heritage in Tyne and Wear in the run up to the 2012 Olympics.

Clearly, there is a rich store of material, expertise and, let it be emphasised, goodwill within the Tyne and Wear community.

Let us hope therefore that this book is just one contribution of many in the years to come.

▲ Undoubtedly one of the finest and most comprehensive collections of club related artefacts and memorabilia in the north east is in the keeping of **Newcastle United Football Club**.

Between 1991–98 and 2006–08 much of this collection – lovingly assembled both by the club and a number of local historians and collectors – was on display in a publicly accessible club museum at **St James' Park**.

And although parts of the collection, as seen here and on page 40, can still be viewed at St James' Park, it is to be hoped that the space and resources can be found to allow the public to enjoy the collection more fully at some

time in the future, either at first hand or via the internet (as has been recently demonstrated by the Lottery funded online Everton Collection).

Similar consideration might also by given by **Sunderland AFC** to the setting up of a collection of club related archives and material, to be displayed either in the form of a museum at the **Stadium of Light** or as an online resource.

In addition, or alternatively, Sunderland might wish to consider potential for a sports-related museum that celebrates not only the football club but all sports on Wearside, perhaps as part of the Stadium Village proposals currently under discussion.

Links

Where no publisher listed assume self-published by organisation or author

Where no publication date listed assume published on final date within title, ie. 1860–1960 means published 1960

Abbreviations:

ACSH – Association of Cricket Statisticians and Historians

IJHS – International Journal of the History of Sport

IRSS – International Review for the Sociology of Sport

RCHME – Royal Commission on the Historical Monuments of England

UP – University Press

Sport general

Bailey S & Vamplew W *100 Years of Physical Education 1899-1999* Warwick (1999)

Brailsford D *A Taste for Diversions: Sport in Georgian England* Lutterworth Press (1999)

Chinn C *Better betting with a decent feller: A social history of bookmaking* Aurum Press (2004)

Collins T *A Social History of English Rugby Union* Routledge (2009)

Holt R *Sport and the British* Clarendon (1989)

Holt R ed. *Sport and the working class in modern Britain* Manchester UP (1990)

Lowerson J *Sport and the English middle classes 1870-1914* Manchester UP (1993)

Vamplew W *Pay Up and Play the Game: Professional Sport in Britain 1875-1914* Cambridge UP (1988)

Tyne and Wear general

Ayris I *Newcastle on Show: the North East Coast Exhibition 1929* in Flowers A & Histon V eds. *Water Under the Bridges: Newcastle's Twentieth Century* Tyne Bridge Publishing (1999)

Barke M & Buswell RJ eds. *Newcastle's Changing Map* Newcastle upon Tyne City Libraries & Arts (1992)

Charleton RJ *A history of Newcastle-on-Tyne from the earliest records to its formation as a city* William H Robinson (1894)

Cookson G *Sunderland: building a city* Phillimore (2010)

Dodds GL *A History of Sunderland* Albion Press (2001)

Faulkner T, Beacock P & Jones P *Newcastle & Gateshead: Architecture and Heritage* Bluecoat Press (2006)

Faulkner T, Beacock P & Jones P *Changing Urban Landscapes: Architecture and Planning in Newcastle and Gateshead since 1945* in Fawcett H ed. *Made in Newcastle: Visual Culture* Northumbria UP (2007)

France L *Open space and public recreation in the 19th century* in Backe M & Buswell RJ eds. *Historical Atlas of Newcastle upon Tyne* Newcastle Polytechnic (1980)

Hinde Hodgson J *Public Amusements in Newcastle* Archaeologia Aeliana 4 (1860)

Histon V *Keys to the City: Walks exploring Newcastle's hidden history* Tyne Bridge Publishing (2007)

McCombie G *Newcastle and Gateshead* Pevsner Architectural Guides, Yale UP (2009)

McCord N *North East England: An economic and social history* Batsford (1979)

Mackenzie E *A descriptive and historical account of the town and county of Newcastle upon Tyne including the borough of Gateshead* Mackenzie & Dent (1827)

Manders F *A History of Gateshead* Gateshead Corp (1973)

Manders F & Potts R *Crossing the Tyne* Tyne Bridge Publishing (2001)

Meikle MM and Newman CM *Sunderland and its origins: monks to mariners* Phillimore (2007)

Morgan A *Jesmond: from mines to mansions* Tyne Bridge Publishing (2010)

Morgan A *A Victorian Panorama: A visit to Newcastle upon Tyne in the reign of Queen Victoria* Tyne Bridge Publishing (2007)

Newcastle-on-Tyne: Sixty Views from old prints and original drawings Frank Graham (1984)

Taylor S and Lovie DB *Gateshead: Architecture in a Changing English Urban Landscape* English Heritage (2004)

Usherwood P, Beach J & Morris C *Public Sculpture of North-East England* Liverpool UP (2000)

Tyne Guide Tyne and Wear County Council (1986)

Chapter 1. Played in Tyne and Wear

Barnstorming through Britain: 1895 and 1896 IJHS 24 (2007)

Bell D *A history of South Marine Park, South Shields* Jargram Publications (2007)

Boddy K *Boxing: A Cultural History* Reaktion Books (2008)

Brennan P *The Munitionettes: A history of women's football in North East England during the Great War* Donmouth (2007)

Brett A & Royal J *Old Pubs of Sunderland* Black Cat Publications (1993)

Brett A & Wood B eds. *North East Boxing Book Number One* Black Cat Publications (1998)

Bute M *The Olympian: the story of a Wearside boxer and his coach* Bute Publications (2008)

Collingwood Bruce J *A hand-book to Newcastle-on-Tyne* Longman (1863)

Gale J *The Blaydon Races* Oriel Press (1970)

Holt R & Physick R *Sport on Tyneside* in Colls R & Lancaster B eds. *Newcastle upon Tyne: A Modern History* Phillimore (2001)

Huggins M *The regular re-invention of sporting tradition and identity: Cumberland and Westmorland Wrestling c.1800-2001* Sports Historian 21 (2001)

Hunt B & Amos M eds. *Northern Goalfields Revisited* (2000)

Jarrett J *Byker to Broadway: the fighting life and times of Seaman Tommy Watson* Bewick Press (1997)

Jarrett J *Hall of Fame* TUPS Books (1999)

Joannou P & Candlish A *Pioneers of the North: The origins and development of football in North-East England and Tyneside, 1870-93* Breedon Books (2009)

Jones M *The Ouseburn Culvert and the City Stadium* Ouseburn Past and Present (Spring 2008)

Lawson WD *Lawson's Tyneside Celebrities* (1873)

Manders F *Palaces of Pleasure* in Flowers A and Histon V eds. *Water Under the Bridges* op cit

Melling J *Sport, Spectacle and Class: Handball in the North East* IJHS Vol 7 No 3 (1990)

Metcalfe A *Organised sport in the mining communities of south Northumberland, 1800-1889* Victorian Studies 25 4 (1982)

Metcalfe A *Leisure and recreation in a Victorian mining community: the social economy of leisure in north-east England, 1820-1914* Routledge (2006)

Moffatt FC *For a Purse of Gold: Northern racing, the story in word and picture* (1986)

Moffatt FC *Northern Sportsman: the development of sport in the north east of England over the past 150 years* (1999)

Moffatt FC *Linament and Leather: Sixty years of the fight game in the north* (1982)

Potts A *The View from the Stands* in Flowers A & Histon V eds. *Water Under the Bridges* op cit

Potts A *Jack Casey: Sunderland assassin* Bewick Press (1991)

Potts A *The Wearside Champions* Bewick Press (1993)

Potts A *Headlocks and Handbags: Wrestling at New St James's Hall* Black Cat Publications (2005)

Richardson MA *The Local Historian's Table Book* (1841-46)

Sinclair H *Cycle-clips: a history of cycling in the north east* Tyne and Wear County Council Museums (1985)

Sinclair NT *Sport* in Milburn GE & Miller ST eds. *Sunderland, River, Town and People: A history from the 1780s* Sunderland Borough Council (1988)

Wilson AR ed. *Football Under the Skin: A historical glimpse of soccer in Tyne and Wear 1879-1988* Tyne and Wear Museums Service (1988)

www.ciswo.org.uk

www.dmm.org.uk

Chapter 2. Town Moor, Newcastle

Baron F *The Town Moor Hoppings: Newcastle's Temperance Festival 1882-1982* Lovell Baines Print Ltd (1984)

Bloyce D *Just not cricket: Baseball in England 1874-1900* IJHS 14 (1997)

Bowden M, Brown G & Smith N *An Archaeology of Town Commons in England* English Heritage (2009)

Cook D *The Many Pavilions: a history of Benwell & Walbottle Cricket Club 1868-2002* (2002)

Halcrow EM *The Town Moor of Newcastle upon Tyne* Archaeologia Aeliana 31 (1953)

Innerd CAM *The North East Coast Exhibition of 1929* Modern History MA dissertation University of Durham (2001)

Joannou P *United, the first 100 years and more: the official history of Newcastle United FC 1882 to 1995* Polar (1995)

Joannou P *Fortress St James: the official story of Newcastle United's Stadium* Ballast (2000)

Lofthouse C *Town Moor, Newcastle upon Tyne: Archaeological Survey Report* RCHME (1995)

Longrigg R *The Turf: Three Centuries of Horse Racing* Eyre Methuen (1975)

Metcalfe A *Potshare bowling in the mining communities of east Northumberland, 1800-1914* in Holt R ed. *Sport and the working class in modern Britain* Manchester UP (1990)

Newcastle United Golf Club: On course for a century 1892-1992

Newcastle-upon-Tyne Royal Mining, Engineering and Industrial Exhibition, Jubilee Year 1887, Official catalogue R Robinson & Co (1887)

Chapter 3. Gosforth

Airey J *Bygone Gosforth* Newcastle City Libraries & Arts (1989)

Bayles FH *The Race Courses of Great Britain and Ireland* Equitable Publishing Syndicate (1907)

Harbottle G & Middleton S *100 years at 'The Park': the Northumberland Golf Club story 1898-1998* (1999)

Hedley A *The Newcastle Rugby Story* Tempus (2000)

Kirkup M *The Pitmen's Derby* Mid Northumberland Arts Group (1990)

Sleight J *The 'City' Centenary 1891-1991* City of Newcastle Golf Club Ltd (1991)

Vamplew W *The Turf: A social and economic history of horse racing* Allen Lane (1976)

Whittaker J *Gosforth Football Club: The early years 1877 to 1883* Roundtuit (2002)

Chapter 4. Hillheads

Bone JL *The Whitley Bay FC Story 1958-1983* (1983)

Harris M *Homes of British Ice Hockey* Tempus (2005)

Hedley A *Rockcliff Rugby Football Club: A Hundred Years of Rugby Football* (1987)

Muckle DS *All the way with Whitley Bay 1958-70* DSM-Falcon (1971)

Chapter 5. Wearmouth

Brett A *Canny Old Sunderland* Black Cat Publications (2007)

Brett A & Curtis P *Sunderland: A History of the Lads* Black Cat Publications (2005)

Curtis P & Brett A *Once upon a time in Sunderland* Black Cat Publications (2009)

Gravell J *From sport to leisure: Billingham to Crowtree* Architects' Journal Vol 168 26 (July 1978)

General websites

www.english-heritage.org.uk
www.gateshead.gov.uk
www.newcastle.gov.uk
www.northtyneside.gov.uk
www.southtyneside.gov.uk
www.sunderland.gov.uk
www.twmuseums.org.uk

Newspapers & journals

Architects' Journal, The Builder, Gateshead Chronicle, Independent on Sunday, Newcastle Evening Chronicle, Northern Athlete, South Shields Gazette, Sporting Man, Sunderland Echo, Sunderland Herald, The Times Online Digital Archive 1785–1985, Whitley Bay Guardian

Hudson J & Callaghan P eds. *Sunderland AFC: The Official History 1879-2000* (1999)
Inglis S *Engineering Archie* English Heritage (2005)
Ruttley J *Mowbray: The People's Park* Holroyd (2002)

Chapter 6. Ashbrooke
Smyth I *The Development of Baseball in Northern England 1935-39* IJHS 10 (1993)
Moses Watts E *To Ashbrooke and Beyond: The History of the Sunderland Cricket & Rugby Football Club 1808-1962* (1963)
www.ashbrookesports.com

Chapter 7. Clubhouses and pavilions
Blaydon Rugby Football Club Centenary Brochure (1988)
Brett A *Caseys, Cups and Canny Lads* Black Cat Publications (2004)
Byrne M *South Shields Golf Club Centenary 1893-1993*
Cain D *A history of Tyneside Golf Club* (2000)
Chapman J *100 years of cricket at Blaydon 1891-1991*
Crickmer C *Grass Roots, a history of South Shields Cricket Club 1850-1984*
Danskin TC *Whitley Bay Golf Club: A brief history 1890-1990*
Draper S *Cricket Grounds of Durham* ACSH (2006)
Evans AC *Benwell Hill Cricket Club 1883-1983* Smith Print Group (1983)
Evans S *Pride in the Lion: The History of Newcastle University Rugby Football Club* NURFC Vice Presidents' Assoc (2007)
Harbottle G *A century of cricket in South Northumberland 1864-1969* Fenwick & Wade (1969)
Linsley SM *The Royal Mining, Engineering and Industrial Exhibition, Newcastle upon Tyne 1887* Tyne & Tweed 46 (1991-92)
Millen T *A History of North Durham RFC 1876-1998* (1999)
Mountford CE *Tynemouth Cricket Club 1847-1996* (1997)
Patterson NH *Lawn tennis by Tyne and Wear* T&G Allan (1921)
Reeder S *Memories of Whitburn in words and pictures* (2007)
Semple S & Charlton E *The Medical Rugby Football Club 1898-1998* (1999)
Stevens BDR *Northumberland's Non-League Cricket Clubs* Smith Print Group (1978)
Sutton P *Wearside Golf Club 18892-1992*

Chapter 8. Grounds and grandstands
Owen R *The Reyrolle Story: A History of A Reyrolle & Co Ltd* Write Good Books (2007)
Rae I & Smith K *Swan Hunter: The Pride and the Tears* Tyne Bridge Publishing (2008)
Twydell D *Appleby Park - North Shields (1896-1992)* in *Gone But Not Forgotten 18* Yore Publications (2001)
Twydell D *Walker Celtic* in *Gone But Not Forgotten 29* Yore Publications (2006)

Chapter 9. Stadiums and tracks
Bamford R & Jarvis J *Homes of British Speedway* Stadia/Tempus (2006)
Esther G *Requiem for Redheugh* Gateshead MBC Libraries Arts & Shipley Gallery Committee (1984)
Genders R & NGRC *The NGRC Book of Greyhound Racing: The complete history of the sport* Pelham Books (1990)
Nicholson R *North East Motorsport* Tempus (2005)
Oliver S *North East Motorsport* History Press (2005)
Thompson G *South Shields FC: The Football League Years* Yore Publications (2000)
www.newcastlespeedwayhistory.co.uk
www.newcastlespeedway.net
www.sunderlandspeedway.co.uk

Chapter 10. Cock Fighting
Egan P *Pierce Egan's Book of Sports and Mirror of Life* (1832)
Jobey G *Cock-fighting in Northumberland and Durham during the 18th and 19th centuries* Archaeologia Aeliana 20 (1992)
Tolson J *Cockfighting* in Collins T, Martin J & Vamplew W eds. *Encyclopedia of Traditional British Rural Sports* Routledge (2005)

Chapter 11. Quoits
Cuthbertson J *Quoits* Tyne and Tweed 35 (1981)
Lawson WD *Lawson's Tyneside Celebrities* (1873)
Lockey WA *Hawkey's Hall Quoit Club 1860-2010* (2010)
Taylor A *Played at the Pub* English Heritage (2009)

Chapter 12. Bowls
Anderson A *Bowls in Sunderland: An illustrated history* Black Cat Publications (2003)
Gosforth Bowling Club: The first hundred years 1902-2002 (2002)
South Tyneside Bowling Association 1892-1992 South Tyneside Libraries (1992)
Summerhill Bowling Club 1916-2008 (2008)
Sykes J *Local Records: Or, Historical Register of Remarkable Events Which Have Occurred in Northumberland and Durham, Newcastle-upon-Tyne and Berwick-upon-Tweed* (1866)

Chapter 13. Real Tennis
Aberdare, Lord *The JT Faber Book of Tennis & Rackets* Quiller Press (2001)
www.jdrtc.co.uk
www.tennisandrackets.com

Chapter 14. Running
Allen W *The Eastenders: Heaton Harriers 1890-1990* (1990)
Lewis R *The Great North Run: The first 25 years and my part in it* Kensington West Productions (2005)

Long S & Merrill A *From dirt track to glory: A story of Gateshead Harriers* (1978)

Moffatt FC *Turnpike road to tartan track: A history of professional footrunning on Tyneside, 1850 to 1970* (1979)

Murray N *The Boys in Red: Elswick Harriers 1889-1989*

Watson D *Champion Peds: Road running on Victorian Tyneside* North East Labour History 28 (1994)

Watson D *Popular athletics on Victorian Tyneside* IJHS 11 (1994)

www.blaydonrace.org

www.newnet.org.uk/elswickharriers

www.greatnorthrunculture.org

www.greatrun.org

www.saltwellharriers.com

Chapter 15. Pigeon Racing
The Homing Instinct Meerkat Films (2008)

www.nehu.co.uk

www.rpra.org

Chapter 16. Rowing
Blake G *One hundred and seventy five years of Durham University rowing* River & Rowing Museum (2008)

Clasper D *Harry Clasper: Hero of the North* Gateshead Books (1990)

Clasper D *Rowing: A way of life - The Claspers of Tyneside* Portcullis Press (2003)

Dillon P *The Tyne Oarsmen* Keepdate (1993)

Gibson P *Southwick-on-Wear Volume 3* Southwick Publications (1991)

Huggins M *Death, memorialisation and the Victorian sporting hero* The Local Historian Vol 38 No 4 (Nov 2008)

Morgan A *A Fine and Private Place: Jesmond Old Cemetery* Tyne Bridge (2000)

Morgan A *Beyond the Grave: Exploring Newcastle's Burial Grounds* Tyne Bridge (2004)

Osborne K *Boat Racing in Britain 1715-1975* Amateur Rowing Association (1975)

Stokes W *Reclaiming the Tyneside scullers* Durham County Local History Society Journal 75 (February 2010)

Weil TE *Beauty and the Boats: art and artistry in early British rowing* River & Rowing Museum (2005)

Whitehead I *The Sporting Tyne: A history of professional rowing* Gateshead MBC (2002)

Whitehead I *James Renforth of Gateshead: Champion sculler of the world* Tyne Bridge Publishing (2004)

Chapter 17. Model Boating
Potts R *Sporting hobbies and social class: the case of model yachting* IJHS Vol 5 No 2 (1988)

Thomson AC *Tynemouth Model Boat Club* (2001)

Chapter 18. Swimming
Bidwell P & Speak S eds. *Excavations at South Shields Roman Fort* Vol 1 Society of Antiquaries of Newcastle upon Tyne with Tyne & Wear Museums (1994)

Campbell A *Report on Public Baths and Wash-houses* Carnegie United Kingdom Trust (1918)

Clarke F *Making a Splash: How Jesmond Pool made history* Jesmond Swimming Project (2009)

Edwards B *Crest of a Wave: FaulknerBrowns on Tyneside* Architecture Today 44 (1994)

Fletcher DR *The Official History of the Northumberland and Durham Counties ASA 1897 to 1997* (1997)

Gordon I & Inglis S *Great Lengths: The historic indoor swimming pools of Britain* English Heritage (2009)

Hodgson N ed. *The Roman Fort at Wallsend (Segedunum): Excavations in 1997-8* Tyne & Wear Museums and Arbeia Society (2003)

Illingworth M A *Newcastle City Hall and Public Baths: An architectural history* Bachelor of Architecture dissertation University of Newcastle upon Tyne (1985)

Love C *An Overview of the Development of Swimming in England, c.1750-1918* and *A chronology of English swimming 1747-1918* and *Local Aquatic Empires: The municipal provision of swimming pools in England 1828-1918* IJHS 24 (2007)

SAVE *Taking the Plunge: The architecture of bathing* (1982)

Smith J *Liquid Assets: The lidos and open air swimming pools of Britain* English Heritage (2005)

Elswick Park and Pool, Newcastle-upon-Tyne Architects' Journal Vol 174 2 (September 1981)

Swimming baths Architects' Journal Vol 138 (Nov 1963)

Swimming baths Architects' Journal Vol 140 (Nov 1964)

www.fenhampool.talktalk.net

www.jesmondpool.co.uk

www.victorianturkishbath.org

Chapter 19. Conclusions
www.beamish.org.uk

www.climbnewcastle.com

www.evertoncollection.org.uk

www.experiencewoodhorn.com

www.heritageopendays.org.uk

www.icon.org.uk

www.twhods.org.uk

Credits

Photographs and images

Please note that where more than one photograph appears on a page, each photograph is identified by a letter, starting with 'a' in the top left hand corner of the page, or at the top, and continuing thereafter in a *clockwise* direction.

All English Heritage and National Monuments Record photographs listed are either © English Heritage or © Crown Copyright, NMR. Application for the reproduction of these images should be made to:
National Monuments Record
Kemble Drive
Swindon SN2 2GZ
Tel 01793 414700

All maps are Ordnance Survey © Crown Copyright

English Heritage/National Monuments Record

Aerofilms Collection: 35; 41c, 118; NMR: 17a, 84b, 114b; Alun Bull: back flap, 1, 4, 8a, 11, 14b, 16ab, 22ab, 23a, 24ab, 33b, 36a, 37b, 47, 48a, 50a, 58, 67ab, 74ab, 83b, 93ab, 98a, 99a, 102, 103ab, 104ab, 105, 106a, 107bd, 108a, 111b, 125b, 134abc, 135abcde, 138bc, 140ab, 141a, 152ab, 153b, 154b, 158ac, 159a, 160abc, 164abc, 165abcd, 166abc, 167a, 173b, 178b, 179ab, 181abc, 184a, 185ab, 191ab, 192b; Dave MacLeod: 27, 63, 85b, 123b, 126b; Bob Skingle: front flap, 76b, 77b, 85a, 95, 104c, 125c, 153a, 174ab, 175ab, 176ac, 177, 186ab, 187

Photographers

Steve Brock: 120bc; Tony Davis: 46ab; Julian Germain: 6; Simon Inglis: back cover a, inside back cover, 9a, 23b, 31c, 36b, 37c, 40c, 44b, 49abce, 69, 70, 71abc, 76a, 84a, 86ab, 87abc, 88abc, 89b, 96a, 110a, 113a, 120a, 121, 122abc, 123a, 142ab, 143abcd, 144, 145abcd, 184b, 189b, 193; Bob Lilliman: 81a, 108b, 110b, 112abc, 126a; Lynn Pearson: back cover bcd, 9b, 12ab, 17b, 34bc, 37a, 48bc, 49d, 54c, 55ab, 56ab, 72a, 94b, 98b, 99b, 100ac, 101ab, 107a, 109, 111a, 131ab, 136a, 139b, 146, 154a, 158b, 162a, 167b, 168, 172b, 173ad, 176b, 190b; Jeff Walton: 150; Matthew Walton: 155abc

Tyne & Wear Museums & Archives

Discovery Museum: 156a; Monkwearmouth Station Museum: 14a; Natural History Society of Northumbria Great North Museum: Hancock: 128ab; Shipley Art Gallery: 13; Sunderland Museum & Winter Gardens: 73, 82b; Tyne & Wear Archives Service: 10, 18ab, 19ab, 33a, 59abcd, 97b, 133b, 136b, 156b

Archives, libraries and agencies

360R: 60b; AirFotos: 54b, 113b, 115b; Architectural Press Archive / RIBA Library Photographs Collection: 43b, 182; Athletics Images / Mark Shearman: 149ac; Beamish Museum: 97a, 132; ©The British Library Board (MapsK.Top.32.57.m): 169; Fiescher Fotos / South Tyneside MBC Local Studies Collection: 125a; Gateshead Council: 127a; Gateshead Council / i2i Photography: 127b; Gateshead Council Collection: 117, 133a, 180ab; Getty Images: 80b; Mary Evans: 26, 137a, 157; Mirrorpix: 28b, 42ab, 45b, 80a, 81b, 83acd, 97c, 124abc, 151ab, 178a, 183a,192a; Mirrorpix / Newcastle City Library:

21b; The National Archives: 51; Newcastle City Library: 15ab, 19e, 21b, 32a, 39ac, 50b, 129, 130a, 163b, 170, 173c, 183b, 188c; Newcastle University / Robinson Library Special Collections (RD 942.82 BRO): 30; North News & Pictures: 45a, 191c; North Tyneside Libraries: 188a; Northumberland Collections Service: 28a; River and Rowing Museum: 159bc; Society of Antiquaries of Newcastle upon Tyne: 38, 130b; South Tyneside MBC Local Studies Collection: 18c, 172a; Sunderland Echo: 2, 72b, 77ac; Sunderland Public Libraries: 92b; University of St Andrews Library: 189a; West Newcastle Picture History Collection: 21a, 139a, 147a

Private collections

Gosforth Golf Club: 60a; Paul Joannou: 39b, 40a, 41ab, 43ac, 64a; Lynn Pearson: 7, 18d, 52a, 54a, 62a, 141c, 190a; John Somerville Collection: 31b, 62b, 114a; Tyne Rowing Club: cover; Ward Philipson Collection: 119

Donated photographs

The publishers wish to thank the following individuals and organisations: Richard Appleby: 115a; Stuart Archer: 61a; Arcot Hall Golf Club: 22c; Michael Armstrong: 94a; Ashbrooke Sports Club: 90ab, 91ab, 92ac; Colin Bradshaw: 66a; Peter Carter: 94c; Paul Cook: 106b; Paul Days: 78ab, 79; Clino d'Eletto: 40b; Fitz Architects: 107c; Ian Gordon: 171, 188b; Heaton & District Model Power Boat Club: 162b, 163a; John Jarrett: 19c; Al Johnston: 200; Duncan Jordan: 66b; Brian Leng: 82a; MCC Library, Lord's: inside front cover; Newcastle Racecourse: 52b, 57; Newcastle United FC: 44a; Newcastle United Golf Club: 34a; Newcastle University / The Centre for Physical Recreation and Sport: 100b; North Shields FC: 112d; Nova International: 148a; Nova International / Suky Best: 149b; Nova International / Scott Heppell: 148b; Colin Percy: 161; Portland Park Bowling Club: 137b, 141b; Rockcliff RFC: 64b, 65; Bob Rowe: 116; Alan Spoors: 147b; Summerhill Bowling Club: 138a; Sunderland AFC: 89a; Miles Templeton: 19d; Ann Watson: 68a; Wearside Golf Club: 20ab; Whitley Bay Ice Rink: 68bc; World Rugby Museum: 61b

Printed sources

Anderson A *Bowls in Sunderland* Black Cat Publications (2003): 139c; Kirkup M *The Pitmen's Derby* Mid Northumberland Arts Group (1990)**:** 32b; Longrigg R *The Turf: Three Centuries of Horse Racing* Eyre Methuen (1975): 31a

Acknowledgements

English Heritage and the *Played in Britain* team would like to thank Gateshead Council, Newcastle City Council, North Tyneside Council, South Tyneside Council, Sunderland City Council and Tyne & Wear Archives & Museums for their generous support. Thanks also go to their very helpful library and archives staff and to the following: Keith Gregson, Tom Almond, Rob Deverson (Ashbrooke Sports Club); John Cleverley (Backworth BC); Brian Thubron (Boldon CC); Alastair Greenfield (Boldon Golf Club); Alex Smith, Alan Walker (Bowmen of Backworth); Andy McKinley (Brandling Park BC); Ian Linsley (Burnmoor CC); Newton Scott (Byker Village BC); John Glendenning (Close House Golf Club); Tim Fay (Gosforth Golf Club); John Plant (Gosforth Homing Society); John Gray (Gosforth RFC); Neil Pattinson (Gosforth Squash Club); Simon Harris, Dr Peter Quinn (Jesmond Dene Real Tennis Club); Alan Lockey (Hawkey's Hall Quoit Club); Tom Clement, Albert Foxton (Heaton & District Model Power Boat Club); Lindisfarne Social Club; Olwyn Hocking (Newcastle CC); Terry Meynell (Newcastle Greyhound Stadium); Anna Skelton (Newcastle Racecourse); Rod Adams (North of England Homing Union); Andy James (Northern RFC); George Leighton (Portland BC); Ian Firth, Peter Merchant (Rockcliff RFC); Peter Jameson (Rockcliffe BC); Jack Martin, Alan Green (Saltwell Park Model Boat Club); Lindsay Allason-Jones, Rob Collins (Society of Antiquaries of Newcastle upon Tyne); Gillian Usher (South Northumberland CC); Mac Stephenson (South Shields Harriers); Percy Young, William Young (Summerhill BC); Philip Curtis, Norman Kirtlan (Sunderland Antiquarian Society); Rob Mason (Sunderland AFC); Patsy Wilkinson (Sunderland Stadium); Anna Flowers (Tyne Bridge Publishing); Colin Percy (Tyne RC); Alex Pattinson, Chris Smith, Brian Lunns (Tyne United RC); Bryan Young (Tynemouth Model Boat Club); Maxie Walsh (Tyneside Ex-Boxers' Association); Marc Jarvis, Colin Shilton (Wallsend Boys Club); Philip Hall, Peter Sutton (Wearside Golf Club); Jim Huxley (Whickham CC); Russell Muse (Whitburn CC); Peter Watson (Whitley Bay CC); Frank Elliott, Clare and Peter Crosby (Whitley Bay Golf Club); Francis Smith (Whitley Bay Ice Rink), the staff of Wallsend Children's Centre and Threshers in Tynemouth.

Further thanks go to Alan Brett, Anne and John Bundock, Paul Days, Chris Foote-Woode, Ian Gordon, Elain Harwood, Jim Henry, Bob Houston, John Jarrett, Tim Jenkins, Paul Joannou, Grace McCombie, Jennifer Morrison, Peter Nicol, Ray Physick, Martin Polley, Jim and Margaret Perry, Archie Potts, Russell Potts, Sybil Reeder, Neil Robinson (MCC Library), John Skinner, David B. Smith, Rosemary Stearman, Maurice Surtees, Steve Troup, Barry Wallace, Graham Walters and Robert Wray.

Finally, the author would particularly like to thank Carol Pyrah, Stephen Allott and Alun Bull at English Heritage, John Dark and James Holland for their good work, and last but not least Sue Hudson and Razzle the dog.

Played in Manchester
Simon Inglis (2004)

Played in Birmingham
Steve Beauchampé and
Simon Inglis (2006)

Played in Liverpool
Ray Physick (2007)

Engineering Archie
Simon Inglis (2005)

Liquid Assets
Janet Smith (2005)

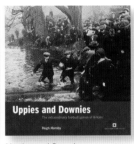

Uppies and Downies
Hugh Hornby (2008)

Great Lengths
Dr Ian Gordon and Simon Inglis
(2009)

Played at the Pub
Arthur Taylor (2009)

Played in Glasgow
Ged O'Brien (2010)

Future titles

The British Olympics – Britain's Olympic heritage 1612–2012 Martin Polley (2011)
Played in London – charting the heritage of the capital at play Simon Inglis (2011)
Bowled Over - the bowling greens of Britain Hugh Hornby (2012)
For more information **www.playedinbritain.co.uk**

▲ As the competing crews in the annual **University Boat Race** head for the finishing line under the Millennium Bridge in May 2010, so we come to the end of our journey around the sporting treasures of Tyne and Wear.

As someone who has lived, worked, walked, run and cycled in the north east for nearly three decades, and thoroughly enjoyed the sporting scene both as a spectator and a player – of hockey most of all – it has been a privilege to visit so many fascinating and welcoming clubs and grounds during the research for this book.

If music be the soundtrack to our lives, then assuredly, sport is the map of mine. And still, I feel sure, there remains much more to learn and to discover about the rich sporting heritage of this extraordinary part of Britain.

So to conclude, there is one message to impart, and that is to urge the reader to step out and enjoy what you have read about at first hand; to experience the buildings and the places, to watch, mingle, and even better, take part.

Lynn Pearson September 2010